Marcel Carné

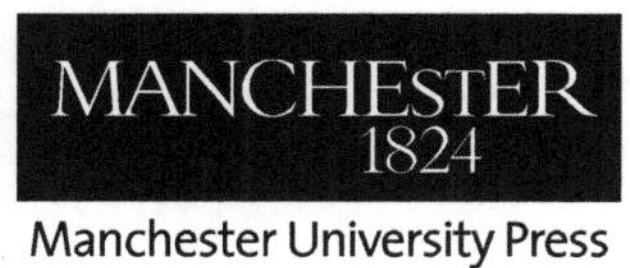

Manchester University Press

FRENCH FILM DIRECTORS

Marcel Carné

JONATHAN DRISKELL

Manchester University Press

Published by Manchester University Press
Altrincham Street, Manchester M1 7JA, UK
www.manchesteruniversitypress.co.uk

British Library Cataloguing-in-Publication Data is available

Library of Congress Cataloging-in-Publication Data is available

ISBN 978 1 7849 9285 9 *paperback*

First published by Manchester University Press in hardback 2012

This paperback edition first published 2016

The publisher has no responsibility for the persistence or accuracy of URLs for any external or third-party internet websites referred to in this book, and does not guarantee that any content on such websites is, or will remain, accurate or appropriate.

Printed by Lightning Source

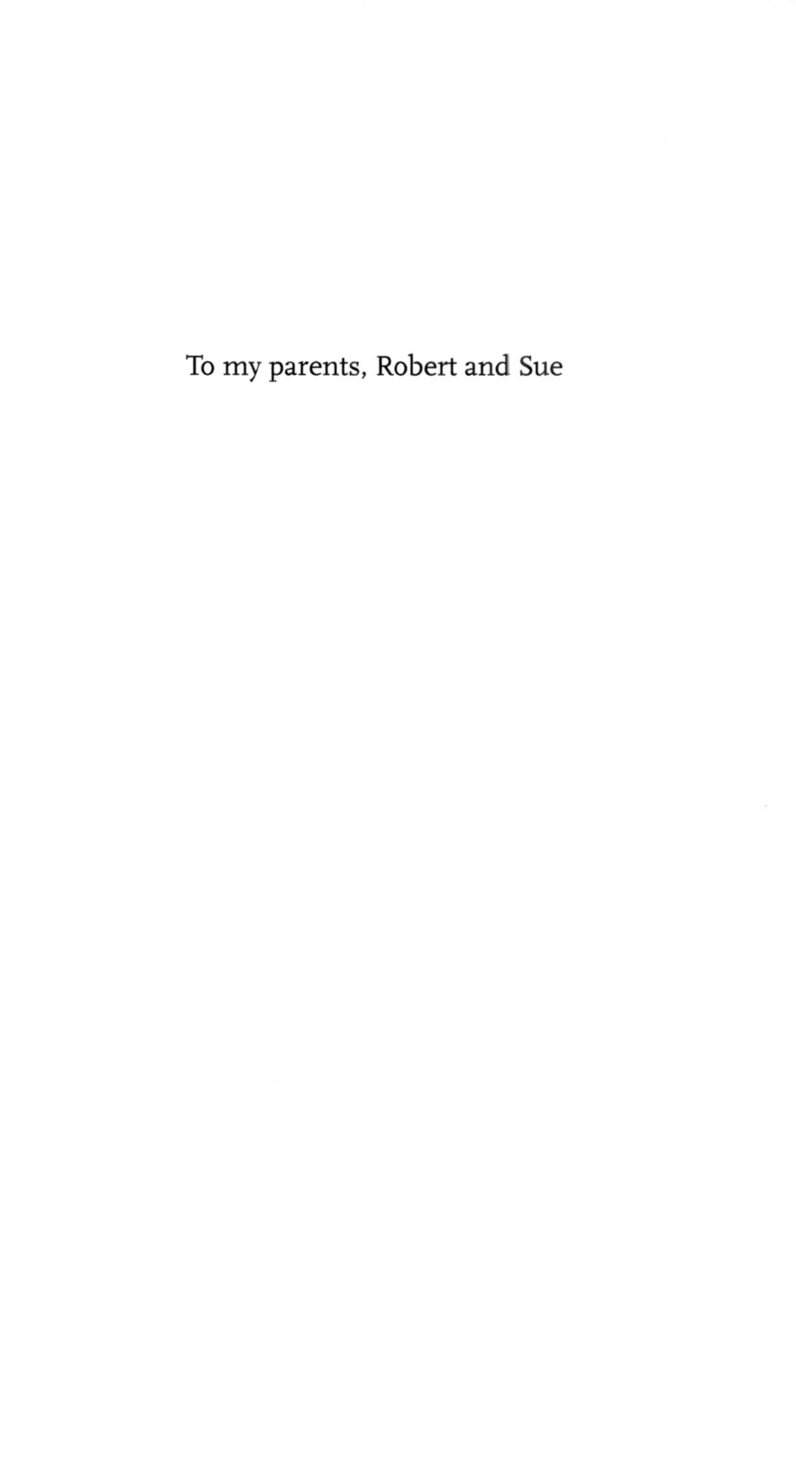

To my parents, Robert and Sue

Contents

List of plates

Series editors' foreword

To an anglophone audience, the combination of the words 'French' and 'cinema' evokes a particular kind of film: elegant and wordy, sexy but serious – an image as dependent upon national stereotypes as is that of the crudely commercial Hollywood blockbuster, which is not to say that either image is without foundation. Over the past two decades, this generalised sense of a significant relationship between French identity and film has been explored in scholarly books and articles, and has entered the curriculum at university level and, in Britain, at A-level. The study of film as art-form and (to a lesser extent) as industry, has become a popular and widespread element of French Studies, and French cinema has acquired an important place within Film Studies. Meanwhile, the growth in multi-screen and 'art-house' cinemas, together with the development of the video industry, has led to the greater availability of foreign-language films to an English-speaking audience. Responding to these developments, this series is designed for students and teachers seeking information and accessible but rigorous critical study of French cinema, and for the enthusiastic filmgoer who wants to know more.

The adoption of a director-based approach raises questions about auteurism. A series that categorises films not according to period or to genre (for example), but according to the person who directed them, runs the risk of espousing a romantic view of film as the product of solitary inspiration. On this model, the critic's role might seem to be that of discovering continuities, revealing a necessarily coherent set of themes and motifs which correspond to the particular genius of the individual. This is not our aim: the auteur perspective on film, itself most clearly articulated in France in the early 1950s, will be interrogated in certain volumes of the series, and, throughout, the director will be treated as one highly significant element in a complex process of film production and reception which includes socio-economic and political determinants, the work of a large and highly skilled team of artists and technicians, the mechanisms of production and distribution, and the complex and multiply determined responses of spectators.

The work of some of the directors in the series is already well known outside France, that of others is less so – the aim is both to provide informative and original English-language studies of established figures, and to extend the range of French directors known to anglophone students of cinema. We intend the series to contribute to the promotion of the formal and informal study of French films, and to the pleasure of those who watch them.

DIANA HOLMES
ROBERT INGRAM

Acknowledgements

I would like to thank: my editors Diana Holmes and Robert Ingram, along with Matthew Frost and the staff at Manchester University Press, for their help with this volume; the librarians at the BFI library and the Bibliothèque Nationale de France; Margaret Flinn, Robbie Lumsden and Philippe Morisson for supplying me with research materials, and Philippe Morisson for information on Carné-related queries; Olga Kourelou and Louis Bayman for discussions, and the latter for Italian translations; Ginette Vincendeau for her advice, comments and suggestions. Finally, I am grateful for all the help I have received from Christopher Driskell, Mariana Liz, and my parents, Robert and Sue Driskell.

1

Marcel Carné's career and reception: the highs and lows

During his long filmmaking career, which stretched from the 1920s to the 1990s, Marcel Carné had a profound impact on French cinema. For many his status as one of France's greatest directors is guaranteed by the continuing popularity of *Les Enfants du paradis* (1945), a film that regularly appears at the top of critics' lists of 'best ever' French films. Others acknowledge his central place within poetic realism, the defining movement in the 'golden age' of French cinema in the 1930s. Carné's *Le Quai des brumes* (1938), *Hôtel du Nord* (1938), and *Le Jour se lève* (1939) encapsulate these dark and fatalistic, yet lyrical and stylised accounts of working-class lives. Carné achieved countless other successes: he made many box-office hits, won festival and industry prizes, and gained recognition in French cultural life through, for example, his induction in 1980 (the first of a French film director) into the Académie des Beaux-Arts. His work is regularly shown in cinemas and on television in France, it is discussed in classes and at conferences, and it has generated much writing, both academic and popular. In short, Carné is a towering figure in French cinema.

But there is another side to the Carné story. In keeping with his films, which are often tales of rejection, alienation, and marginalisation, Carné at many points in his career occupied a less harmonious position within the French film industry and public sphere. His troubles include the controversy surrounding his decision to continue making films under the Nazi Occupation and his high-profile disappointments, particularly *Les Portes de la nuit* (1946) and *Juliette ou la clef des songes* (1951). The lengthy list of Carné's incomplete films also emphasises that, despite his successes, his career was not free from obstacles, whether financial or censorial. One of the ways that his trajectory contained highs and lows was through the changing critical reception of his work. While his films were initially highly acclaimed by the French critical establishment, his reputation was badly damaged in the 1950s by the *Cahiers du Cinéma* critics, who launched an assault on his postwar cinema. In order to understand Carné's cinematic significance more fully it is necessary to begin by considering in greater detail the exact nature of these highs and lows – the trajectory of his career and critical reception.

A long and difficult career

For Carné the 1930s was a period of great success: he achieved impressive box-office results and was discussed favourably by many of the nation's critics. The early years of sound film witnessed a conflict between figures such as Marcel Pagnol and Sacha Guitry, who believed the new medium should be used to create 'filmed theatre' – filmed versions of plays, often using a minimum number of sets and with performers taken directly from the stage show – and those, most notably René Clair, who argued that cinema must remain aesthetically advanced, pursuing the visual innovations of silent cinema and using sound creatively. Within this context, Carné (and his early collaborator, the poet-turned-scriptwriter Jacques Prévert) was singled out as an important 'cinematic' filmmaker, along with such figures as Jean Renoir, Jacques Feyder, Julien Duvivier, Jean Vigo, and, of course, René Clair. Their innovative approach to film aesthetics made these directors a source of national pride in the 1930s, a view enshrined in the numerous books on this period that centre on their work, such as Georges Sadoul's *French Film*, published in 1953. From this perspective, Carné's main contribution was his role in the formation and development of poetic realism, and his involvement in the strong populist strain of cinema that was prevalent at this time. Although there was controversy surrounding the bleakness of his poetic realist films, an issue that will be explored in Chapter 2, Carné went into the Occupation period as one of France's most celebrated directors.

During the Occupation his public persona went from strength to strength. In part this was because many of the significant figures of the 1930s left France at this time, creating a vacuum that was filled by established personalities like Carné and new talent such as

Jacques Becker, Claude Autant-Lara, Henri-Georges Clouzot, and Jean Delannoy, all of whom would continue to be important in the postwar 'tradition of quality'. Within this context Carné experienced a rapid rise to become *the* most celebrated director in the country. Such faith in him was consolidated by his two wartime films that were widely acknowledged as masterpieces: *Les Visiteurs du soir* (1942) and *Les Enfants du paradis*. The former was seen by many as expressing a nationalistic opposition to the occupying forces, the latter, actually released just after the Liberation of Paris, represented for many the pinnacle of French culture. This period will be discussed in Chapter 3.

However, while the period of the Occupation marked the apex of Carné's career, the immediate postwar years would signal the beginning of what has for a long time been seen as a decline. When Carné was criticised in postwar trials for collaboration, because of his decision to continue making films under the occupying forces, his public image was badly damaged. His first postwar release, *Les Portes de la nuit*, didn't improve the situation: in comparison with the films of the Occupation it was a critical failure (though, as we will see, not such a commercial failure as is frequently made out), and it marked the end of the Carné-Prévert partnership. Despite this setback, Carné continued to make films into the 1950s and became closely associated with the tradition of quality, with a number of highly successful works, such as *La Marie du port* (1950) and *Thérèse Raquin* (1953). On the other hand, some of his output at this time was badly received – *Juliette ou la clef des songes*, for example, was a resounding failure. During the same period Carné's reputation as a filmmaker became the subject of debate. In discussing what he referred to as the 'Carné question', the eminent critic André Bazin came to his defence – with qualifications – as we shall see in Chapter 4, and Jean Quéval (1950 and 1952) and Bernard G. Landry (1952) wrote the first books devoted to Carné's work.

Others were less enthusiastic towards Carné, particularly critics from *Cahiers du Cinéma*. Although other figures such as Jean Aurenche and Pierre Bost received more vicious criticism, Carné was, as Turk (1989: 392) states, 'jabbed ... relentlessly throughout 1954 and 1955'. Such hostility needs to be contextualised within broader notions of cinema emerging at this time. The *Cahiers* critics developed a defence of Hollywood cinema, which had not been available during the war, claiming it to be superior to French production, aside from the work of a small elite, including Max Ophüls and Jean Renoir. They saw the tradition of quality, or 'cinéma de papa' ('father's cinema') as they called it, as outdated and over-reliant on literary form and sources. Within this view of cinema Carné was found lacking. The nature of this criticism and the reasons behind it will be explored in Chapter 5.

The *politique des auteurs* developed by *Cahiers du Cinéma* was eventually superseded by other approaches to authorship and other agendas within the discipline (for example, *Screen* theory in the 1970s). Nevertheless, many of its biases as well as the cinematic canon it established endured, with negative results on Carné's reputation. Although he continued to make films and achieved a number of popular hits in the 1950s, culminating in the national sensation of *Les Tricheurs* (1958), his critical reputation did not improve. Carné's final films, from *Du mouron pour les petits oiseaux* (1963) onwards, remained completely outside the critical radar. While Carné's ultimate decline cannot solely be explained by the negative criticism he received, his career, as Jill Forbes (1993) remarks, never really recovered from the *Cahiers* critics' attack.

From the Young Turks to Edward Baron Turk

With the establishment of Film Studies as an academic subject, Carné didn't fare much better and until the late 1980s received little serious attention. By contrast, Renoir, the 'godfather of the new wave', was examined at length in a huge number of books and articles – for the *Cahiers* critics his work typified the 'auteur' as expressive individual and creative genius. Despite this a slow trickle of work examining Carné emerged, including in 1972 a special issue of *Les Cahiers de la Cinémathèque* devoted to Carné and in 1979 a book in Italian by Roberto Nepoti. In addition, Carné's autobiography (1996), first published in 1975, is, with its bitter and polemical tone, an important contribution to the critical debates on his work. In the 1980s a shift within Film Studies from the auteurism of the 1960s and *Screen* theory of the 1970s towards a greater concern for historical issues brought about increased interest in Carné, who was discussed by Dudley Andrew (1983) in his chapter on poetic realism in Mary Lea Bandy's *Rediscovering French Cinema*, which also included a reprint of Bazin's 1951 article 'Carné et la désincarnation' ('The disincarnation of Carné') – a discussion of Carné's postwar work and reception. Other important pieces include Richard Abel's (1988) edited volume *French Film Theory and Criticism*, which provides English translations of some of Carné's articles on film, written as a journalist, as well as broader discussion of the director's significance within the period's cinema. However, it was not until 1989 that the first comprehensive academic study of Carné was undertaken by Edward Baron Turk in his monograph *Child of Paradise: Marcel Carné and the Golden Age of French Cinema.*

The fact that this work has remained, until now, the only academic English-language study of Carné says as much about the exhaustiveness and high quality of Turk's research as it does about his subject's critical neglect. In contrast to the *Cahiers* critics' dismissal of Carné as a mere 'metteur en images' ('image renderer'), Turk finds great complexity, artistry, and self-expression in his cinema. Drawing upon methodology developed in post-*Cahiers* Anglo-American criticism, Turk implements a sophisticated psychoanalytical and gender-based approach, explaining Carné's films through reference to biographical information taken from his memoirs, discourses about the director's homosexuality, extensive archival research and an interview he conducted with the director himself.[1] For Turk, Carné's films enact his attempt to return to the moment of pre-Oedipal bliss that he experienced with his mother, before she died of pneumonia when he was five years old. He argues that this childhood trauma and sudden banishment from the 'paradise' his early years signified was responsible for Carné's subsequent feelings of loneliness, marginalisation, and alienation, which are explored as key themes in his cinema. An important part of this is his 'masochistic aesthetic', a concept borrowed from Gaylyn Studlar (1988), centring upon the intensification of these painful emotions. This is channelled through, for example, the use of 'primal scenes' – recurring scenes in which a character witnesses intimacy between somebody they love and another person, which heightens his or her sense of loneliness and rejection. Beyond such psycho-aesthetic concerns, Turk also advances comprehensive discussion of the politics of Carné's cinema in relation to important moments, such as the Popular Front and, importantly, the Occupation. In addition, the book makes key arguments about

---

1 This interview can be listened to on the website Marcel-Carné.com. http://www.marcel-carne.com/.

Carné's representations of gender, arguing that his work is characterised by continuing efforts to undermine and disrupt conventional patriarchal attitudes, particularly through his use of androgyny. Such elements are an index of Carné's homosexuality and represent his attempts to challenge patriarchy's oppressive gender norms.

Since the publication of Turk's book, Carné has become the subject of increased academic attention, which is particularly focused on his poetic realism and the films he made during the Occupation. While this work is varied in its agenda, and as such these pieces will be dealt with in their specificity in the chapters that follow, in the more recent work there is a strong tendency, in keeping with the turn to history in Film Studies, to position his work within broader contexts – an approach at odds with the *politique des auteurs*, which conceptualised the auteur as *transcending* history. Typifying this approach is Dudley Andrew's *Mists of Regret* (1995), which analyses Carné's work in relation to a range of contextual issues as part of a broader discussion of poetic realism. Carné's work with Prévert also receives detailed consideration in a 2001 special issue of *CinémAction*. Moreover, and very importantly for this volume, recent work has further challenged previous conceptions of Carné by moving beyond the established canon. For example, Ginette Vincendeau in 'Paradise regained' (1997) argues for the importance of Carné's postwar work, critically neglected since the *Cahiers* critics made their vitriolic attacks against it. In addition to the fact that many of these films were extremely popular with contemporary audiences, they provide fascinating insight into how France was changing in the 1950s. Other recent examples of work on the postwar cinema include articles on *L'Air de Paris* (1954) by Dyer (2000) and Dhoest (2003), which explore its homosexual content. Since 2005 there has also been an excellent website called Marcel-Carné.com, which contains a huge amount of information on the director's work, including copies of many rare archival documents. Nevertheless, Carné is still a surprisingly under-investigated director; there is thus much to be gained from a re-examination of his work, in particular his neglected postwar work.

Aims and approach

A central concern throughout this book will be to examine how Carné's recurring themes (loneliness, alienation, marginalisation, transcendence) are expressed through his distinctive style. Examining these elements throughout his career will shed light on how his work related to the changing cinematic context and on whether he was as reliant on collaborators, such as Prévert, as critics have claimed.

I will also consider Carné's films within the broader social and political context. One key area will be his political agenda, as well as how this position evolved and how it is explored in his work. At the same time, I will be attentive to how Carné's films are not necessarily coherent political 'statements' emanating from the director, who as we shall see frequently avoided direct political engagement, but instead contain a range of complex and sometimes contradictory representations and ideologies, which in part stem from the conflicted periods in which he worked. A final concern here will be Carné's treatment of gender, considering the extent to which such representations relate to his sexuality as a gay man, are the influence of his collaborators, such as Prévert, or are symptomatic of broader changes in French society.

My concern in this book is also to reinvestigate Carné's highly contested position within French film history, and in particular how his films relate to major moments of French cinema such as poetic realism, the tradition of quality and the French new wave – here I will explore, in particular, what was at stake in the bitterly antagonistic attitude of the new wave critics towards him. The book also re-examines how Carné fitted into both popular and artistic French cinematic traditions, and his identity as a 'populist filmmaker', an area that has not received sufficient analysis. Important sources here have been his reception in the popular film press, and his use of genre and of many of the period's biggest stars. Finally, by redressing the neglect of Carné's postwar work, I highlight its value in bringing about greater understanding of Carné's cinema *per se*, but also its relationship with broader social, political and cinematic contexts. Nevertheless, before doing this, I need to start with his most canonical period, that of his great poetic realist films.

References

Abel, R. (1988), *French Film Theory and Criticism, 1907–1939, Vol. II 1929–1939*, Princeton, NJ; Guildford, Princeton University Press.

Andrew, D. (1983), 'Poetic realism', in M. L. Bandy, ed., *Rediscovering French Film*, New York, Museum of Modern Art, pp. 114–19.

Andrew, D. (1995), *Mists of Regret: Culture and Sensibility in Classic French Film*, Princeton; Chichester, Princeton University Press.

Bandy, M. L., ed. (1983), *Rediscovering French Film*, New York, Museum of Modern Art.

Bazin, A. (1983), 'The disincarnation of Carné', in M. L. Bandy, ed., *Rediscovering French Film*, New York, Museum of Modern Art, pp. 131–5.

Carné, M. (1996), *Ma vie à belles dents*, Paris, L'Archipel.

Dhoest, A. (2003), 'How queer is *L'Air de Paris*? – Marcel Carné and queer authorship', *Scope: An Online Journal of Film and TV Studies*, May, online at www.scope.nottingham.ac.uk/article.php?issue=may2003&id=258§ion=article&q=dhoest (25 October 2010).

Dyer, R. (2000), 'No place for homosexuality: Marcel Carné's *L'Air de Paris*', in S. Hayward and G. Vincendeau, eds, *French Film: Texts and Contexts*, 2nd edn, London, Routledge, pp. 127–41.

Forbes, J. (1993), 'Surreal eye in the city', *The Guardian*, 20 August, pp. 8–9.

Landry, B.-G. (1952), *Marcel Carné: sa vie, ses films*, Paris, Éditions Jacques Vautrain.

Nepoti, R. (1979), *Marcel Carné*, Firenze, La Nuova Italia.

Quéval, J. (1950), *Marcel Carné*, London, British Film Institute.

Quéval, J. (1952), *Marcel Carné*, Paris, Les Éditions du Cerf.

Sadoul, G. (1953), *French Film*, London, The Falcon Press.

Studlar, G. (1988), *In the Realm of Pleasure: Von Sternberg, Dietrich, and the Masochistic Aesthetic*, Urbana, University of Illinois Press.

Turk, E. B. (1989), *Child of Paradise: Marcel Carné and the Golden Age of French Cinema*, Cambridge, Mass.; London, Harvard University Press.

Various (1972), 'Revoir Marcel Carné', *Les Cahiers de la Cinémathèque*, 5.

Vincendeau, G. (1997), 'Paradise regained', *Sight and Sound*, 7:7, pp. 12–16.

2

Poetic realism

The period from the late 1920s to the end of the 1930s was crucial in Marcel Carné's career: he entered the French film industry, made films now considered his masterpieces, and achieved significant box-office success. In discussing these accomplishments, I will consider the main developments in his career, from his early work as a journalist, amateur filmmaker, and assistant director, to his production of his first feature films, *Jenny* (1936) and *Drôle de drame* (1937), and will finish with his contributions to poetic realism at the end of the decade, *Le Quai des brumes*, *Hôtel du Nord*, and *Le Jour se lève*.

The seemingly contradictory term 'poetic realism' describes a popular and critically respected film movement that emerged in France in the 1930s, which centred on pessimistic, fatalistic stories about working-class characters and places. With a stylised use of film language, especially through the *mise en scène* and lighting, these films infused depictions of quotidian milieu with a lyrical quality, 'poetry arising precisely from the everyday', as Vincendeau (2004: 148) puts it. This loosely defined group of films, which was identified by critics and not announced by a manifesto, emerged from a range of cultural developments, including nineteenth century realist literature, crime fiction, avant-garde cinema of the 1920s, and 1930s populist culture (music, photography, novels), as well as, for some writers, the broader social developments of the time, such as the fall of the Popular Front and the approaching war – though, as we shall see, this issue is complex. A number of the decade's most prestigious figures contributed to the movement, such as Jean Renoir, Julien Duvivier, Jacques Feyder and, of course, Marcel Carné (not to mention key stars, scriptwriters, cinematographers, set designers, and composers). Significantly for this book,

Carné's work is absolutely central to the movement, as Vincendeau (2004: 148) explains: 'The supreme examples [of poetic realism] are the films of Marcel Carné and Jacques Prévert – *Quai des brumes* (1938) and *Le Jour se lève* (1939)'. While later critics, such as those working for the *Cahiers du Cinéma*, would have harsh opinions about Carné's postwar work, his poetic realism has remained ensconced within the canon of French film. Throughout this chapter I will be concerned with charting the main developments that led towards the production of these films, and with explaining what was specific to Carné's own particular inflection of poetic realist cinema.

Carné's early career

Unlike many of the other top French directors of the decade, such as Jean Renoir, Jacques Feyder, and René Clair, Marcel Carné came from humble origins. He was born in Paris on 18 August 1906 and lived in a working-class area near the Square des Batignolles, in the seventeenth arrondissement. His mother died when he was young and he was brought up by his father, a cabinet maker, and, later, by his aunt and grandmother. While his father wanted Carné to follow him into a career as a craftsman, Carné had other ideas. From a young age he had been interested in film and his autobiography discusses his early attempts to recreate moving images with a magic lantern he owned. He attended many films and other forms of popular entertainment, such as cabaret shows – his love of these would be evident in films that he would go on to make, a number of which starred former music-hall performers.

However, despite Carné's desire for a career in cinema, his modest background meant that breaking into such a line of work would be extremely difficult. By contrast, Jean Renoir was wealthy: he sold canvases painted by his father, the French Impressionist Pierre-Auguste Renoir, enabling him to self-fund his early projects. Nevertheless, in the early years of the 1930s, Carné managed to work in the film industry, in a range of capacities, developing his ideas about film, and learning the skills that would one day enable him to make his own feature films. Between 1929 and 1935 he worked as a journalist, made a short documentary called *Nogent, Eldorado du dimanche* (1929), and assisted the directors René Clair and Jacques

Feyder. Consideration of these formative years not only sheds light on the activities he undertook before his career as a director, it also gives us our first insight into the development of key aspects of his filmmaking identity, particularly his working methods, his ideas on style and his thematic concerns.

Before his filmmaking career began, Carné spent a number of years as a successful journalist, writing for *Cinémagazine* and *Vu*, and working as assistant editor on a trade magazine called *Hebdofilms*. This came about when he entered a film review competition organised by *Cinémagazine* with a piece on René Clair's *Les Deux timides* (1928). Not only did he win the competition, he was also hired as a permanent film reviewer, a job he kept until 1933. Carné's articles give insight into his ideas about film aesthetics and the direction cinema should take. Most obviously, his writing reveals his main filmmaking influences, which include Fritz Lang, F. W. Murnau, Joseph Von Sternberg, Carl Theodor Dreyer, and Jacques Feyder, as well as French directors, such as Abel Gance, Jean Grémillon, and René Clair. In a variety of ways, each of these figures influenced the development of Carné's cinema, particularly, as we shall see, his poetic realism.

In the early 1930s a key issue concerned the coming of sound. On the one hand, this innovation brought about the development of filmed theatre. These cheaply produced films were very popular with audiences, in large part owing to the centrality of dialogue and use of established stage performers whose vocal skills were showcased. For some filmmakers, such as Marcel Pagnol, and, later, Sacha Guitry, both of whom started their careers writing and directing plays, this was a positive development in cinema, which capitalised on the spoken word and enabled a larger number of people to enjoy their theatrical entertainment. However, others, most notably René Clair, were strongly opposed to this point of view, believing that the cinema should remain 'visual at all costs' (Clair, 1988: 39). While Clair's and Pagnol's contributions to this debate, which they published in articles, are most well known, other writers, including Carné, also got involved. For instance, in 'La caméra, personnage du drame' ('The camera, a character in the drama') (Carné, 1929), Carné articulated his desire for cinema to retain its inventiveness and medium specificity, arguing for the expressive possibilities of the mobile frame and criticising the restricted approach of filmed theatre: 'Pour la réalisation des talkies, la caméra est retenue prisonnière dans une cabine dépourvue de résonance' ('To make talkies, the camera is kept prisoner in a sound-proof cabin') (Carné, 1929). While Clair was an important creator of 'cinematic' films in the early 1930s, Carné would become one of the directors who towards the end of the decade was famed for exploring the possibilities of the cinematic medium.

Carné's opposition to filmed theatre also had a political dimension, particularly through his strong populist stance, evident in one of his most famous pieces, 'Quand le cinéma descendra-t-il dans la rue?' ('When will the cinema go down into the street?') (Carné, 1988). In 1930s French cinema there was an increased interest in populist themes and imagery, with films focusing on working-class milieux and characters. Such developments were part of a broader populist culture of the period, evident through the songs of realist singers, the literature of writers like Pierre Mac Orlan and Eugène Dabit, and the photography of Brassaï and André Kertész. In his article Carné highlights and criticises filmed theatre's emphasis on high society (most famously articulated in the work of Sacha Guitry), arguing instead for a cinema centring on the lives of ordinary people. In one well-known passage he states:

> Populism, you say. And after that? Neither the word nor the thing itself frightens us. To describe the simple life of humble people, to depict the atmosphere of hard-working humanity which is theirs, isn't that better than reconstructing the murky and inflated ambience of night clubs, dancing couples, and a nonexistent nobility, which the cinema has kept on doing as long as they've been so abundantly profitable? (Carné, 1988: 129)

While the populist culture in France in the 1930s brought working-class themes to the fore, its politics was diverse. At one extreme was a voyeuristic interest in the criminality that took place in the 'lower depths', at the other an attempt to celebrate working-class life, though even this had little interest in challenging the inequalities in society. While the above passage shows Carné's sympathy for ordinary people, a closer consideration of the article reveals important aspects of his political viewpoint. It begins with him stating:

> First, set your minds at ease. There's nothing revolutionary in this title, it simply represents the increasingly anxious questioning of someone who is irritated at seeing the current cinema turn its back on life and lock itself in an airtight chamber, the better to admire sets and artifice. (Carné, 1988: 127)

Here, then, we can see that, while Carné is interested in representing the lives of ordinary people, his motivation is more aesthetic than political. This is related to his interest in urban milieux, especially Paris, a preoccupation that would continue throughout his filmmaking career, and, in particular, the realism and authenticity that such spaces bring to films, something he considers to be absent from the 'façades' created in filmed theatre, which would tend to focus on bourgeois life (Pagnol's films are a notable exception). For Carné, the authenticity of the streets stemmed from their 'atmosphere' – he stresses the city's 'picturesque' and, though he doesn't use the word, 'poetic' qualities. Through this he expresses a yearning for some form of authentic, transcendent experience, a yearning that would be present throughout his career: as we shall see, the search for transcendence is one of Carné's key themes. Because of his interest in 'atmosphere', Carné advocates – and some may consider this surprising in the context of an article about 'going down into the streets' – the use of studio filming, which would give greater control to the director. As Carné explains: 'René Clair's Paris, which is so true to life, so accurate, stirring, and sensitive, in reality is a Paris of wood and stucco reconstructed at Epinay. Yet so great is René Clair's talent, so subtle are his gifts of observation, that, in a fake milieu and with characters miraculously seized from life, he can give us an interpretation of life which is more real than life itself' (Carné, 1988: 128). This, then, highlights what would become fundamental aspects of Carné's filmmaking identity. While being opposed to filmed theatre, preferring populist films focusing on urban milieux, Carné's interest was more aesthetic than revolutionary, with him seeing such spaces as indexes of authenticity and sites of atmosphere.

Nogent, Eldorado du dimanche

Carné became increasingly interested in the idea of making films, rather than writing about them. Even before producing his first feature film, he had made progress in this direction, making, along with Jean Aurenche and Paul Grimault, a number of early advertisement designed to be shown before films, as well as, more significantly, a short silent film entitled *Nogent, Eldorado du dimanche*.[1] The project

---

1 For years many considered the film to have been lost, though, as Turk (1989: 28) highlights, some copies were in circulation. When *L'Avant-Scène Cinéma* found out that Carné had his own copy, the journal decided with his permission to distribute it.

became possible when Carné, who had been studying filmmaking at night school, bought a small 16mm film camera and some film stock, with the financial help of a friend, Michel Sanvoisin (who is listed as one of the film's collaborators).

Although *Nogent, Eldorado du dimanche* was made three years before Carné articulated his views on populism in his writing, they are already in evidence, as are stylistic qualities that would define his later work. Lasting seventeen minutes, the film is a documentary about Parisian workers spending their Sunday – their only day off – in a suburb called Nogent. Aside from the opening shots of deserted Parisian streets, the film is not concerned with an urban milieu, focusing instead on the still semi-rural Nogent, a paradisiacal setting, as the film's title indicates, consisting of a river, meadows, cafés, and a communal dance hall. Nevertheless, Carné's concern for celebrating the lives of ordinary people is very much in evidence, particularly from the fact that they are shown to exist so harmoniously within such an idealised setting. The location has powerful precedents, and antecedents, in French culture, through the work of French Impressionist painters, such as Pierre-Auguste Renoir, whose *Le Déjeuner des canotiers* ('Luncheon of the boating party') focuses on a similar idyll, and it would resurface later in a number of significant films, such as Julien Duvivier's *La Belle Équipe* (1936), about five friends who build a riverside café. However, in Carné's cinema emphasis on such a setting is atypical. While the notion of 'paradise' would continue to be important in his work, as discussed at length by Turk (1989), who sees its invocation as a central Carné theme, his films become, for the majority of his career, more pessimistic. Although escape from the city would be a recurring subject in his films, it would be positioned as a distant dream his characters struggle, but ultimately fail, to realise.

Carné presents a highly romanticised vision of his working-class characters. In part this stems from the numerous instances of actual romance that the film depicts, with images of lovers lying together in a meadow and a couple of men 'chatting up' two women whom they meet. Such romanticism also comes from Carné's emphasis on the vitality and authenticity of these ordinary people. The beginning of the film crosscuts between static shots of deserted Parisian streets and a rapidly moving train, transporting people to Nogent, associating the masses with energy, and articulating the joy and freedom of their escape. Vitality is also conveyed through the depictions of people engaging in boating, going on funfair rides and dancing. The shots of young men diving into the river are also particularly striking. Shot from a range of angles, and edited in a way that dwells on their bodies in moments of flight, the emphasis is upon displaying their physiques. While the images share similarities with the famous diving board scene from Leni Riefenstahl's Nazi propaganda film, *Olympia* (1938), Carné's emphasis on such physical perfection is part of his celebration of the working classes. In addition, the depictions of male physiques here and elsewhere are early instances of Carné's destabilisation of conventional notions of gender, positioning men as objects of the gaze, making such images an early filmic index of his sexuality. While the working-class men are celebrated for their virility, the film provides a vision of pure and innocent femininity, especially through the shots of a young woman collecting flowers in a field. Throughout Carné's cinema, particularly in his films of the 1930s, we will see similar depictions of innocent ingénues. The working class, then, are presented as lively and authentic, engaging with passion in simple pleasures, as opposed to the expensive leisure activities of the bourgeoisie.

In terms of film style, compared to Carné's later films, *Nogent, Eldorado du dimanche* can seem unusual. For one thing, he would make only one more documentary, and that was his final film *La Bible* (1977), which he reluctantly made when he could no longer find the finances to make another feature film. Whereas his later work would in large part be distinctive because of his precision and control over the finished product, *Nogent, Eldorado du dimanche*, is, as would be expected from a self-financed amateur production, much rougher around the edges. For instance, the fact that the camera could take only six seconds of film at a time meant that the film does not possess some of the longer takes found in Carné's later work. In addition, Carné tries out a number of innovative formal techniques, such as underwater shots of fish swimming, point of view shots from a helter-skelter, and the aforementioned images of men diving. Such features reveal a first-time director keen to experiment with the medium, while also, more significantly, highlighting his desire to create a type of film in which the director exerts a significant amount of control over the film's formal properties. The final image of the film, a low-angle shot of a blind accordionist, underlines this sense of Carné's tight formal control. The smile on his face and his powerful position within the frame emphasises the overt formalism of the piece and that somebody – Marcel Carné – is in control of the reality that has unfolded. Combined with the film's populism, this overt formalism marks it out as a precursor to poetic realism, which would adopt a highly stylised view of working-class milieux.

Carné's apprenticeship

If Carné's interest in formal control is evident in *Nogent, Eldorado du dimanche*, and made explicit in his advocacy of studio filming in his writing, it would have been a dominant issue in his work as an assistant for René Clair and Jacques Feyder, with both directors adopting this approach in their filmmaking. Carné's work as an assistant overlapped with his journalism and filming of *Nogent, Eldorado du dimanche*, but of the three activities it is the one that brings us most up to the present – his final work in this role was in 1935, just before his feature film debut with *Jenny*. He secured his first job as an assistant when he was invited to a meal at a friend's house, which was also attended by Françoise Rosay, a major star of French cinema, and wife of Jacques Feyder. At this meal Carné impressed Rosay with his opinions on film and she suggested that he meet her husband. This led to him assisting on *Les Nouveaux Messieurs* (Jacques Feyder, 1929), followed by work on *Cagliostro* (1929) directed by Richard Oswald and *Sous les toits de Paris* (1930) by René Clair, which came about because of Clair's admiration for *Nogent, Eldorado du dimanche*. He then worked as assistant on three more Feyder films, *Le Grand Jeu* (1934), *Pension mimosas* (1935), and *La Kermesse héroïque* (1935). This period was important for Carné because it enabled him to learn from two of the top directors of the 1930s. Unsurprisingly there are striking connections between their films and Carné's, in terms of both style and subject matter.

As we have already seen, from Carné's article 'Quand le cinéma descendra-t-il dans la rue?', Clair's films contain a strong populist dimension, with *Sous les toits de Paris* centring on working-class characters and spaces – his later films *A Nous la liberté* (1931), *Le Million* (1931), and *Quatorze juillet* (1933) would also be concerned with the lives of the ordinary people of Paris. Feyder, too, made a number of films centring upon such milieux, such as in *Crainquebille* (1923) and *Pension mimosas*, and it is clear that taken together these films would have had a significant impact on the development of Carné's ideas about populism.

Clair's and Feyder's influence is also important as they are both credited as the figures who did the most (along with Jean Vigo and a few others) to challenge the filmed theatre aesthetic. For instance, while filmed theatre tended to utilise static shots of sets, taken from the position of the theatrical fourth wall, Clair's *Sous les toits de Paris* begins with a long mobile shot, moving from a Parisian rooftop down into the streets, where a street singer (Albert Préjean) entertains a group of onlookers. Carné's article on the mobile frame highlights his interest in such virtuoso movements, and, as we will see, it was a technique that he would draw upon when he came to make his own feature films. Feyder's and Clair's work was crucial to the development of poetic realism because of their combination of populist themes and iconography with an overtly formalistic aesthetic. While Clair's films present an idealised, poeticised reality, they are too light-hearted to be considered as belonging to the poetic realist canon. Feyder, on the other hand, produced work that contained the essential pessimism and fatalism that critics have seen as being at the core of poetic realism. This is especially the case with *Le Grand Jeu*, which Carné worked on, a film about a man who flees heartbreak in Paris by joining the Foreign Legion. We can see, then, that Carné's apprenticeship gave him exposure to techniques and ideas that he would adopt and develop as the decade progressed.

Through his journalism, his production of a short film, and his work as an assistant for Clair and Feyder, aspects of Carné's filmmaking identity were thus beginning to emerge. In particular, we can see a keen interest in populist cinema, especially the creation of atmosphere, coupled with the desire for transcendence to a world above the façades of daily life. In addition, *Nogent, Eldorado du dimanche*, with its objectification of male bodies, provides an early example of Carné's unconventional approach to representing masculinity. While his populist celebration of the masses indicates left-wing sympathies, his early work hints at a tendency to prioritise aesthetics. These are productive areas to investigate further as we turn to consider his first feature films.

An emerging talent

The Popular Front formed in the mid-1930s in response to a growing threat of fascism in France. This danger had become evident on 6 February 1934 when various anti-parliamentary, far-right groups held a demonstration in the Place de la Concorde, which culminated in a bloody riot. The Popular Front, a coalition between the three main left-wing parties of the time, the Socialists, the Radical Socialists and the French Communist Party, went on to win the parliamentary elections of 1936. In addition to its united stance against fascism, it aimed to bring about better conditions for the nation's workers, and would result in key legislation including the introduction of paid holidays and the forty-hour working week. While the coalition only lasted a little over a year, it also had a profound cultural impact, bringing a wave of optimism to the lives of ordinary people in France.

The cinema of this period has been closely examined by film scholars. It has been explored through consideration of the avant-garde political cinema, or *cinéma engagé*, produced at this time (Buchsbaum, 1988) and in relation to the key film stars of the moment, such as Jean Gabin (Vincendeau, 1985) and Danielle Darrieux (Driskell, 2009). However, one of the main ways it has been discussed is through an examination of the political films of Jean Renoir (O'Shaughnessy, 2000), particularly *Le Crime de Monsieur Lange* (1936), *La Vie est à nous* (1936), and *La Marseillaise* (1938). Although his output at this time is less overtly political, Carné, who held strong left-wing beliefs, though he never joined the Communist Party, is also an interesting figure to consider in relation to these events. For one thing, he was directly involved when he was accidentally caught up in the riot on 6 February 1934, while walking home from the studio after a day working as Feyder's assistant. More significantly, at the instruction of the French Communist Party he filmed footage of a Popular Front event on Bastille Day in 1935, which was used in *La Vie est à nous*, a collective film supervised by Jean Renoir. Before the job was given to Renoir, it was offered to Carné, but because he had just signed a deal to make *Jenny* he was unable to commit himself. In his autobiography, Carné expresses annoyance that the French Communist Party didn't allow him to produce the film once he had completed *Jenny* and that he was not credited for the Bastille Day footage: 'ni Renoir ni le Comité central ne virent la nécessité d'indiquer le nom de celui qui les avait tournés' (Carné, 1996: 68).[2] Such annoyance relates to Carné's antagonistic attitude to Renoir, who he felt, as a member of the bourgeoisie, was less well qualified for the task – the two would be rivals for the immediate future. While Carné didn't have much involvement with *La Vie est à nous*, both *Jenny* and *Drôle de drame* have interesting connections with the political moment. A consideration of these films also introduces us to Carné's approach to film production and to his distinctive aesthetic.

Jenny

Carné's feature debut was made possible by his friendship with Françoise Rosay, who agreed to star in his first film, thus making it appealing to potential investors. It also included Albert Préjean, a big star of the period, with whom Carné had worked on *Sous les toits de Paris*. The other main performers, Charles Vanel, Lisette Lanvin, Jean-Louis Barrault, and Robert Le Vigan, were all significant figures in the decade's cinema, particularly Barrault who would later have the starring role in Carné's classic, *Les Enfants du paradis*. It was also at this time that Carné began to form his highly talented *équipe* (team). Whereas *Nogent, Eldorado du dimanche* had been made with just a few people, Carné was used to working, after his work with Feyder and Clair, with large crews that included some of the most talented technicians in the industry. Two members who joined Carné at this time were the composer Joseph Kosma and the cinematographer Roger Hubert. However, the most important individual to mention here is the scriptwriter Jacques Prévert. Before working in the cinema, Prévert had worked as a poet, had been involved in the Surrealist movement, before falling out with its leader André Breton, and, along with his brother Pierre and a number of other writers and performers, formed the radical theatre troupe the Groupe Octobre. Their experimental works, which were often very quickly written, rehearsed and performed, were aimed at a popular audience of workers and explored left-wing agendas. His first move towards the cinema was also with the Groupe Octobre, a thirty-five-minute anarchic comedy directed by his brother called *L'Affaire est dans le sac* (1932). His political credentials were stressed further when he wrote the script for Jean Renoir's *Le*

---

2 'neither Renoir nor the central committee saw the necessity to indicate the name of the person who had shot it'.

Crime de Monsieur Lange, a film that also included in its cast members of the Groupe Octobre.

For his first feature film Carné was asked to adapt a novel by Pierre Rocher called *Prison de velours*. He considered this source material to be of limited artistic value, so he approached Prévert, whom he believed would be able to rescue the project. After reading the novel Prévert shared Carné's assessment, but agreed to work on it. The story centres on Jenny (Rosay), a middle-aged woman who owns a bar/brothel in the sixteenth arrondissement of Paris called 'Chez Jenny'. She also has both a partner, Benoît (Vanel), and a lover, Lucien (Préjean). Her life is disrupted when her daughter Danielle (Lanvin), who had been living in London as a concert pianist, returns to live with her. Although Jenny tries to keep her secret life hidden, Danielle one day visits Chez Jenny, where she sees her mother drinking champagne, surrounded by men. While she is there, one of the establishment's seedy regulars, L'Albinos (Robert Le Vigan), makes advances towards her, but she is rescued by Lucien. This starts a romance between the two, though neither is aware of the other's relationship with Jenny. However, Jenny finds out, and in the end, in order to protect her daughter, must allow them to leave Paris to start a new life without revealing the truth. The film finishes with Jenny alone and defeated, having lost both her daughter and her lover.

As Carné's debut feature, it was his first opportunity to put forth his cinematic vision. In doing so he followed the trajectory established in his earlier work, pursuing a highly 'cinematic' approach to the medium. Indeed, Lucien Wahl (1936: 6) wrote in his review of the film: 'Ce drame où l'on parle est un film ci-né-ma-to-gra-phique' ('The drama that I'm talking about is a ci-ne-ma-to-gra-phic film'). This is evident from the film's first shot, a long virtuoso camera movement, following Danielle along a London street as her boyfriend breaks up with her. As we have seen from his article 'La caméra, personnage du drame', Carné was a big fan of this type of shot. In addition, by 'going down into the street', this opening also highlights the film's realism, another aspect of its distinctive style. This was complimented at the time by Georges Sadoul, who commented upon how the film's 'talent, craft, and dialogue have been placed in the service of an uncompromising *realism*' (Sadoul, 1988: 220).

Fundamental to this is the continuation of Carné's interest in populist cinema. This is evident from the centrality of Lucien, played by Préjean, a star whose persona revolved around working-class roles. That Carné and Prévert wanted Lucien to possess this identity is even clearer from the fact that Jean Gabin, who had a strong working-class persona, was initially sought for the role, though he was unavailable because he was filming Duvivier's *La Belle Équipe* (Carné, 1996: 85). Sadoul (1988: 220) also points out that an important aspect of the film's realism is the dialogue written by Prévert, which was complimented by other writers for its naturalness and absence of theatricality: 'Le dialogue est important ... nous sommes donc loin du théâtre' ('The dialogue is important ... we are therefore far from the theatre') (Wahl, 1936: 6). As with Carné's early work, the film's populism is particularly evident from its use of ordinary working-class milieux with scenes taking place in Montmartre as well as in an industrial area next to a river. Here Lucien and Danielle talk to each other following his rescue of her from Chez Jenny. With the sun shining on the water, and a contrast between the early morning mist and the solid buildings and factories, the industrial setting possesses the 'atmosphere' that interested Carné. In addition, as Sadoul's comments above indicate, the film is consistent with Carné's approach to realism, particularly because of its emphasis on 'craft'. However, while *Jenny* is carefully put together, it should be noted that Carné would exhibit even greater formal control in subsequent productions, especially through the use of elaborate sets. All in all, though, *Jenny*'s populist imagery and atmosphere mark it out as an important precursor to Carné's poetic realism.

A third important aspect of the film's aesthetics is the use of melodrama, a key aspect of Carné's cinematic identity, which stems from the film's exploration of the relationship between a mother and her daughter, as well as the pathos that comes from the ensuing love triangle and the mother's ultimate self-sacrifice. This aspect of the film was viewed negatively by some critics of the period, such as Georges Sadoul, who wrote:

> Some have reproached *Jenny* for its subject. And undoubtedly they're not wrong. An aging woman who is holding on to her last lover and whom fate has given her own daughter as a rival is a typical subject of tragedy that threatens to turn into melodrama, if only the heroines were transported into the milieu of pimps and barkeeps on Montmartre. Yet no one, despite a certain family resemblance in subject and milieu, would dream of comparing *Jenny* to *Rigolboche*, a pitiful balloon inflated for an old hag like Mistinguett. (Sadoul, 1988, 219)

Such attitudes are part of a general bias against melodrama because of the way these films place emphasis on female subject matter. Indeed, the profound misogyny of Sadoul's viewpoint is evident from his comments on *Jenny* and, to an even greater degree, *Rigolboche* (Christian-Jaque, 1936). However, Vincendeau argues that the critically revered movement, poetic realism, is in actual fact a highly melodramatic form, with its emphases on 'fate, coincidence, circularity, and nostalgia' (Vincendeau, 1989: 52), something that goes unacknowledged by critics like Sadoul. This is a crucial issue: Carné's poetic realist films, which I will discuss shortly, all contain strong melodramatic elements, which, moreover, accounts to a significant degree for the huge popularity of his work at this time.

The film's subject matter and aesthetics bring the working class to the fore in the cinema at a time when the Popular Front was seeking to do the same thing in politics. While *Jenny* does not deal overtly with these events, and is described by Andrew (1995: 219) as 'a shamelessly commercial production', it contains clear left-wing ideas. This was identified by the fascist film critic Lucien Rebatet, writing under his pen name, François Vinneuil (cited in Turk, 1989: 69): 'I believe Monsieur Carné is "on the left", at least for the moment. *Jenny* thus confirms all our suspicions about the depressing influence of Socialist ideology on artists, even when they pretend to make apolitical works.' The film's politics are most immediately evident through its articulation of a number of anti-bourgeois sentiments. For instance, Chez Jenny, a place of decadence and debauchery, is situated in the affluent sixteenth arrondissement and is frequented by lecherous, seedy characters, like L'Albinos, who, as Turk highlights, was based on 'the international armaments contractor Sir Basil Zaharoff (1850–1936)', and who 'reduces to cash transactions all that is most precious to Prévert: love, beauty, and women' (Turk, 1989: 59). While Carné was opposed to filmed theatre, with its use of stifling and artificial interiors, he uses these elements in *Jenny* for its melodramatic scenes and to present the bourgeoisie as inauthentic. This aspect of the film is in opposition to its populist narrative, which centres on the sincerity of the working-class Lucien and the young, innocent Danielle. An important scene in this respect occurs when the couple go into the countryside together, where they run amongst trees, laughing and kissing. This conflates their romance with nature, beauty, and, importantly, youth, with Lucien's affections having shifted from Jenny to her daughter Danielle. This emphasis on youth was also discussed in the press at the time, in part in relation to the film, in part owing to the youthful team who had created it: 'Atmosphère de jeunesse. Le scénariste, les dialoguistes, le metteur en scène, le directeur technique, l'administrateur du film, tous des moins de trente ans!' (Doringe, 1936: 5).[3] The film's idealised celebration of young romantic love stems from various factors. To some extent we can see the influence of Prévert, whose poetry explored these themes. This made him a productive partner for Carné who, in *Nogent, Eldorado du dimanche*, as we saw, represented the freedom and romance of working-class characters entering a paradisiacal environment. The scene in the countryside also relates to key ideas from Popular Front culture, which celebrated nature and leisure – brought about by the newly won holidays and the reduction in the working week – and youth. This latter point is illustrated by Jean-Paul Le Chanois's statement: 'In 1936 we were 20. But in 1936 everyone was 20' (Le Chanois cited in Jackson, 1988: 113). The scene represents, then, a convergence between the thematic concerns of the film's authors and dominant ideas in the broader culture of Popular Front France.

While the Popular Front stood united against fascism and sought to improve the conditions of the nation's workers, it was far less concerned with addressing the unequal position held by women in French society at the time. For instance, women still did not have the vote, a situation that was unchanged by the Popular Front government. At the same time, the Prime Minister Léon Blum made some steps towards creating female equality by including in the government for the first time in the nation's history three female undersecretaries, Cécile Brunschvicg, Irène Joliot-Curie, and Suzanne Lacorre. Women also became involved in the Popular Front in huge numbers, with many joining the street protests and strikes. Nevertheless, the period was ideologically conflicted, representing a clash between the continuation of conservative values and the emergence of more emancipated forms of femininity. Such tensions are evident in *Jenny*, a film that presents a fascinating insight into notions of gender at this time. To some extent, Danielle is typical of the increased visibility of the period's modern woman – an up-to-date and more liberated form of womanhood. With her youthful beauty and tall, slim

---

3 'Atmosphere of youth. The scriptwriter, the dialogist, the director, the technical director, the film's administrator, are all under thirty years old!'

physique, she possesses the characteristic appearance of the modern woman, and at the beginning of the film lives an independent life in London. However, her modernity is undercut by her weak and passive qualities, evident when her visit to Chez Jenny ends with Préjean having to rescue her. This develops into a narrative that in certain respects conforms to one of the dominant trends of the period. As Vincendeau (1988), and Burch and Sellier (1996), have argued, 1930s French cinema consistently presents romantic narratives involving mature men and young women, creating quasi-incestuous relationships between a symbolic father and daughter. This is evident from *Jenny* in which Préjean, who at the beginning of the film, as Jenny's lover, could easily be a stepfather for Danielle. Such a narrative is indicative of the social realities of the time, during which such unions were advocated. It also highlights the power of the period's patriarchy, with such narratives emphasising the strength of men in contrast to the vulnerability of young women.

Where the film's representation of gender is less typical is that it places a woman, and an older woman at that, at the centre of the narrative: there were very few films at this time featuring female protagonists. In *Jenny* this produces a mixed ideological outcome. On the one hand, as Vincendeau (1989: 51) explains, a film centring on a female protagonist can deal with 'a woman's point of view' or even portray 'a woman's subjectivity and desire'. This is certainly the case with *Jenny*, which deals at length with its protagonist's dilemmas and desires, and, surprisingly for this time, represents its older female character as a sexually desiring subject, with both a partner and a lover. The progressive possibilities of this are enhanced by Rosay, a star who frequently played strong women, such as in *La Kermesse héroïque*, in which she, as the wife of the mayor of Flanders, shows much greater diplomatic skills than her weak and ineffectual husband. On the other hand, in *Jenny*, ultimately, the older woman is left alone and miserable, while the older man and the young woman live happily ever after. In the final scene, following the departure of Lucien and Danielle, Jenny's misery is conveyed by the way she sadly walks away along a bridge into the distance, just as the steam from a train below engulfs her – a 'poetic' effect that would be used again by Carné in *Le Quai des brumes*. While the film could be seen to be exposing the unfairness of this state of affairs, it is also, some might say sadistically, extracting as much pathos from the situation as possible. Jenny also takes the conservative and, as Vincendeau (1989: 54) points out, nostalgic, role of the self-sacrificial mother, who puts her daughter's happiness first at the expense of her own. Nevertheless, while the film's ideologically conflicted attitudes to femininity are symptomatic of the period's tensions, by focusing on an older female protagonist the film also presents us with an instance of Carné's unconventional approach to gender – we will see the significance of this develop in subsequent films.

Although *Jenny* contains interesting connections with the events in the broader political sphere, it does not present the overt political discourse that can be found in some films of the period, such as Renoir's *Le Crime de Monsieur Lange*. While the film is populist, it does not have any 'revolutionary intent'; Carné is more concerned with exploring his thematic and aesthetic concerns, particularly realism, authenticity, and atmosphere. By 'going down into the streets', and introducing a strong sense of pessimism and entrapment Carné took a step closer towards the aesthetic that would define his later poetic realist masterpieces. However, with its emphasis on outdoor shooting and the absence of an unrelenting fatalism, *Jenny* is still distinct from the works that would follow.

Drôle de drame

Carné's film was a box-office and critical success, and, although he was initially discussed in the press as Feyder's assistant, he was soon established as an up and coming director. Because Carné and Prévert had a positive experience working together, they teamed up again and set to work on a piece that was to be called *L'Île des enfants perdus*. This film, about a youth detention centre in Belle-Île-en-Mer in Brittany, was to star Danielle Darrieux, the top female star of the period. However, because it dealt with controversial subject matter, criticising the juvenile justice system, it was abandoned through fear of censorship. Nevertheless, it highlights a few of what were, or would become, Carné's key concerns, such as his desire to work with top stars and his exploration of the theme of youth. Moreover, although the film would have been another opportunity for an exploration of his aesthetics – according to Carole Aurouet (2005: 68) it had the 'imprint' of poetic realism – it is clear, from the fact that it was abandoned for censorship reasons, that it was also going to deal with controversial social issues. While Carné has been criticised for his films being more interested in aesthetics than politics, we shall see a number of examples of him dealing in a direct way with contemporary issues, often in a controversial way. *L'Île des enfants perdus* would have been such a film.

When this project fell through, the producer Édouard Corniglion-Molinier suggested they select a scenario from one of the novels to which he had the rights. They chose Joseph Storer Clouston's *The Lunatic at Large: His First Offence* (1912), which would become *Drôle de drame*. In making this film Carné further established his famous filmmaking *équipe*, particularly through the addition of the German cinematographer Eugen Shüfftan and celebrated set designer Alexandre Trauner. With Trauner's assistance Carné moved towards the studio filmmaking that would become central to his filmmaking. In doing so, and with the camerawork of Shüfftan, who had worked on German Expressionist films such as *Metropolis* (Fritz Lang, 1927), Carné also moved a bit closer towards his conception of poetic realism. Although the film does not fit within the canon of poetic realism strictly speaking – it is far too light-hearted – some of the exterior scenes, set in London's Limehouse area, contain the atmospheric qualities of these films; the high contrast between light and dark, and the slightly distorted sets, make these brief scenes a taste of what was to come. In addition, Carné hired Maurice Jaubert, the decade's most celebrated composer and another key contributor to the poetic realist aesthetic (see Ben McCann, 2009).

Also made during the Popular Front, *Drôle de drame* has interesting connections with the broader political context but, while developing aspects of Carné's aesthetic, it was different in many ways from *Jenny*. Although the source material was a serious police story, Carné and Prévert transformed it into a comedy. It centres on Irwin Molyneux (Michel Simon), who secretly publishes crime novels under the penname Félix Chapel in order to keep his wife, Margaret Molyneux (Françoise Rosay), in the luxury to which she is accustomed. However, he gets his stories from his maid, Eva (Nadine Vogel), who in turn is provided with the stories by the dreamy, romantic, milkman, Billy (Jean-Pierre Aumont). This somewhat bizarre equilibrium is disturbed when Irwin's cousin, the Bishop of Bedford (Louis Jouvet), who is fiercely opposed to the work of Chapel, comes to stay with him, not realising his cousin's secret identity. While he is critical of Chapel's stories on moral grounds, we see him looking at a signed photograph of a scantily clad woman he visits in a disreputable establishment, signalling his hypocrisy. The final main character is William Kramps (Jean-Louis Barrault), a murderer of butchers as a result of his love of animals, who now has his sights set on killing Félix Chapel. What follows is a complex and convoluted tale of misrecognition and mistaken identity.

This brief overview of the film's characters already hints at some of its differences from *Jenny*, particularly in terms of tone; whereas *Jenny* is a realist melodrama, *Drôle de drame* is a Surrealist comedy. To some extent, *Jenny* also contains Surrealist elements, particularly through the inclusion of a hunchback character, played by Jean-Louis Barrault. However, this is explored much more fully in *Drôle de drame*, and in this respect Prévert, as a former member of the Surrealists, appears to have exerted a higher degree of influence on the film than Carné (though it should be noted that *Nogent, Eldorado du dimanche* has Surrealist elements, as does *Juliette ou la clef des songes*; both of these were made without Prévert).

Apart from the highly improbable plot, the film's Surrealism is evident from some of the bizarre occurrences in the story, such as a brief romance between the bourgeois Margaret Molyneux and the insane Kramps, as well as a scene depicting detectives investigating the Molyneux household, believing that Margaret has been murdered: we see them playing table tennis, lounging on the sofa, and generally exuding an anarchic atmosphere. As with *Jenny*, Surrealism stems to a certain extent from the characters Prévert created. In this respect, one of the most obvious additions is Buffington (Henri Guisol – a member of the Groupe Octobre), a journalist who claims to be able to solve cases in his sleep. In between brief moments of consciousness, he spends the majority of the film sleeping on the couch at the Molyneux household, before waking at the end, and revealing that Margaret Molyneux is hiding in the closet, thus proving the validity of his working methods. Other unusual characters include William Kramps, whose love of animals but murder of butchers places him outside conventional modes of behaviour. But the film's Surrealism also comes from Carné's visual tricks: there are stop-motion animations of Irwin Molyneux's carniverous plants as they eat the food he gives them, and, when Buffington wakes from his slumber to reveal where Margaret Molyneux is hiding, he suddenly lifts into an upright position. We will see similar devices in his later films, particularly in the fantasy cinema he produced from the war onwards.

While *Drôle de drame* does not squarely belong to the poetic realist canon, Surrealism of this type has an important place in the movement's development. In *Mists of Regret*, Andrew discusses the influence on poetic realism of the European avant-garde, particularly German Expressionism, French Impressionism and Surrealism. As he argues, poetic realism's dreamy, bizarre qualities owe much to Surrealism and the Surrealists, such as Prévert, who contributed to it directly. In this respect, *Drôle de drame* is a significant work in the development of Carné's poetic realist aesthetic.

The film's aesthetics also play an important role in defining its political position, though, as with *Jenny*, Carné and Prévert did not make an overtly political film. But while *Drôle de drame* does not contain any direct references to the period's politics (it is set in London in the late 1890s), or visualise any revolutionary activity, it dramatises a tension between bourgeois repression and rigidity, and freer, more romantic attitudes, which are associated in the film mostly with the working class. As with *Jenny* the film contains anti-bourgeoisie sentiments, evident through the representation of Irwin and Margaret Molyneux. To some extent, the portrayal of Margaret as a sexually desiring character, whom Kramps falls in love with, makes her another instance of Carné challenging conventional attitudes to gender. Again he draws upon Rosay's active persona and performance style, for instance in her enactment of Margaret's power over her husband. On the other hand, she is demanding and shallow, making her an embodiment of more negative stereotypes, particularly as she is in contrast with Eva, who is young, intelligent and sensitive. Moreover, by being emotionally cold (aside from her fling with Kramps) and concerned only with money and appearances, she presents the bourgeoisie in negative terms. Similarly, the film contains anti-clerical sentiments through its corrupt and hypocritical clergyman, the Bishop of Bedford.

In contrast to these stifling qualities, represented by the bourgeoisie and clergy, there is a strong sense of characters aspiring towards freedom. The cast includes members of the Groupe Octobre, such as Henri Guisol, which hints at the film's radical dimension. Through their involvement and their liveliness and spontaneity, we get a sense of the energy and challenge to boundaries that defined the Popular Front. Also, in keeping with the Carné films already considered, the working-class characters, Billy and Eva, are a repository for positive values: creativity, romance, and authenticity. Whereas the inauthentic bourgeois characters are portrayed in theatrical styles of acting (Simon, Rosay, and Jouvet all began their careers on the stage), Aumont and Nogel act with more nuance and naturalism, which facilitates the communication of their sincerity. However, although Billy and Eva are presented as a positive vision of ordinary people, others of the working class are shown in a more negative manner. As hysteria mounts surrounding the apparent murder of Margaret Molyneux, which Irwin has been accused of, the masses are presented as capricious and gullible. They become a scary mob, besieging the Molyneux house and throwing stones through the windows. Such a representation is unusual in Carné's films, which normally celebrate the ordinary people. This highlights the limitations of viewing *Drôle de drame* as a piece of overt political cinema; instead it is, as with many Carné films, contradictory in its political outlook.

All in all, *Drôle de drame* is something of an oddity in Carné's cinema, and particularly in the 1930s when his work has primarily been discussed in relation to poetic realism. The film's fate at the box-office has been the source of debate for critics at the time and since. As Serge Veber (1937: 5) pointed out in his review for the film: 'Voici un film qui sera sans doute passionnément discuté. Certains le trouveront outrancier dans la bouffonnerie, d'autres apprécieront sa fantaisie débridée.'[4] Many have seen the film as sub-standard, as discussed by Guylène Ouvrard (2001: 59): 'L'idée que ce film, aujourd'hui considéré comme un chef d'œuvre, reçut à l'époque un accueil désastreux est communément répandue.'[5] However, by returning to the film's contemporary reception Ouvrard argues that, while it was criticised by the influential figures Henri Jeanson, François Vinneuil, and Georges Sadoul on aesthetic or political grounds, many critics were very enthusiastic about it.

Carné's early career thus shows his desire to create socially engaged cinema, while his films are politically contradictory and on the whole shy from engaging directly with the politics of the Popular Front era. It was also during this early formative period that Carné and Prévert first worked together. Through the heightened realism, injection of Surrealism, and move towards studio filmmaking of *Jenny* and *Drôle*

---

4 'Here is a film that will undoubtedly be passionately discussed. Some will find its buffoonery excessive, others will appreciate its unbridled fantasy.'

5 'The idea that this film, today considered a masterpiece, had at the time a disastrous reception is commonly spread.'

de drame, we can see a clear development towards the poetic realism that Carné's work was about to fully embrace, and to which I now turn.

A poetic realist 'trilogy'

Marcel Carné's three final films of the decade, *Le Quai des brumes*, *Hôtel du Nord*, and *Le Jour se lève*, were his most popular and critically respected works of the 1930s and, while not an official trilogy, taken together represent the blossoming and crystallisation of his version of poetic realism.

Le Quai des brumes

The first of these was based on the novel *Le Quai des brumes* (1927) by the populist writer Pierre Mac Orlan, who described his work as dealing with the 'fantastique social' (Andrew, 1995: 260), a blend of the ordinary social world and a sense of the extraordinary; we can thus already see its suitability as source material for poetic realism. Indeed, one of his other novels, *La Bandera* (1931), had already been adapted into a poetic realist film a few years earlier by Julien Duvivier. Carné proposed filming *Le Quai des brumes* to producer Raoul Ploquin and Jean Gabin, who had starred in *La Bandera* (Julien Duvivier, 1935), and both were keen to collaborate. While Mac Orlan's source novel played a central role in shaping the film, Gabin's stardom is another key intertext. At this time he was the nation's biggest star, which not only meant that he played an important role in making the film attractive to investors and audiences; he also brought a hugely popular persona to the film. Since *La Bandera* he had developed a 'mythic' identity as an ordinary, working-class male tragically pursued by fate – for Bazin he was 'Oedipus in a cloth cap'. Because *Le Quai des brumes* was a Gabin star vehicle, an exploration of his contribution to the film is an important consideration. In addition, the film contains a number of other top stars, such as Michel Simon, Pierre Brasseur, and, importantly, Michèle Morgan, who, largely on the strength of this film, would become the top female star of the late 1930s. An analysis of the role of these stars highlights their importance to the film's poetic realism as well as, more generally, the central role of stardom within Carné's films.

The story follows an army deserter called Jean (Gabin), who arrives in a dark, wet and misty Le Havre with the intention of boarding a boat and escaping to some far corner of the world. While there he becomes romantically involved with Nelly (Morgan), a young and beautiful, but melancholic woman, who spends her time trying to evade the advances of Lucien (Brasseur), a small-time gangster, and Zabel (Simon), her foster father, who, it is revealed, has killed her last boyfriend through jealousy. Jean has a series of confrontations with these men and in each case asserts his stronger masculinity, usually in a manner that humiliates his opponent – at a fairground he slaps Lucien in the face to the guffaws of onlookers. Although Jean manages to get a passport, clothing and a place on a ship leaving for Venezuela, he does not manage to escape. The film concludes with him returning onshore to see Nelly one last time. Upon arriving, he fights and kills Zabel, whom he had found trying to rape Nelly. However, as he once more makes his way to the ship he is shot in the back by Lucien. A tearful Nelly holds him as he dies.

In *Le Quai des brumes* we witness Carné's first full articulation of his poetic realist vision; while we have already seen examples of him blending realism with poetic qualities, in this film the tension between these elements is pushed to an extreme. Firstly, the film's heightened realism is created in several ways, and central amongst these is Carné's populist aesthetic, focusing on ordinary people and ordinary places. Here Gabin is particularly important, because, as Vincendeau (1985) has argued, a key aspect of his persona is his 'authenticity', which stems from his identity as, and performance of, an ordinary, working-class character. Although he had begun his career on stage he 'unlearned' this style of acting when he began working in films, using instead an understated and spontaneous type of performance and delivery of dialogue, which enhanced his image as 'authentic'. This style of acting is also shared by Michèle Morgan, who entered the cinema directly, but is in stark contrast to the performances of Simon and Brasseur, who both began their careers in the theatre. In addition, fundamental to the film's authenticity is its *mise en scène* and particularly the extremely detailed sets by Alexandre Trauner, which recreated in the studio authentic depictions of spaces found in the outside world, such as the dark, cobbled streets of Le Havre.

At the same time, such realism is balanced with a strong poetic dimension. Early images of the towering hull of a ship, the murky rain-swept streets, the thick fog, and the hazy interior of Panama's bar, create the 'atmosphere' that is central to the poetic realist aesthetic. While Carné's studio approach facilitated *Le Quai des brumes*'s realism through its concentration upon the details we find in the real world, it was also adopted to enhance the film's poetic qualities. In part this relates to the sets themselves, which are so detailed that they take on greater significance, particularly as Carné adopts a slow pace of editing, encouraging audiences to become absorbed in the milieux and sensitive to their subtle moods and tones. In part it is because the sparsely decorated sets contain objects that take on symbolic meanings, such as a ship in a bottle at Panama's, which stands for the film's central problematic: the impossibility of escape. By filming in a studio, Carné and his crew of talented technicians also attained greater control over the film's *mise en scène*. Here Eugen Shüfftan's cinematography is particularly important, with his use of complex high-contrast lighting and a range of filters enabling him to transform the spaces, while retaining their essential realism. In *Making Pictures* (Imago, 2003: 212–13) for instance, it is observed that Shüfftan's use of fog filters in the early scenes achieves a powerful effect, with the deep blacks taking on the appearance of smudged charcoal. Such noirish features, and the involvement of Shüfftan, who learned his trade in Germany in the 1920s, highlights the profound influence on Carné, and poetic realism more generally, of German Expressionism, a movement devoted to such dark depictions.

In contrast to Carné's earlier work, *Le Quai des brumes* is completely devoted to immersing its audience within a profoundly bleak view of the world. The early scenes present us with dark and lonely streets and an all-pervading fog, which comes to stand for the protagonist's negative state of mind: we learn he is haunted by his experiences of fighting and killing in the colonies and, as he explains what it is like to kill somebody to a lorry driver who has picked him up hitch-hiking, he looks into the distance, eyes wide, lost in the horror of his memories. He is also now, as an army deserter, a social outcast. Such marginalisation and the loneliness that comes with it, which would become key recurring Carné themes, is starkly visualised in the scenes that follow: on arriving in Le Havre, Jean walks through the dark empty streets, hunched over, his hands in his pockets, withdrawn within himself, and followed by a stray dog, which reflects his own predicament; he then meets Quart Vittel (Raymond Aimos), a homeless man, who takes him to Panama's, a bar frequented by outcasts and misfits and, significantly, placed on the outskirts of the town and at the water's edge. Above all, though, the film's pessimism is conveyed through its sheer claustrophobia and sense of entrapment, fundamental features of poetic realism. Here Carné's polished aesthetic enhances such confinement, placing the film in contrast to the work of a director such as Renoir, whose camera movements and improvisation generate a sense of spontaneity and a world beyond the frame. This confinement is created through Carné's controlled camerawork and classical style, and by his use of studio sets, even for many of the scenes set in exterior locations. These narrowly delimited spaces are made more constrictive through the use of shadows and fog, which consistently threaten to engulf the protagonist. For instance, as Jean stands outside Panama's, bar-like shadows are cast across him, providing a visualisation of his entrapment (a technique that would be taken up in the coming years in Hollywood's film noir).

But the film isn't *entirely* bleak: as with all poetic realist films there is the hint that the protagonist may be able to escape his or her predicament.[6] In *Le Quai des brumes* this is most obviously conveyed through Jean's attempts to take a boat to Venezuela; he is given clothing and a passport and makes friends with the doctor of a ship. He even boards the boat, just before it is about to depart. However, the importance of this escape diminishes as another, more appealing, form of escape becomes apparent, which is represented by Nelly and the notion of romantic love. What Jean is ultimately fleeing from is not the military police, whom we don't see at any point in the film. Instead, he hopes to escape from other negative forces, such as the darkness and grotesquery that Zabel represents. Zabel's unattractive appearance – Jean compares him at one point to a scolopendrid (a centipede-like creature) – is heightened through Simon's 'large' theatrical performance style. A key scene in this respect occurs when he enters Panama's. As everyone looks at him suspiciously because he has blood on his hands, he talks about how surgeons have clean white hands despite having them in blood all day. As he says this, he wriggles his fat fingers with a smile on his face, as though he is taking pleasure in imagining such an experience. In contrast to Zabel are the values embodied by Nelly, who represents a beacon of hope

---

6 An example of a female-centred poetic realist film is *L'Entraîneuse* (Albert Valentin, 1939), starring Michèle Morgan.

for Jean, evident from her first meeting with him. As he enters the backroom at Panama's, where he is to be given some food, he sees her standing by the window; she turns around, revealing that she is an exceptionally beautiful young woman. Her pale white face presents her as a bright object in what has so far been a very dark film, but also it places her as a symbol of purity, in contrast to the sordidness and corruption of Zabel. Her unpretentious, though stylish, clothing and Morgan's nuanced acting stress her sincerity in contrast to the lying, inauthentic people that Jean will meet.

Whereas Zabel and Lucien, along with Jean's experiences of war, represent the imperfections and suffering involved in life, Nelly embodies transcendence from these pains, indeed, transcendence from the physical world, and all the misery it can bring. As a consequence, she takes on metaphysical significance, contrasting with the physicality of Zabel, which is conveyed by his association with blood and by Simon's bulky body and 'large' acting style. Morgan's paleness, slim physique, and statuesque acting present her as an ethereal, otherworldly presence, something that's also suggested by the transparent raincoat that she wears, which metaphorically hints at her mysterious absence of corporeality. Following Jean and Nelly's meeting, a brief image suggests that Nelly may indeed provide Jean with the escape he seeks. We see the two of them looking out of the window at Panama's. Filmed from outside the building they are confined within the window frame, with its horizontal and vertical slats encaging them further: the implication is that they are trapped; but trapped *together* – an interesting example of Carné's use of 'poetic' film language to underscore the points he is making. We then cut to a point of view shot of what they are looking at: it is dawn, the fog has cleared, and we can see the sea stretching off into the distance. This shot is held for only a few moments, but the meaning is clear: Nelly can help clear the fog in Jean's mind, and, together, they may be able to escape. The unity of the couple and the authenticity they stand for is enhanced when one has knowledge that Jean Gabin and Michèle Morgan enjoyed a real-life romance at the end of the 1930s. Their on-screen chemistry certainly appealed to the public; they were known as the nation's 'ideal couple' (Morgan, 1978: 88) and starred together in two more prewar films, *Le Récif de corail* (Maurice Gleize, 1938) and *Remorques* (Jean Grémillon, 1939–41). Their partnership in *Le Quai des brumes* introduces what would be a key Carné theme – redemption and transcendence through idealised romantic love (even though the couple is ultimately doomed).

While the poetic realism of Duvivier and Renoir contains a tension between freedom and escape, there is less emphasis in their films on romance. In *La Bandera*, Pierre Gillieth (Gabin) has a relationship with Aïcha (Annabella), a native woman, but this soon diminishes in importance. In keeping with Duvivier's penchant for 'men's stories', Gillieth, a murderer who has fled France, seeks redemption through his brotherhood with his fellow Legionnaires and the film culminates with him dying a hero's death in combat. In *Pépé le Moko* (Julien Duvivier, 1937), Pépé is clearly attracted to Gaby, but she doesn't represent the escape into an otherworldly ideal that Nelly does. As Vincendeau argues (1998: 51), Gaby's appeal is ultimately that she represents Paris, where Pépé longs to return, which is evident from their shared knowledge of the city and from her jewels, which make her shine like the city of lights. Similarly, in Renoir's poetic realist film *La Bête humaine* (1938) Jacques Lantier (Gabin) is fascinated by Séverine Roubaud (Simone Simon), but her appeal is not transcendent; she becomes an animalistic (specifically catlike) *femme fatale*. The idealisation of women in a romantic narrative is, then, a distinctive part of the Carné–Prévert poetic realist film.

Carné's particular take on poetic realism, especially its unrelenting darkness, creates a distinctive and much discussed political dimension which has generated a range of interpretations. Right-wing critics in France dismissed the film as decadent and diseased, and there was concern amongst many that its defeatist attitude, with a narrative centring on an army deserter, was severely demoralising. It was even claimed when France was defeated by the Germans a couple of years later that *Le Quai des brumes* and Jean-Paul Sartre were to blame! On the other hand, Renoir was also critical of the film, describing it, by contrast, as fascist (Carné, 1996: 102). While he didn't elaborate on his reasons for claiming this, it is likely it was related to the fact that the Aryan Gabin, who at the beginning of the film is dressed as a soldier, kills Zabel, a character who could be seen as possessing Jewish qualities – his name sounds Jewish, and with his dark features and beard he possesses a stereotypically Jewish appearance. It is unlikely that Carné intentionally inserted such meanings into his film, but possible that he inadvertently drew upon stereotypes that were prevalent in France at the time. Renoir's criticisms can also be seen to be related to a personal rivalry with Carné, and it is possibly significant that *Le Quai des brumes* won that year's Prix Louis Delluc ahead of Renoir's *La Bête humaine.*

If we consider *Le Quai des brumes*'s representations of gender, we can understand its position more fully, though this too adds layers of contradiction. To some extent the film exhibits conservative notions of femininity. Whereas Duvivier's films and Renoir's *La Bête humaine* draw upon the sexist stereotype of the highly sexual and dangerous woman, Carné–Prévert draw upon a different – though arguably equally sexist – stereotype, that of the virginal, ethereal woman, embodied in *Le Quai des brumes* by Michèle Morgan. On the other hand, Morgan also stresses more progressive ideas. While she is ethereal, she is also a modern woman, a more empowered and grounded form of femininity: she is glamorous, wears a Chanel overcoat and has the tall, slim physique of the modern woman. Indeed, this was a key part of her persona in French cinema at this time (Driskell, 2008). In one scene, following Gabin's discovery that she has put some money in his pocket without him realising, which she has done because she knows he is broke, he states that it is not right to accept a woman's money. She replies: 'L'argent des hommes, l'argent des femmes, c'est pareil' ('A man's, a woman's, what's the difference?'). Because she is presented in a positive manner, Carné can be seen to be endorsing such progressive views. At the same time, this is part of a more general blurring of genders, with Morgan's modern femininity being marked by androgyny, evident from her slimness, her short hair, and her functional, pared down clothing, which, dominated by the overcoat, is not overtly feminine. This, then, is a key instance of Carné's articulation of androgynous gender identity in his films.

Carné also challenges conservative notions of gender through his take on the period's quasi-incestuous narratives, between mature men and young women. While such relationships are presented in many of the decade's films in ways that emphasise the strength of the older male generation, *Le Quai des brumes* is one of a group of films (along with *Le Jour se lève* and Renoir's *Le Crime de Monsieur Lange*) which present this older male in a negative way: Zabel is, as Burch and Sellier discuss, one of the period's 'mauvais père[s]' ('bad father[s]') (1996: 26). Although Jean's relationship with Zabel adds a progressive dimension, showing him challenging a corrupt older generation, it also emphasises the ultimate futility of this, with Jean's death signifying a failure of the younger working-class man to alter the status quo. While the film's defeatism was criticised for the way it emphasised male weakness, it should be noted that it also, within such a patriarchal context, placed a refreshing emphasis on male vulnerability, which was central to Gabin's persona at this time. As Vincendeau (1985) argues, a tension between the passive/feminine and the active/masculine is at the core of Gabin's identity: he usually displays strong masculinity in his films, but ultimately lacks sufficient power to alter his fate. Carné's melodramatic cinema, with its emphasis on transcendent love, was well suited to drawing upon the more passive and romantic side of Gabin's persona. Combined with Morgan's androgyny, this heightening of male sensitivity is typical of Carné's disruption of gender.

Despite its mixed political reception, Carné's film, as the winner of the prestigious Prix Louis Delluc, was critically well received. It was also the second most popular film of the year, after *Snow White and the Seven Dwarfs* (David Hand, 1937), highlighting an important part of Carné's success, his ability to appeal to both a critical and a popular audience.

Hôtel du Nord

The year 1938 was a busy time for Carné and before the year's end he had also released *Hôtel du Nord*. Following his successful adaptation of populist literature with *Le Quai des brumes*, he turned to another author he admired, Eugène Dabit and his novel *L'Hôtel du Nord* (1929), which follows the lives of a number of residents in the eponymous establishment. Carné had shown an interest in this work since an early stage in his career, mentioning it in his article 'Quand le cinéma descendra-t-il dans la rue?' in which he praises Dabit's ability to convey the atmosphere of ordinary working-class life (1988: 129). In making the film, Carné retained a number of members of his *équipe*, such as Trauner and Jaubert, but, more significantly, some key individuals were not involved. *Hôtel du Nord* was the first feature film Carné made without Prévert, who was working in Hollywood at the time. Carné considered joining him there so they could work on the script together, but instead decided to collaborate with Henri Jeanson, with assistance from Jean Aurenche. Jeanson was one of the top scriptwriters of the period, who had worked on a number of classics, such as Duvivier's *Pépé le Moko*, and Aurenche would go on to be one of the most important scriptwriters of the tradition of quality. Because the film was not a Carné–Prévert collaboration it is a useful benchmark in the debate about whether Carné's films without Prévert are of a lower quality. It is true that *Hôtel du Nord* is the least celebrated of the poetic realist films that he made in the late 1930s – it has not been discussed to the same extent as *Le Quai des brumes* and *Le Jour se lève*. However, it was still a successful film, commercially and critically. It was also well received in the popular film press, with countless articles appearing in magazines like *Pour Vous*, in large part owing to the presence of Annabella, a huge star of the time.

Indeed, the film's stardom is very important. Aside from Jouvet and Aumont, both popular stars of the time, who had already appeared in *Drôle de drame*, the film is notable for its use of Annabella and Arletty. Nowadays, Arletty is the star who is best remembered, something that is evident from a plaque that stands outside the actual Hôtel du Nord on the banks of the Canal Saint Martin (the original novel is based on a building that still exists); the plaque mentions Arletty and Jouvet, but not Annabella (or Aumont). Arletty's performance in the film was her 'big break' and her role was expanded during shooting because Carné was so impressed by her performance. However, at the time Annabella was by far the bigger star, and it was because of her involvement that the film received financial backing. For the last year she had been working in the UK and then Hollywood, where she had made a number of films for Fox and its British subsidiary, New World Pictures. She returned to France to make *Hôtel du Nord*, before going back to Hollywood until after the war. Of great importance to the film is the way these two stars function together, with Arletty, who began her career on stage, drawing upon her theatrical form of stardom, and Annabella, who went directly into working in films, embodying more cinematic values.

The story begins with Renée (Annabella) and Pierre (Aumont), the film's 'doomed lovers', arriving at the Hôtel du Nord with the plan of committing suicide together. In the opening scenes we are also introduced to the other main characters, Raymonde (Arletty), a prostitute, and Edmond (Jouvet), her pimp/boyfriend and a former gangster, who has assumed a new identity to prevent his former criminal friends from finding him. Renée and Pierre take a room in the hotel, but their suicide attempt goes wrong: he shoots her, but cannot bring himself to turn the gun on himself. He flees from the hotel and then turns himself in to the police. Renée survives and is taken to hospital to recover, before returning to the hotel, where she is given a job as a waitress. While there she causes quite a stir, with many of the male inhabitants becoming infatuated by her beauty. Edmond falls in love with her and the couple decide to run away to the colonies together, but, although Edmond boards the boat, Renée changes her mind at the last minute and returns to Paris. A little later, during Bastille Day celebrations, Edmond finds Renée back at the hotel where she is doing her final shift before leaving with Pierre, who is about to be released from prison. She warns him that some men, criminal accomplices from his past life, are waiting for him, but he still goes to his room, where he is killed. The film finishes with Pierre and Renée leaving the Hôtel du Nord, in a reversal of the film's opening scene.

Hôtel du Nord is notable for its expression of Carné's populist concerns, as pointed out by Vincendeau (1999), and by Andrew and Ungar (2005). Dabit had based his populist book on the experience of living in the original Hôtel du Nord, which his parents owned. The book and film differ in a number of ways, most obviously through their characters. Dabit's novel does not feature Raymonde, Edmond, Renée, and Pierre, and centres instead on a political activist called Bénitaud. Nevertheless, the film retains the novel's strong populism, something that is most immediately established through its setting – the area around the Canal Saint Martin, at the time a working-class area in Paris's tenth arrondissement. Carné and Trauner recreated one side of the canal at the Billancourt studio. This huge construction consisted of bridges, a road, and the fronts of buildings, such as the Hôtel du Nord, which were integrated with actual nearby Parisian rooftops. The great care the filmmakers took in recreating this milieu is one of the main signifiers of their affection for it, the wealth of detail testifying to their rich experience of such places. This also positions the film in contrast to Carné's earlier expressions of filmic populism, which, through necessity, involved more location shooting. The importance of the sets to the film's appeal is also evident from the fact that they became a key selling point. They were discussed in film magazines and the producer Joseph Lucachevitch even held a press conference there, as Trauner explained: 'The idea behind it was that the set had been expensive, but at least he would get some free publicity out of it' (cited in Bergfelder, Harris, and Street, 2007: 280).

The use of such large sets is significant in that they would become an important part of Carné's image in the years that followed.

The film's populist identity is also created by its host of picturesque characters. These consist of a number of key 'types', such as the prostitute, the pimp/criminal, the romantic couple, including a *midinette* (a romanticised, young working-class woman), the cuckold, and various workers (the lock keeper, hotel proprietors and merchants). As Chion (2008: 28) discusses, the dialogue these characters speak also plays an important role in generating the film's populism, something that is particularly evident with Raymonde. Throughout the film she speaks in a strong working-class Parisian dialect, and accent, liberally using slang and making a number of grammatical errors, which serve a comic function, but are also meant to stress her authenticity and down-to-earth persona. This style of speaking is strikingly demonstrated in a famous scene, in which she loses her temper with Edmond, who has stated that he is going to leave her because he needs a change of atmosphere. Her angry response, and one of the most famous lines in French cinema, is: 'Atmosphère, atmosphère? Est-ce que j'ai une gueule d'atmosphère?' ('Atmosphere, atmosphere? Does my mug look like atmosphere?'). Here, then, she counters Edmond's pretentious sentiments with her more direct, down-to-earth and witty response.

Fundamental to this scene and, indeed, the film's populism is Arletty's memorable performance. Her character, Raymonde, who embodies the liveliness and vitality of the working classes, is placed at the centre of the hotel's community. In the opening scenes we see her sat at a dining table, surrounded by the hotel owners, their family, and other residents, as she dominates the conversation, making everyone laugh with her sarcastic worldview. While she displays a strong sense of freedom and agency, through her wit and intelligence, she is also constrained in her relationship with Edmond, who dominates her and at one point even gives her a black eye. Arletty was well suited to this role, having played other feisty, but downtrodden, working-class women on stage. Here her physical appearance is important: while attractive, she does not possess the idealised, otherworldly beauty of Annabella and her voice, her most famous feature, is piercing, with a shrill Parisian accent. Combined with her physical acting style, a product of her time on stage, these qualities present Raymonde as a grounded, if charismatic, member of the community. With her energy, wit and stoicism, she is a celebration of the working class, an embodiment of the 'hardworking people' whom Carné discusses in 'Quand le cinéma descendra-t-il dans la rue?' – even though her character is moulded through the sexist stereotype of the 'tart with a golden heart'.

Hôtel du Nord, then, is one of Carné's fullest expressions of his interest in populism. However, at the same time, the film contains key features of poetic realism. A number of writers, such as Vincendeau (1999) and Andrew (1995), argue that in particular respects *Hôtel du Nord* departs from the poetic realist aesthetic, particularly through its light-heartedness. At the same time, they highlight ways in which it belongs to the movement. For instance, it contains a strong sense of the 'elevated' and 'transcendent' qualities that we have already seen in *Le Quai des brumes*, which comes in part from the film's poeticised reality, particularly its populist *mise en scène* and 'atmosphere'. In addition, Carné creates formal patterns, with, for example, the opening shot, a virtuoso camera movement that follows Renée and Pierre as they approach the hotel, being repeated in reverse at the end of the film. This reveals its underlying order and Carné's control of the film's reality.

Within the narrative there are also other developments that mark the film out as belonging to poetic realism, in particular the issue of fatalism. Here Jouvet's narrative is significant. He feels trapped, which becomes evident when he complains to Raymonde that he needs a change of 'atmosphere', and at the end of the film displays the kind of fatalistic behaviour that is fundamental to poetic realism. In conventional plot terms, it is unclear why he faces his former accomplices and, more to the point, why he hands them his gun when he finds them asleep in his room. However, like other poetic realist protagonists he feels compelled to destroy himself when he cannot find the escape he seeks.

The romance narrative involving Renée and Pierre is also important to the film's poetic realism, especially the early scene in which the couple are about to commit suicide, which presents their love in the highest romantic terms (the planned joint suicide evokes the story of Mayerling, which two years earlier had been made into a hugely successful film starring Danielle Darrieux and Charles Boyer). The tragic Renée–Pierre romance provides the flipside to Carné's populist representation of the city, embodied by the comic Raymonde–Edmond couple. While the elaborate construction of the Canal Saint Martin contributes to a celebration of Paris, the film's poetic realism, as in *Le Quai des brumes*, presents the city in a gloomier way, emphasising in particular the darkness and loneliness of the urban space. At the same time, as with Nelly in *Le Quai des brumes*, Renée herself signifies the 'something higher' that Carné's poetic realism seeks to evoke. During the film she comes to represent a fantasy for many different characters: for the owners of the hotel she is an ideal daughter figure; for Adrien (François Perier), a gay character, she is an unthreatening female; for Kenel (Andrex) she is an erotic ideal; and, most importantly, for Edmond she represents a spiritual ideal, coming to signify the change of atmosphere he seeks.[7] As Raymonde later says to Renée: 'Ah, vous êtes une atmosphère pas ordinaire!' ('Ah, you're not an ordinary atmosphere!').

This characterisation is enhanced by the fact that Renée is played by Annabella. Though she is now largely forgotten, she was the top female star of the early 1930s, having appeared in Abel Gance's *Napoléon* (1927) and René Clair's *Le Million* and *Quatorze juillet*, and she was still extremely famous in the late 1930s, having recently worked in Hollywood. She was initially cast by Gance owing to her photogenic appearance, and it is this quality that ensured her continued success throughout the decade. While Carné was not keen on her as a performer, he was impressed with the use that Clair had made of her in *Quatorze juillet*, in which she plays a delicate *midinette* searching for love. In many ways, her role in *Hôtel du Nord* is a reprise, though she is a much darker version of this character. Whereas her youth, beauty and romanticism in *Quatorze juillet* represent positive values that unite the community, in *Hôtel du Nord* she is ultimately a divisive force, unwittingly tempting men with her looks and leading Jouvet to his death. Annabella's recent work in Hollywood helps us to understand further her importance to the film. Her status as one of Fox's current stars would have been in people's minds when the film was released in France. In an issue of *Pour Vous* from the end of 1938, which includes publicity for *Hôtel du Nord*, there is also an advert for Fox which has, under the headline 'Les vedettes de la 20th Century-Fox vous souhaitent un joyeux Noël!' ('The stars of 20th Century-Fox wish you a Happy Christmas'), images and names of a number of Fox stars, including Annabella (Anon, 1938: 23). Her status as a Hollywood

---

7 This was pointed out to me by Ginette Vincendeau.

star, plus the glamour and beauty that came with this, plays a significant role in the film, helping her to embody the 'transcendence' that defines her character.

These qualities are particularly evident in the scene in which Renée and Pierre carry out their suicide pact. Here she is lit with soft, glamorous lighting, and is filmed from a range of angles. Whereas Arletty is generally shown in wide shots, stressing her place within the broader community, Annabella is presented through a number of close-ups, which emphasise her photogenic appearance. Attention is further directed to her beauty through her 'neutral' accent and low-key performance style. This scene has come up for repeated criticism, with Veber (1938: 6) at the time of the film's release stating: 'Une scène trop longue, au début, entre Annabella (pas meilleure que d'habitude) et Aumont, que j'aime mieux brun, est déjà écourtée à l'heure où j'écris ces lignes. C'était le seul reproche qu'on pouvait adresser à ce film magnifique.'[8] It is alleged that Jeanson sabotaged the scene, with weak dialogue, in order to 'highlight the broad and racy repartee written for Arletty and Jouvet' (Turk, 1989: 140). On the other hand, Annabella clearly brings much to the film's poetic realism. She is transcendent in contrast to the earthly and grounded Arletty, and whereas Raymonde belongs within the hotel's community, Renée comes from 'elsewhere', arriving at the hotel at the film's beginning and leaving in the final scene. This mirrors her real-life trajectory, with her coming from Hollywood and returning there after making the film. Consequently, Annabella's glamour enhances a key aspect of Carné's version of poetic realism, with its emphasis on idealised romantic love.

Through *Hôtel du Nord* we can see how poetic realism and populism bring about a range of ideological effects. The writer of the original novel, Dabit, was a regular participant in the left-wing Association des Écrivains et des Artistes Révolutionnaires (Association of Revolutionary Writers and Artists). Such an allegiance is evident from the novel's strong political dimension, particularly through its conclusion, which involves the hotel being bought by a company who knock it down to build offices. Carné's (1938) discussion of the film in an article written at the time suggests he also saw his film as political,

---

8 'A scene that's too long, at the beginning, between Annabella (no better than usual) and Aumont, whom I prefer dark haired, has already been shortened as I write these lines. This is the only fault that can be found in this magnificent film.'

with him stressing the importance of representing poor people's lives: 'Pourtant, ne nous a-t-on pas appris que le fait de n'être pas riche ne constituait pas une offense à la société? "Pauvreté n'est pas vice!", cela fait partie des axiomes qu'on enseigne à la jeunesse des écoles.'[9] Indeed, Andrew and Ungar (2005: 285–8) discuss Carné's use of shots of homeless men filmed at the actual Canal Saint Martin. His dramatisation of Renée and Pierre's struggle also has a social dimension, with their desire for suicide being linked with their financial troubles. The fact that Raymonde and Edmond both want to escape from Paris also suggests the limitations of life in working-class Paris. However, other elements emphasise the film's contradictory attitudes. Its representation of the area around the Canal Saint Martin is a nostalgic celebration of the lives of the ordinary people of Paris; it is about preserving this milieu, rather than exploring the hardships of working-class life.

At the same time, the film is more progressive when it comes to gender in spite of the use of female stereotypes already discussed. For instance, while it presents a nostalgic vision of working-class Paris, Annabella brings elements of modernity, rather like Michèle Morgan in *Le Quai des brumes*, through her glamour and invocation of Hollywood stardom. In addition, Arletty's Raymonde is a sympathetic character who possesses a degree of empowerment. This is evident through the witty defiance she shows as a response to Edmond's abusive control over her. Although this is not always successful – she receives a black eye at one point for answering him back – it represents a degree of resistance.

Moreover, for the first time in one of his films, Carné includes an explicitly gay character, Adrien, who is also gay in Dabit's novel. In the film his sexuality is conveyed at a few points. For instance, when Madame Lecouvreur (Jane Marken) asks if a girl is visiting, when he tells her he is tidying his room, he says in a slightly uncomfortable way, 'Non, un camarade' ('No, a friend'). Another strong hint of his sexuality is given later in the film during a conversation he has with Renée – he says hello to a young man passing them, who replies, 'Je t'ai même pas regardé quand je t'ai vu avec une mademoiselle' ('I didn't even look at you when I saw you with a girl'). While Adrien is very much a peripheral character, he provides a generally positive

---

9 'However, haven't we learned that not being rich is not an offence against society? "Poverty isn't a vice!", this is one of the axioms that one teaches young people in school.'

representation of homosexuality. He is pleasant and attractive, and is part of the hotel's community. Moreover, with his sexuality being so understated, it is presented as something natural. Andrew and Ungar (2005: 283) explain: 'Dabit portrays Adrien as a mystery whom Madame Lecouvreur fails to fathom. For Carné, he is merely a lodger who happens to be gay.'

Hôtel du Nord was another major success for Carné. Although it was not 'lionized by critics the way its predecessor had been' (Andrew, 1995: 3), it received positive reviews and was nominated for the Prix Louis Delluc. It was also a commercial success, achieving significant exposure in *Pour Vous* and getting decent audiences. This stood Carné in good stead for making his next film, which would be his last of the 1930s, and perhaps *the* definitive poetic realist film, *Le Jour se lève*.

Le Jour se lève

This next project came about in a rather unusual way, with his neighbour, Jacques Viot, a gallery owner, presenting him with a synopsis a few pages long of an idea for a film. Carné liked it and it was decided that Viot and Prévert would develop the proposal into a full-length screenplay. Once completed, the familiar Carné team was assembled, including Trauner and Jaubert, as well as Curt Courant, a celebrated German cinematographer, who had worked on other poetic realist films, such as *La Bête humaine* and *La Maison du Maltais* (Pierre Chenal, 1938). An impressive cast was also assembled, including Jules Berry, Jacqueline Laurent, Arletty, and, most importantly, in his second film with Carné, Jean Gabin. The film focuses almost entirely on his character, François, delving deeply into his subjectivity and experiences, also making the film, to a great extent, an exploration of the Gabin persona. Indeed, the front cover of the film's press book states: 'Le public a désigné la vedette no. 1 Jean Gabin. Marcel Carné l'a définitivement consacré dans *Le Jour se lève*.'[10]

Told in three flashbacks from the point of view of François as he sits in his room, *Le Jour se lève* follows the events that lead him to murder an older man called Valentin (Berry). The first of these shows him falling in love with a young flower seller called Françoise (Laurent), with whom he begins a relationship. However, when one evening she tells him that she has an engagement and cannot see him, he follows

10 'The public has designated Jean Gabin as the no.1 star. Marcel Carné has permanently sanctified him in *Le Jour se lève*.'

her to a *café-concert*, where he learns that she is seeing Valentin, a trainer of performing dogs. While there he also meets Clara (Arletty), who quits as Valentin's assistant part-way through the show. Back in the present, we see that the police have now surrounded François's room, before being led into the second flashback, where we learn that his is now seeing Clara. However, Valentin visits and tells François that he is actually Françoise's father and not her lover. François then visits Françoise where they talk together in a greenhouse and swear their love for each other, but not before Françoise states that what Valentin has told him is wrong – he is not her father. In the third flashback Valentin arrives at François's, where after a quarrel François shoots him. Back in the present, the police are closing in on him. Just as they are about to throw teargas through his window, he shoots himself. The teargas lands on the floor next to his corpse and spreads, as his morning alarm goes off.

A desire to represent the quotidian is still very much in evidence in *Le Jour se lève*. It presents us with familiar character types, including the concierge, various neighbours in François's apartment block, and, of course, François himself, who as a factory worker is a classic poetic realist hero, not to mention a typical Gabin character. Here it is also important to mention Clara, particularly as she is played by Arletty – as we have seen in *Hôtel du Nord* her persona, performance style, and voice helped to stress her identity as an ordinary working-class woman, albeit an exceptionally witty and charismatic one. At the same time, *Le Jour se lève* deploys a range of techniques to *transform* this ordinary milieu, particularly to facilitate an exploration of François's interiority. In this respect, the most notable device is the flashback. Although this was not an entirely new technique, as it had been used by the French Impressionist filmmakers in the 1910s and 1920s and, more recently, by Jean Renoir in *Le Crime de Monsieur Lange*, its use was still quite rare, especially as an extended structural device as in *Le Jour se lève*. A reason for this is that there was concern that such a technique would confuse audiences, which Carné discussed in an interview in *Pour Vous*: 'L'unité de style ne m'a pas désavantagé: j'ai suivi carrément et fidèlement l'action de mes interprètes, et il me semble bien que le public n'a pas été désorienté' (Frank, 1939: 5).[11] Whereas the avant-

11 'The unity of style hasn't disadvantaged me: I have followed firmly and faithfully the action of my performers, and it really seems to me that the public hasn't been disorientated.'

garde French Impressionist filmmakers were not concerned by such possible disorientation and were aiming at an elite audience, Carné's attempt to integrate this innovative device in a mainstream narrative film highlights a key aspect of his filmmaking, his desire to combine aesthetic innovation with box-office appeal. In order to explain his use of flashbacks Carné inserted a title card at the beginning of the film, stating that the protagonist is remembering recent events as he sits in his room. He also uses long, slow dissolves combined with an eerie musical accompaniment that lead us from the present to the past, and back again. Such a technique has an important effect, heightening our engagement with François's subjectivity: as we enter into his mind, we see events and memories from his point of view.

The interrogation of his subjectivity is enhanced further through a particular use of the film's settings. On the one hand, the *mise en scène* stresses the film's realism, particularly through the depiction of working-class contexts: the *café-concert*, the factory, the apartment block, and François's room. However, as with other poetic realist films, such sets are designed and filmed in a way that heightens the film's 'poetry'. For instance, while François's building is an elaborate and accurate recreation of the type of place a worker would live, it also serves a poetic function. As the film progresses, François, who lives in a room on the top floor, is shown to be separated from the people below, stressing his loneliness and isolation from the community. His room also serves an important dual function. It is furnished with mundane items, including a mirror, bed, chair and wardrobe, and contains other objects that we see him accumulating during the course of the film, such as a brooch and a teddy bear. However, because each of these objects relates to past moments, which we see in the flashbacks, the room comes to represent his mind and the objects within his memories. As Maureen Turim comments, such an interpretation is strengthened through awareness that the French word for memories is 'souvenirs': 'This word-play reminds us of how objects become invested with memories, for in Prévert's poetic condensation of *souvenir*, objects and memories are inseparable' (Turim, 2000: 66).[12]

This heightened emphasis on François's subjectivity brings a new element to the fatalistic dimension of poetic realism. On the one hand,

---

12 For a fuller discussion of this, see also André Bazin (1979).

Le Jour se lève uses familiar ways of conveying its sense of entrapment. As with other films of this type, such as *Le Quai des brumes*, the main character is trapped owing to his position as a working-class male. This is stressed throughout the film, with the audience being reminded on a few occasions of the difficult conditions that he has to endure as a factory worker and the effect these have on his health. The fact that he inhales sand at work vividly creates the sense of suffocation that poetic realism seeks to create. Spatial confinement is also important in conveying his entrapment, particularly in the scenes set in his room. After shutting himself inside, by pushing his cupboard in front of his door, François walks up and down like a trapped animal. His occasional outbursts of anger – either shouting at the people gathered below his window, or throwing a chair against the mirror – stress his entrapment and frustration even further. Carné intensified this confinement by the creation of a four-walled set, which the cast and crew could enter and exit only with the use of a ladder. Entrapment is also conveyed through Jaubert's music – as Bazin (1979: 6) discusses, one of the film's themes is 'sentimental', the other, which uses basses and percussion instruments, is 'dramatic' and 'oppressive'. Moreover, the use of the flashback structure makes clear – even more than in other poetic realist films – that the main character is doomed from the very beginning of the film, and, by presenting the narrative through François's memories, it conveys explicitly something that is often just implied in poetic realism, namely that the main source of entrapment is the protagonist's own mind.

As with Carné's other poetic realist films there are hints that escape is possible. The scene that best represents the potential for this is the greenhouse scene, in which François and Françoise declare their love for each other. In a shot showing the couple approaching the greenhouse, we can see the steam from a nearby train as it departs from its station, a family walking in the opposite direction to François and Françoise, and there is a hurdy-gurdy playing traditional music. These elements help to immediately establish a feeling of optimism, with the departing train connoting freedom, and the family and music, representing a nostalgic, cosy worldview. The greenhouse, with its abundance of flowers and plant life, represents a paradise of sorts, a point explored by Turk (1989: 168). Carefully composed, beautiful images show the couple surrounded by flowers and, at one point, Françoise reclines amongst them, bathed in soft light. However, it is stressed that this is no more than a moment of freedom and escape; we know the couple are in actual fact very much confined. This is in part clear from the scene's dramatic irony, with François talking about a future together we know they will not have (we have seen François in the present, his room surrounded by police). This is further underscored by situating the action in a greenhouse, which while representing nature does so in a way that emphasises artificiality and confinement: with its glass walls and roof, it presents very much an illusion of freedom.

This poetic realist aesthetic has been discussed at length in relation to the period's politics. Turim (2000: 63) points out that early discussions saw the film as a renunciation of the Popular Front. With François placed high up in the apartment block, above the crowds below, Carné provides a vivid depiction of his isolation from other people, placing the film in contrast to films such as *La Belle Équipe*, in which Gabin is at the centre of the community. Additionally, François's fatalism and ultimate suicide are in stark contrast to the desire for collectivity that is at the heart of Popular Front cinema. On the other hand, Turk (1989) discusses ways in which the film may be seen to possess a left-wing stance, emphasising, in particular, its sympathetic representation of the doomed proletariat, François. We see him in the factory carrying out tough manual labour, and we learn that his work has a negative effect on his health, with the sand from the machines damaging his lungs. When François's alarm goes off moments after he has committed suicide, this suggestively links his death with the beginning of the working day. The film also provides a vision of the oppressive forces threatening the proletariat, particularly through the riot police, who for Turk represent 'Fascist henchmen' (1989: 162). When they arrive at the apartment block we witness as they form a line and roughly push members of the community away from below François's window. Turk also argues that, while Valentin is not of the bourgeoisie, his rich clothing and theatrical mannerisms suggest bourgeois qualities.

Another tendency is to read the film as symptomatic of the gloomy period at the end of the 1930s. This is suggested by Sadoul's comments on the film: 'At a time when the world stood on the threshold of a new war, the French cinema seemed to have been injected with a fatalistic despondency. Carné was sunk in a quasi-metaphysical confusion' (Sadoul, 1953: 85). This agenda is explored in depth by Turk, who sees the film as an allegory for contemporary events – though his argument is in places a little far-fetched. He writes (1989: 152): 'The very name of its protagonist, François, imparts an allegorical dimension to the picture, and François's moving plight may well be read as an expression of the state of hopelessness to which the French were succumbing in 1939.' In addition, he (1989: 158) sees the backward tracking camera at the end of the film as 'a symbolic anticipation of France's acceptance of defeat in World War II'.

Other writers on the film's ideological significance and relationship with its context, such as Burch and Sellier (1996), and Turim (2000), pursue different lines of enquiry. For instance, Turim explores the film's psychoanalytic and melodramatic basis, and Burch and Sellier analyse its representations of gender. One of Burch and Sellier's main concerns is to discuss the film in relation to the decade's Oedipal narratives. With Valentin having an ambiguous relationship with Françoise, who is positioned as both lover and daughter, the film is a key instance of the quasi-incestuous narratives that were so prominent in French cinema of the 1930s. Importantly, with its use of a 'mauvais père' – Valentin is, as Bazin (1983: 134) highlights, 'demoniacal' – the film is challenging such relationships. At the same time, as with *Le Quai des brumes*, because François dies, the film pinpoints the difficulty of the younger man usurping the older male. For Burch and Sellier the significance of this in relation to the broader social context is clear: 'Constat désespéré de l'impuissance des fils face au cynicisme des pères, qui annonce la défaite et la confiscation du pouvoir par Pétain' (Burch and Sellier, 1996: 73).[13]

In terms of the film's representations of femininity we can see Carné and Prévert using a similar dichotomy as in previous films, between the Madonna and the whore. In the role of the 'whore' is Clara, who is defined by her physicality. When she first talks to François she makes sexually direct comments, stating, 'Ils en parlent tellement qu'ils oublient de le faire' ('Men talk about [love] so much, they forget to make it'), and, when they begin a relationship, it is presented as being largely based upon sex. She takes a room near his, and we see him as he goes to visit her on his day off. When he arrives she is naked, washing herself, emphasising her physicality. Indeed, this was

---

13 'Desperate acknowledgement of the powerlessness of sons in the face of the cynicism of the fathers, which announces the defeat and the confiscation of power by Pétain.'

originally filmed as a nude scene, which was censored, though stills from it remain and appear in Turk's book (1989: 167) amongst others. In contrast to this physicality is the ethereal, spiritual Françoise. As with Nelly and Renée, she is mysterious, setting her apart from her quotidian surroundings and down-to-earth women like Clara. When we are first introduced to her she is associated with flowers, through her profession as a flower seller and her flowery dress. While Laurent's performance has been criticised, particularly in comparison with Arletty's,[14] she possesses, like Morgan and Annabella, a form of 'cinematic' stardom, which placed emphasis on her youth and beauty rather than acting, qualities that made her ideal for the embodiment of the mysterious woman that she plays. Although this tension between Clara and Françoise, based on the notion of the Madonna and whore, is very important to *Le Jour se lève*, Burch and Sellier argue that the film also offers another way of seeing gender, writing:

> Toute la complexité du film réside sans doute dans ce balancement entre le point de vue de François, qui, à travers les retours en arrière, structure le film, et les éléments signifiants qui relativisent ce point de vue, et peuvent inciter le spectateur à s'interroger sur les causes profondes de la tragédie que vit le jeune homme. (Burch and Sellier, 1996: 69)[15]

Central to this 'relativising' of François's perspective is the unconvincing nature of his relationship with Françoise. To some extent they are presented as being a good match for each other, with her representing his 'double': aside from the 'e' in Françoise, they have the same name (when they first meet it is their name day) and both are orphans. On the other hand, while François is fixated on Françoise, it is suggested that François and Clara would make a better couple. In part this is because of the differences in performance. As has been noted, viewers tend to prefer Arletty's portrayal more than Laurent's. But also, in many respects the two women do not conform to the stereotypical roles of the Madonna and the whore. Clara may be sexual,

14 Turim (2000: 71), for example, refers to the 'comparative weakness of Jacqueline Laurent's performance'.

15 'All the complexity of the film resides without doubt in this balance between François's point of view, which, through flashbacks, structures the film, and the signifying elements that relativise this point of view, and can provoke the spectator to question the deep causes of the tragedy that the young man experiences.'

but unlike the period's *garce* (bitch), frequently portrayed by Viviane Romance and Mireille Balin, she is a sympathetic and compassionate character. Even at the end of the film, although upset at François choosing Françoise over her, she is kind to Françoise when she faints in the crowd outside and becomes delirious. In addition, Françoise is not quite as 'pure' as she may seem as it is implied that she has had a sexual relationship with Valentin. Indeed, in tension with Françoise's identity as an innocent *midinette*, there is the suggestion she is an aspiring modern woman, evident from her slim, androgynous appearance, her clothing, with her changing from the flowery dress she wears with François to a sleeker, more glamorous garment when she goes to meet Valentin, and her use of a compact mirror, a symbol for the modern woman, capturing her desire for a glamorous appearance and an active, mobile life.

Despite these other dimensions to the female characters, which problematise the distinction between the Madonna and the whore, François ultimately cannot see beyond his idealised view of Françoise. When Valentin hints that he has slept with her, François shoots him, an expression of his disgust that her purity has been 'soiled' by her union with the older man and that his ideal has been ruined. Like other poetic realist protagonists, then, when he cannot attain the transcendence and thus escape he seeks, he opts for self-destruction.

While contemporary reviews for the film were mixed, and it went on to be banned by the Daladier government and then the Germans under the Occupation because of this bleak subject matter, its subsequent success is less equivocal. André Bazin (1979) wrote enthusiastically about the film in the years following the war, and since then *Le Jour se lève* has become probably the most important example of poetic realism as well as one of the most celebrated French films of all time.

Having considered Carné's poetic realist films of the late 1930s, we can now understand more fully the nature of his contribution to the movement. His great emphasis on the use of studio sets, with – uncharacteristically for poetic realism – very little location shooting, generated a form of realism based upon an abundance of detail and observation, while also making his films particularly claustrophobic. Whereas other poetic realist filmmakers would tend to include moments of exhilaration and release (Pépé running down the steps of the Casbah or singing on its rooftops in *Pépé le Moko*, or the expansive train journeys in *La Bête humaine*), Carné's films provide just subtle hints that escape is possible, and conceptualise it more abstractly as a form of transcendence that's only achievable through idealised romantic love. In contrast to other poetic realist films, centring on 'man's stories' (as in Duvivier's work) and on dangerous, sexually attractive women (as in *La Bête humaine*), Carné's idealism celebrates emotional sincerity and sublimated sexuality, which entails an exploration of male sensitivity and the creation of mysterious and ethereal women. In keeping with this, his films examine the emotional side of the Gabin persona and use 'cinematic' female stars whose glamour and aura facilitate the creation of the transcendent women they play. In focusing so fully on male sensitivity Carné adopted an unconventional approach to gender, which challenged the period's patriarchal norms – this aspect of his filmmaking would develop further in the following years.

Another important aspect of Carné's poetic realism in the 1930s is that he was able to achieve commercial and critical success, balancing the demands of both 'art' and 'entertainment'. As we have seen, he made finely crafted, aesthetically innovative films (with mobile frames, flashbacks and elaborate sets), which deployed a range of cinematic techniques, making them popular with critics during a period in which the 'threat' of filmed theatre was on many cinephiles' minds. They were also 'popular', partly in the sense that they were populist celebrations of the lives of ordinary people and partly in that they were enjoyed by large numbers of people. Here Carné's use of stars is particularly important: as we have seen, they play a significant role in contributing to the meanings of his films, not to mention their commercial appeal.

As well as being hugely popular in the 1930s, the films Carné made at this time have become cult classics, especially in France. For instance, dialogue from these works often appears in lists of the most popular film lines, such as 'bizarre, bizarre' from *Drôle de drame*, 'T'as d'beaux yeux tu sais' ('You have beautiful eyes you know') from *Le Quai des brumes*,[16] and, in particular, 'Atmosphère, atmosphère' from *Hôtel du Nord*. The latter lent itself to the name of the perfume Arletty launched (Atmosphère) and is the name of a bar on the Canal Saint Martin (L'Atmosphère), near where Raymonde

---

16 This is referenced, for example, in the title of the Agnès Varda short film about the old Cinémathèque Française, *T'as de beaux escaliers, tu sais* (1986).

delivers the line. Indeed, the cult status of Carné's films is evident from the renovation, owing to popular demand, of the actual Hôtel du Nord in 1993, in what is now an affluent area of Paris: it has become a trendy restaurant, with a website that makes many references to the film (when the cursor moves over one image of Arletty, we hear her famous line). The lasting appeal of the film is also evident from *Le Fabuleux destin d'Amélie Poulain* (Jean-Pierre Jeunet, 2001), which contains numerous nostalgic references to the cinema of the 1930s, a period that for many is encapsulated by Carné's work, including a scene with Amélie skimming stones on the Canal Saint Martin, not far from the Hôtel du Nord. In the next chapter, which focuses on Carné's work during the Second World War and its aftermath, I will consider the issues raised in this chapter further. Indeed, it was during the Occupation that Carné made two of his most critically respected *and* popular films.

References

Andrew, D. (1995), *Mists of Regret: Culture and Sensibility in Classic French Film*, Princeton; Chichester, Princeton University Press.

Andrew, D., and S. Ungar (2005), *Popular Front Paris and the Poetics of Culture*, Cambridge, Mass.; London, Belknap.

Anon. (1938), 'Les vedettes de la 20th Century-Fox vous souhaitent un joyeux Noël!', *Pour Vous*, 525, December, p. 23.

Aurouet, C. (2005), 'Prévert et Carné: *La Fleur de l'âge*', *Positif*, 535, pp. 68–72.

Bazin, A. (1979), '*Le Jour se lève* … poetic realism', in Le Jour se lève *a Film by Marcel Carné and Jacques Prévert*, London, Lorrimer Publishing, pp. 5–12.

Bazin, A. (1983), 'The disincarnation of Carné', in M. L. Bandy, ed., *Rediscovering French Film*, New York, Museum of Modern Art, pp. 131–5.

Bergfelder, T., S. Harris, and S. Street (2007), *Film Architecture and the Transnational Imagination: Set Design in 1930s European Cinema*, Amsterdam, Amsterdam University Press.

Buchsbaum, J. (1988), *Cinema Engagé: Film in the Popular Front*, Urbana, University of Illinois Press.

Burch, N., and G. Sellier (1996), *La drôle de guerre des sexes du cinéma français, 1930–1956*, Paris, Nathan.

Carné, M. (1929), 'La caméra, personnage du drame', *Cinémagazine*, 28, 12 July.

Carné, M. (1938), 'Ce qu'on ne verra pas dans *Hôtel du Nord*', *Cinémonde*, Christmas special.

Carné, M. (1988), 'When will the cinema go down into the street?', in R. Abel, *French Film Theory and Criticism, 1907–1939, Vol. II 1929–1939*, Princeton, NJ; Guildford, Princeton University Press, pp. 127–9.

Carné, M. (1996), *Ma vie à belles dents*, Paris, L'Archipel.

Chion, M. (2008), *Le Complexe de Cyrano: La langue parlée dans les films français*, Paris: Éditions Cahiers du Cinéma.

Clair, R. (1988), 'Talkie versus talkie', in R. Abel, *French Film Theory and Criticism, 1907–1939, Vol. II. 1929–1939*, Princeton, NJ: Guildford, Princeton University Press, pp. 39–40.

Doringe (1936), 'Autour de *Jenny*, du *Grand Refrain* et de *Ma femme*', *Pour Vous*, 386, 9 April, p. 5.

Driskell, J. (2008), 'The female "metaphysical" body in poetic realist film', *Studies in French Cinema*, 8:1, pp. 57–73.

Driskell, J. (2009), 'Female Cinematic Stardom in 1930s French Film', PhD dissertation, King's College London.

Frank, N. (1939), '"*Le Jour se lève* est le film qui m'a coûté le plus d'efforts"', *Pour Vous*, 552, 14 June, p. 5.

Imago, The Federation of European Cinematographers (2003), *Making Pictures: A Century of European Cinematography*, London, Aurum.

Jackson, J. (1988), *The Popular Front in France: Defending Democracy, 1934–38*, Cambridge, Cambridge University Press.

McCann, B. (2009), '(Under) scoring poetic realism' – Maurice Jaubert and 1930s' French cinema', *Studies in French Cinema*, 9:1, pp. 37–48.

Morgan, M. (1978), *With Those Eyes*, with the collaboration of Marcelle Routier, trans. Oliver Coburn, London, W. H. Allen.

O'Shaughnessy, M. (2000), *Jean Renoir*, Manchester, Manchester University Press.

Ouvrard, G. (2001), 'L'insuccès de *Drôle de drame*: un mythe?', *CinémAction*, 98, pp. 59–65.

Sadoul, G. (1953), *French Film*, London, The Falcon Press.

Sadoul, G. (1988), 'Apropos several recent films', in R. Abel, *French Film Theory and Criticism, 1907–1939, Vol. II. 1929–1939*, Princeton, NJ; Guildford: Princeton University Press, pp. 218–23.

Turim, M. (2000), 'Poetic realism as psychoanalytical and ideological operation: Marcel Carné's *Le Jour se lève* (1939)', in S. Hayward and G. Vincendeau, eds, *French Film: Texts and Contexts*, 2nd edn, London, Routledge, pp. 63–77.

Turk, E. B. (1989), *Child of Paradise: Marcel Carné and the Golden Age of French Cinema*, Cambridge, Mass.; London, Harvard University Press.

Veber, S. (1937), 'Une farce de grande classe: *Drôle de drame*', *Pour Vous*, 467, 27 October, p. 5.

Veber, S. (1938), '*Hôtel du Nord*', *Pour Vous*, 527, 21 December, p. 6.

Vincendeau, G. (1985), 'Community, nostalgia and the spectacle of masculinity', *Screen*, 26:6, pp. 18–38.

Vincendeau, G. (1988), 'Daddy's girls (Oedipal narratives in 1930s French films)', *Iris*, 8, pp. 70–81.

Vincendeau, G. (1989), 'Melodramatic realism: On some French women's films in the 1930s', *Screen*, 30:3, pp. 51–65.

Vincendeau, G. (1998), *Pépé le Moko*, London, British Film Institute.

Vincendeau, G. (1999), '*Hôtel du Nord*', *Sight and Sound*, 9:3, pp. 41–2.

Vincendeau, G. (2004), 'Forms 1930–1960: The art of spectacle', in M. Temple and M. Witt, eds, *The French Cinema Book*, London, British Film Institute, pp. 137–52.
Wahl, L. (1936), '*Jenny*', *Pour Vous*, 409, 17 September, p. 6.

3

The Second World War and its aftermath

In the final years of the 1930s people in France and elsewhere were anticipating another war in Europe. Despite Neville Chamberlain and Édouard Daladier's controversial attempts to appease Hitler at the 1938 Munich agreements, the French and British finally declared war against the Germans in September 1939. After a lengthy period during which there was no fighting, referred to in France as the 'drôle de guerre' ('phoney war'), the conflict between the French and Germans finally began in May 1940 and lasted until France surrendered in June. Aside from the devastating effect this had on the French nation as a whole, these developments naturally impacted upon its cinema. In Paris the Nazis seized large parts of the industry, especially from Jews, and banned 'undesirables' from working in film (for example, Jews and Communists), while also forming a large vertically integrated studio called Continental Films. Many members of the film community left the country, such as Jean Renoir, René Clair, Jacques Feyder, Jean Gabin, and Michèle Morgan. As would be expected, these events had a significant effect on Carné. Because he was still only thirty-three when war was declared, he was called up to serve in the army. However, when the Nazis took France, he resumed his filmmaking career, with spectacular, but, as we shall see, controversial, results.

While Carné in the 1930s was already becoming an important figure in the film industry, with the coming of war his standing improved further. In part this is because most of the other top filmmakers of the 1930s left the country, making him the most prestigious director remaining in France. In addition, during this period he made two critically and commercially acclaimed films, *Les Visiteurs du soir* and *Les Enfants du paradis*, the latter considered by many to be his masterpiece. At the same time, the war was a controversial period for Carné, as it was for many others, whose work and activities under German occupation have been seen by some as constituting collaboration with the enemy. In this respect, Carné's work during the war fits in with Evelyn Ehrlich's (1985) broader conception of French film of this period as a 'cinema of paradox': on the one hand the film industry was sullied through its association with Nazi Germany; on the other, it was a 'golden age' for French cinema, in which the industry thrived and some of the nation's masterpieces were made. This chapter will explore Carné's involvement with the film industry under German occupation, and his creation of two classics, before moving on to consider his first postwar film, *Les Portes de la nuit*, which deals with the aftermath of war. In doing so, this chapter enables me to challenge the usual break that is assumed between Carné's wartime films and his post-Liberation work, while exploring his complex engagement with this troubled period of French history.

The first issue we must consider is the fact that at the beginning of the Occupation Carné worked for Continental Films. This German-run studio in Paris was designed to make films for the French public. It was created from various German-seized assets and was run by Alfred Greven, who was appointed by Joseph Goebbels. Films made by Continental were not concerned with overt propaganda. Instead, as Goebbels himself stated, they were supposed to be 'light and frothy entertainment' designed to pacify the populace. Carné's position at the top of the industry meant he was an appealing director for the Nazis, who wanted to sign up the nation's most prestigious directors. As a result Continental Films approached him with a contract, which he signed, beginning work on *Les Bottes de sept lieues* and *Les Évadés de l'an 4000*, a science fiction film. When approached by Continental, Carné was told that other major directors, such as Christian-Jacque, Jean-Paul Le Chanois, Henri Decoin, Léo Joannon, and Georges Lacombe, had all signed to make films, which persuaded him to join. However, he later found out that these directors had not signed, but had agreed to contracts because *he* had. Realising his error Carné managed to get out of his contract, claiming that certain obligations had not been fulfilled by Continental. Even so, after the war this brief involvement with the studio became a huge controversy, as did the fact that he continued making films in France during the Occupation. While his move from Continental was a potentially dangerous one, which could have spelt the end of his career (or worse), Carné managed to get a deal to make another film, a hugely opulent production for the producer André Paulvé, *Les Visiteurs du soir*.

Poetic, not realist

Les Visiteurs du soir

A brief consideration of *Les Visiteurs du soir*'s production background immediately highlights ways in which the wartime context affected Carné's filmmaking. As we have seen in the last chapter, he developed a familiar *équipe* and often used the same cast members from film to film. However, this setup was affected by the war. His set designer, Alexandre Trauner, who was Jewish, and thus banned from working in the film industry, went into hiding in Prévert's house in the South of France, where he stayed for most of the war, working clandestinely on both films Carné made at this time. While Carné's involvement with Continental became a black mark against his name, he has argued that his role in helping to hide Trauner was an act of resistance against the Nazi regime, and one that put him at considerable personal risk (Carné, 1996: 159). Another member of the Carné *équipe*, Maurice Jaubert, died from injuries sustained during a battle at Azerailles and was replaced by Joseph Kosma, who in the 1930s composed music for a number of Renoir films, including *La Bête humaine* and *La Grande Illusion*, as well as Carné's *Jenny*. The war also affected Carné's casts, with a number of his regular players leaving the country. Most significant amongst these was the absence of Jean Gabin and Michèle Morgan, who both went to Hollywood, Gabin later joining the Free French Forces until the Liberation of France. On the other hand, a number of Carné's leading players remained, including Arletty and Jules Berry, who both appear in *Les Visiteurs du soir*.

Les Visiteurs du soir is also significant for giving insight into developments in Carné's aesthetics. Most strikingly, the film belongs to the period's 'cinéma fantastique' – films dealing with magical, otherworldly subject matter. Key examples of this genre include *Le Baron fantôme* (Serge de Poligny, 1943) and *L'Éternel Retour* (Jean Delannoy, 1943), both of which involved the work of Jean Cocteau, an important contributor to the genre. Such films were well suited to this period as their emphasis on fantasy meant they avoided dealing with the present context of occupied France. Taking place almost exclusively in and around a castle in medieval France, *Les Visiteurs du soir* begins with Dominique (Arletty) and Gilles (Alain Cuny) arriving at the castle and mingling with the people there. Unknown to the inhabitants of the castle, they are representatives of the Devil and have arrived to disrupt the planned wedding between Renaud (Marcel Herrand) and Anne (Marie Déa). In order to do this Dominique seduces Renaud and Gilles attempts to seduce Anne. However, because of Anne's beauty and innocence, Gilles actually falls in love with her, a love she reciprocates. To resolve the situation, the Devil himself (Berry) arrives and chains up Gilles in the castle's prison. In response to her pleading, the Devil tells Anne that he will set Gilles free, but will erase his memory. However, when the lovers are reunited Gilles instantly falls in love with her again. Out of anger the Devil turns them to stone, but despite this, their hearts continue to beat.

This synopsis highlights some clear departures from Carné's work of the 1930s. Most strikingly, while poetic realism, a genre that largely declined during the war, is concerned with ordinary, quotidian milieux, which are rendered in a 'realist' way, *Les Visiteurs du soir* deals with a fantastic representation of another time and place. In addition, poetic realism's strong metaphysical dimension is made more extreme with *Les Visiteurs du soir*, which is explicit in its use of supernatural content. Whereas the main characters of those films were the working classes, in *Les Visiteurs du soir* Carné focuses instead on royalty, the Devil and his messengers. In this respect, then, the 'realist' part of poetic realism is minimised. However, at the same time, there are some revealing continuities with Carné's earlier work, particularly through the recurrence of familiar thematic concerns. First of all, by placing the Devil, *the* embodiment of evil, in opposition to the beautiful and pure Anne, Carné draws upon his usual Manichean worldview. Also, as with his poetic realist films, *Les Visiteurs du soir* is concerned with the issue of fate. Indeed, even more than in his earlier works, the characters are manipulated by a force beyond their control, in this case the Devil himself. Moreover, as discussed in the last chapter, the theme that is most distinctive in the Carné–Prévert version of poetic realism is that of intense, idealised romantic love. But, whereas this represented the possibility of salvation, it was ultimately never enough to save the characters from their destinies. By contrast, the ending of *Les Visiteurs du soir* provides a more extreme celebration of romantic love, with the continuing heartbeats presenting love as the ultimate power in the universe, even stronger than the Devil.

One of the most striking ways in which the film departs from Carné's 1930s films is through its 'look'. Bazin writes in his article, 'Carné et la désincarnation' (1983: 134–5): '*Les Visiteurs du Soir* marked the transition from "realism" to idealism, from immanence to transcendence.' This is evident from the beginning of the film, particularly through the use of setting and sets. As with many of the 'prestige' films of the time, the space in which the action takes place is 'closed off' from the broader world, a hermetically sealed bubble, comparable to the seemingly isolated town in *Le Corbeau* (Henri-Georges Clouzot, 1943), one of the most famous films of the war. This is not too dissimilar to Carné's earlier work, with both *Le Quai des brumes* and *Hôtel du Nord*, and to a certain extent *Le Jour se lève*, taking place in narrowly defined spatial areas. But whereas these films are set in ordinary milieux, from the beginning of *Les Visiteurs du soir* we are placed within a fantastic and opulent setting: the castle is a bright, white building, which was designed for the film by Trauner and enthusiastically discussed in the period's fan magazines (Jehander, 1942: 7). Once inside the castle we witness the large banquet hall, which is ornately decorated and filled with people in lavish period costumes. Much of this is inspired by a medieval book called *Les Très Riches Heures du duc de Berry*, which contains tableau images depicting similar scenes.

The way these settings are photographed is also important. For instance, Carné utilises the restrained style he adopts in his poetic realism of the 1930s. However, while this is used in *Le Jour se lève* to enter into the mind of François, giving us great intimacy with the character, in *Les Visiteurs du soir* the style is more 'distant', in keeping with the cinema of the period. One of the main ways this is evident is through the use of much wider shots, which add to the tableau aesthetic, particularly when, as happens a couple of times in the film, the action is paused in a freeze-frame, a device motivated by the narrative – the Devil's messengers have the power to make time stand still: we see banqueters at a table, dancers in the middle of a medieval dance, lovers in a flowery garden. We have already seen that in *Drôle de drame* Carné was interested in using trick photography; this is even more the case in *Les Visiteurs du soir*. In addition to freeze-frames, at a number of points in the film objects magically transform. Near the beginning Dominique's clothing changes from the male outfit she has been wearing to a long dress. Later, when the Devil first arrives at the castle, he makes some snakes magically appear. Most significantly, at the end of the film, the lovers turn into a statue. This, then, is a clear move away from the realism of poetic realism, towards a much more fantastical type of film.

Carné's shift from the realism of the 1930s can be understood further through a consideration of stardom and performance. To some extent there are continuities with his earlier work, in so far as he uses Arletty and Jules Berry, and, while Marie Déa was new to him, she plays an ingénue role that is similar to the parts played by Lisette Lanvin, Michèle Morgan, Annabella and Jacqueline Laurent: while her character is not an 'ordinary' girl in the way these others were, she is young, beautiful, performs in a 'cinematic' and understated way and is central to the film's romance narrative. On the whole, though, performances in *Les Visiteurs du soir* exhibit the greater 'distance' I have been describing, particularly as, aside from Déa, the majority of the film's performers had begun their careers on stage. Here Alain Cuny is particularly interesting. Whereas Gabin's performances in the 1930s have the appearance of spontaneity and immediacy, which contributes to his 'authenticity', Cuny is, by contrast, much more restrained and distanced in his acting (some would say wooden), which means that he adds to the film's abstract, even 'poetic' quality. Indeed, an article in *Ciné-mondial* (G. B., 1944: 9) stated: 'Et avec lui naît ce que l'on peut appeler le "comédien poétique"' ('And with him is born what you would call the "poetic actor"'). The use of Arletty and Berry stresses these points further. In many respects Berry's performance is a continuation of his characterisations in the 1930s, and the role clearly works well with his persona – he played a number of villains in his films of the 1930s, particularly Batala in *Le Crime de Monsieur Lange* and, of course, Valentin in *Le Jour se lève*. At the same time, he is even more demoniacal than in his earlier works, the role affording him the opportunity to perform at new histrionic heights. Arletty, however, is hugely different from how she was in her films for Carné in the late 1930s. As we have seen, in those films she plays, with effective theatrical bravado, down-to-earth, ordinary, working-class women who are defined precisely in opposition to the fragile, enigmatic heroines played by the 'cinematic' stars, Annabella and Laurent. Here, by contrast, she is defined by her otherworldly quality, evident from her performance, which is much cooler and more statuesque than in her previous films, her physical appearance, and the way she is filmed: she is now glamorously lit and photographed.

This consideration of Carné's style shows how his approach to filmmaking went through significant changes at the coming of war. In particular there is a shift from the realist to the transcendent; from the intimate to the distanced. However, Carné uses this approach to explore issues (fate, romance, and idealisation) and stylistic features (his 'closed' aesthetic, his perfectionism) that were already important to him. We can see, then, that the war didn't simply constrict him, it actually presented him with important new possibilities. This is also evident from a consideration of his engagement with the broader social context.

Les Visiteurs du soir is an interesting film to consider in relation to the issue of whether Carné's work contains discourses that support or challenge the Nazi Occupation. His critics believed that he should not have made films during the war. Others, including Carné himself, have felt that it was his patriotic duty to make entertaining films, to help people deal with the period's harsh realities. Indeed, the film's huge success highlights the audience's need to escape from the grim austerity of the war into a lavish, opulent, spectacular world. As Bazin (1983: 132) put it: '*Les Visiteurs du soir* presided over that inner escapism in which French cinema sought its temporary salvation.' In doing so, the film stressed the continuation of important values, as pointed out at the time by Pierre Heuze (1943: 4), who complimented the film's expression of eternal ideas such as love, and discussed the importance of beauty during 'les nuits les plus désespérées' ('the most hopeless nights'), clearly a reference to the wider troubles. In addition, Carné's decision to continue to work can in itself be seen as an act of defiance, showing his ability to create 'great art', to continue France's celebrated cultural tradition, despite the conditions. During the war a number of films emphasised the importance of France's heritage, a point explored by Evelyn Ehrlich:

> Filmmakers wanted to present subjects that glorified French culture and history, whether adaptations of classic novels (e g. the many films based on Balzac); biographies of cultural heroes (Berlioz, the nineteenth-century opera star Malibran, a pioneer aviator in *Le Mariage de Chiffon*); films that took place in periods of French political dominance (*Madame Sans-Gêne, Le Destin fabuleux de Désirée Clary*, both set in the Napoleonic era); or myths and legends that were part of

the French heritage (*L'Éternel Retour*, *La Fiancée des ténèbres*). (Ehrlich, 1985: 102)

The period's prestige films, such as *Les Visiteurs du soir*, contributed to the impression that this heritage extended into the present, despite the Occupation. However, perception of this as an act of resistance has to be carefully qualified; by producing a successful film Carné was also supporting an industry now under German control. Such questions were not limited to the film industry of course and historians of the period continue to discuss the many nuances in the word 'collaboration' (Jackson, 2001).

Turning to the film itself enables us to consider these issues further. One of the main ways that critics have explored the politics of *Les Visiteurs du soir* is through consideration of its possible use of allegory. From this perspective, the castle can be seen as France and the outside forces, the Devil and his messengers, as the occupiers. In particular, the Devil has been seen as standing for Hitler owing to his malevolent role in the occupation of the castle. In this light, *Les Visiteurs du soir* may be understood to contain messages of resistance, most obviously through the couple's stand against the Devil at the end of the film, frequently interpreted as representing the continuing spirit of the French nation. Sadoul (1953: 99) writes: 'Beneath the stone of the joint statue in which they are imprisoned, their hearts beat in unison one, two, three ... it was an image of captive France herself.' Even at the time, this was discussed in relation to the contemporary situation, with Pierre Heuze (1943: 4) writing: 'Un cœur qui bat dans la pierre peut être une œuvre d'art, et certes les [*sic*] *Visiteurs du Soir* l'ont prouvé, mais quand une œuvre d'art fait battre tous les cœurs, nos cœurs d'hommes, de Français, est-ce qu'elle ne porte pas en elle la plus magnifique des forces créatrices?'[1] Such a quotation certainly suggests that for many at the time the film captured a spirit of resistance. On the other hand, the film can be seen as overly resigned to the situation. Because the characters ultimately accept their fate and do not fight back against the Devil, they can be seen as complicit with the Occupation. Such allegorical interpretations are an important part of how the film has been discussed, though it is generally accepted

---

1 'A heart which beats in stone can be a work of art, and indeed *Les Visiteurs du soir* proves it, but when a work of art makes every heart beat, our French men's hearts, doesn't it contain within it the most magnificent of creative forces?'

that they are unsatisfactory as they are so polyvalent (Ehrlich, 1985).

A clearer challenge to the status quo comes from a consideration of Carné's treatment of gender. To some extent the women embody conservative stereotypes, with Arletty playing a seductive *femme fatale* who brings death and destruction to the castle, and Déa embodying the opposite, a pure, innocent ingénue. However, in other respects, the film, even more than Carné's work in the 1930s, contains elements that disrupt traditional notions of gender. Déa is more in control than previous ingénues, with her taking an active role in her relationship with Cuny, particularly when he is chained up – it is she who negotiates his release. More important, though, is Dominique, the role played by Arletty, who has a huge amount of control over the men in the castle. Central to her identity is her androgynous quality, evident from her gender-neutral name, the male clothing she wears at the beginning of the film, when masquerading as a man, and the fact that Arletty is the actor playing her – she provides a mesmerising, cool, and charismatic performance that makes the men around her look stupid. The potential that all this has for injecting a 'queer' dimension into the film is realised through a couple of ambiguous scenes showing Renaud (Herrand) and Baron Hughes (Ledoux) attracted to Dominique while she is still dressed as a male.

Indeed, the film's disruption to notions of gender is also evident from the male characters, who are all 'demasculinised' in a variety of ways. In the last chapter I argued that Carné placed great emphasis on the exploration of the vulnerable side of Gabin's persona; such an exploration of male vulnerability is even more extreme in *Les Visiteurs du soir*. In particular, Cuny is significantly different from Gabin through his restraint, his softly spoken speech and his more feminised beauty. As was pointed out at the time in one discussion of Cuny: 'Servi par un masque d'une impénétrable beauté, torturé et serein tout à la fois et par une voix envoûlante et feutrée.'[2] (G. B., 1944: 9). We see an expression of his romanticism when he arrives at the castle, where he sings a ballad to Anne in an extremely heartfelt way: the camera slowly moves into his face as he looks at her, emphasising his intensity, along with his soft features and pale eyes. The film's other males also contribute to this disruption to traditional masculinity, as Reader explains:

2 'Helped by a mask of impenetrable beauty, both tortured and serene, and by a spellbinding and subdued voice.'

It is, however, the varyingly 'demasculinized' males that do most to destabilize the polarities of gender. Baron Hugues has led a lonely, brooding existence since his wife's death; Renaud shows little sign of attraction towards Anne, a perception doubtless abetted by knowledge of Marcel Herrand's homosexuality ... Even the Devil, thanks to Berry's mannered performance, is lacking in the machismo we might feel entitled to expect. (Reader, 2001: 71)

The film's challenge to traditional notions of gender is related to various factors. To some extent, it is part of a broader crisis in masculinity discussed by Burch and Sellier, who argue that in the cinema of the Occupation women are given more prominence, fathers recede into the background, and male protagonists are more passive. This is evident with Cuny, a clear instance of what they refer to as an 'homme doux' ('soft/sensitive man') (1996: 155), a more vulnerable and sensitive form of masculinity that arose during this period. At the same time, the film's articulation of gender ambiguity is very much a continuation of Carné's opposition to conventional notions of gender. Through the film's 'camp visual and verbal universe' (Reader, 2001: 70), androgynous characters, and ambiguous relationships, *Les Visiteurs du soir* was Carné's most overt exploration of gay themes to date. This was enabled by the wartime context of the cinéma fantastique through which he could explore subject matter that would otherwise have been too controversial. Consequently, in *Les Visiteurs du soir* Carné challenges the homophobia and traditional gender roles advanced by Nazi and Vichy society. Thus while the film can be seen in a number of ways to support the occupying regime, through the representation of gender there are clear signs of resistance.

Les Visiteurs du soir, then, manifests a number of changes in Carné's filmmaking. The shift in his style, from the 'realism' of poetic realism towards a greater emphasis on 'poetic' qualities, is to some extent typical of the time, but is also a change that plays very much to Carné's strengths, enabling him to explore his carefully crafted, highly controlled approach to film form. The context also brought about changes in how Carné treated gender and sexuality, enabling him to explore unconventional attitudes, which were already beginning to emerge in his films from the 1930s.

Les Visiteurs du soir was very favourably received, with Didier Daix (1942: 7), for example, referring to it as 'sans doute le plus beau film actuel' ('without doubt the most beautiful film of the moment'), as well as 'le plus important [film] qu'on ait réalisé depuis la guerre' ('the most important [film] that has been made since the beginning of the war'). Seen by many as an act of patriotism, it also found great popularity with the French public, and, following this success, Carné was widely regarded as the nation's top filmmaker: an article in *Ciné-mondial* in 1944, discussing the period's 'star' directors, listed Jacques Becker, Christian-Jaque, Jean Delannoy, Claude Autant-Lara, and Marcel Carné, who was the first to be mentioned and the one discussed in most depth (Pol, 1944a: 5). Consequently, expectations for his next film were very high; the critics and public would not be disappointed.

Art, entertainment and the masses

Les Enfants du paradis

Following his success with *Les Visiteurs du soir* and then a failed attempt to film an adaptation of Émile Zola's *Nana* (1880), Carné decided to take a break in Nice with Prévert, where one day they by chance ran into Jean-Louis Barrault. In the course of their conversation, Barrault told Carné and Prévert his idea for a film, inspired by a viewing of Charlie Chaplin's *The Great Dictator* (1940), focusing on the life of the nineteenth-century mime artist Jean-Gaspard Deburau. Carné and Prévert were taken by the idea, and it was decided that the three of them would make the film, with Carné directing, Prévert providing the script, and Barrault taking the role of Deburau. In 1942 Carné had discussed his desire to move away from the scale and opulence of *Les Visiteurs du soir* and make a much smaller film, with just three sets and only four actors (Renald, 1942: 3). However, it seems the temptation to embark upon another full-scale spectacle was too great. The film that was made, *Les Enfants du paradis*, was a hugely ambitious work. Lasting just over three hours, the film took almost two years to complete, involved the construction of the largest set in French film history to date, drew upon countless technical personnel and extras, and used so much in the way of resources that, according to Trauner, it could not have been completed without the use of the black market. Carné and his crew persisted and the film was finally completed, premiering on 9 March 1945 in the Palais de Chaillot.

Les Enfants du paradis's epic narrative is told in two parts, each with a separate title and each lasting around an hour and a half: the first part is called *Le Boulevard du Crime*; the second, *L'Homme blanc*. In the first half of the film, we are introduced to the main characters whose stories interconnect in a variety of ways. Baptiste Deburau (Jean-Louis Barrault) is an aspiring mime who is given the opportunity to appear in a play at the Théâtre des Funambules, where his father performs, and is an instant success. One of the other performers there, Nathalie (María Casarès), is in love with him, but he is in love with Garance (Arletty), a streetwise Parisian woman, who is also being pursued by Pierre-François Lacenaire (Marcel Herrand), a dandy criminal, Frédérick Lemaître (Pierre Brasseur), an aspiring actor, and, later, Édouard (Louis Salou), the Count de Montray, who offers Garance protection when she runs into trouble with the police at the end of *Le Boulevard du Crime*. Although Garance offers herself to Baptiste in his room, he declines; the situation departs from his romantic worldview. In *L'Homme blanc* several years have passed; Baptiste is the greatest mime in Paris and Lemaître is the city's top actor. Returning from travelling abroad with the Count, Garance goes to see Baptiste perform, but learns he is now married to Nathalie and that they have a child together. When he discovers she is back in Paris he pursues her and they spend the night together. However, in the morning Nathalie arrives and Garance leaves, entering a sea of people assembled for carnival. Baptiste runs after her, but she disappears from view.

Les Enfants du paradis, widely considered the defining film of Carné's career, is also an extremely important work in the history of French cinema and in a number of film polls has been voted 'the greatest French film of all time'. In 1979 Carné received a special César to honour it as 'the best French film in the history of talking pictures'. Its importance is also evident from the amount of scholarly writing it has generated. There have been discussions by, amongst others, Chris Darke (1993), Jean-Pierre Jeancolas (2000), Ben McCann (2006), a chapter by Dudley Andrew in *Mists of Regret* (1995), a BFI Classic by Jill Forbes (1997), and a monograph by Geneviève Sellier (1992). Moreover, Turk (1989) devotes a huge proportion of his book on Carné to the film. Why is it so important?

In many analyses, *Les Enfants du paradis* is presented as Carné's masterpiece denoting its status as a piece of 'great art', and thus an instance of formal and stylistic brilliance. Discussing the film in the immediate postwar period, Sadoul wrote (1953: 102): 'The "stylistic" tendency of the Occupation was crowned by a masterpiece, *Les Enfants du paradis*, the richest and most perfect film by Carné and Prévert, a true treatise on style.' Turk also regards the film as Carné's masterpiece, exploring it as the ultimate expression of his filmmaking, the truest manifestation of his themes, and the platonic ideal that his other films fell short of, to varying degrees: 'It is, at once, a realization of his artistic vision and an indicator of his subsequent inability to revitalize that vision' (Turk, 1989: 219). As a thematically and aesthetically complex film, the 'artistic' importance of *Les Enfants du paradis* should not be neglected. However, I would like to argue that its importance also stems from the significant popular appeal it had in 1945. It was a huge hit, receiving favourable reviews in the film press, performing well at the box-office, and playing at the Madeleine-Cinéma for a full year. As I have been arguing, a key aspect of Carné's identity as a filmmaker is that he could balance the demands of 'art' and 'entertainment'. In this respect *Les Enfants du paradis*'s importance goes further. Not only is it the Carné film that most fully illustrates his capacity to create hugely popular, artistically respected works; the film's story is also very much *about* this, focusing on the lives of celebrated theatrical performers who establish a profound bond with their audience, made up of the ordinary people of Paris. The film's title alludes to this group: the 'paradis' is the name of the upper balcony, where the poorest people would sit. Conversely, the 'enfants' are the actors, the children of the masses who perform for them. To take this point further, it is also significant that the film is celebrating the melodramatic genre, as discussed by Andrew (1995: 324), and stars, both of which are important elements to the popularity of Carné's cinema. Consequently, through its exploration of the popular and the 'artistic' *Les Enfants du paradis* dramatises a key aspect of Carné's identity. In order to discuss this further I will consider two key dimensions of the film's aesthetics: its use of features associated with poetic realism and its status as a spectacular costume film, both of which stress to varying degrees the art/entertainment dichotomy.

One of *Les Enfants du paradis*'s distinctions is that it has been seen as the culmination of poetic realism. Even at the time of the film's release, it was being marketed for its 'poetic' and its 'realist' qualities, as indicated by this passage from one of the film's press books: 'L'évocation d'une époque aussi mal connue et aussi extraordinaire que celle-là ne pouvait manquer de séduire – en raison des difficultés qu'elle comporte – le seul metteur en scène capable d'en retrouver l'atmosphère à la fois réaliste et poétique.'[3] A clear continuity with the prewar work is that it contains themes central to Carné and Prévert's distinctive articulation of poetic realism. Most importantly it has a strong romance narrative; even more than in the earlier films, *Les Enfants du paradis* explores the great emotions involved in the relationship between the central characters, with idealised romantic love representing the possibility of transcendence from the pains of everyday life. At the same time, the film explores the flipside to this: marginality, despair, isolation, states that are dramatised in particular through Baptiste, both on and off the stage. In this respect his mime performances are particularly striking, in which he uses his whole body to stoop and contract, conveying the melancholia that is weighing him down. Finally, the film contains a strong sense of fatalism, especially through the character of Baptiste, who at many points is passive and resigned; he is unable to grasp the opportunity to be with Garance when he has it, and suffers as a consequence.

Les Enfants du paradis also balances its concern for realism and poetry in a different way to the 1930s films. Whereas those films dealt with the present in an 'immediate', and often controversial, way, *Les Enfants du paradis* is set many years in the past – around the 1830s. However, despite this distance, like the earlier work, *Les Enfants du paradis* places great emphasis on the authenticity of *detail*. When designing the sets for *Les Enfants du paradis*, which he did while in hiding, Trauner conducted a significant amount of research, using pictures of Paris in the nineteenth century. The resulting designs for the elaborate Boulevard du Crime are thus hugely detailed. In addition, the crowd scenes show the importance of the costumes, which were similarly extensively researched.

As with earlier poetic realist films, this (in this case 'historical') reality is poetically transformed. In an article about the top directors of the war, the contemporary critic Alain Pol (1944a: 5) referred to Carné as 'un maître incontesté de l'atmosphère' ('an undisputed master of atmosphere'). As with their earlier work, Carné and Prévert explore a

---

3 'The evocation of a period that is as little known and as extraordinary as that cannot fail to appeal – because of the difficulties that attend it – to the only director capable of recreating its atmosphere in a way that is at once realist and poetic.'

world of symbols and abstractions, with the moon, the flowers, and the rag and bone man all becoming recurring motifs. Importantly, though, in *Les Enfants du paradis* Carné and Prévert introduce a new way of imbuing the everyday with the poetic, which is through the exploration of the theme of life as art/theatre. To some extent this is established by the film's self-reflexivity, with the film opening with a curtain being raised, revealing the Boulevard du Crime. Within the film itself there are numerous instances of life and art being blurred. In large part this is because a number of the film's characters take pleasure in playing on the theatricality of life, something that's particularly apparent with Lemaître, whose numerous conversations appear to be like mini-performances, enhanced by Pierre Brasseur's histrionic style. In his first scene, we witness him attempting to seduce two women (one of whom is Garance), in quick succession, using exactly the same chat-up lines – it is as though he is drawing on a pre-written script. Similarly, Baptiste turns life into theatre at the beginning of the film when Garance is accused of stealing a watch and is about to be arrested (in actual fact it is Lacenaire who stole it). Because Baptiste is a witness, he gives his 'statement' to the police in the form of a mime, much to the amusement of onlookers. In addition, his decision not to sleep with Garance ultimately comes from his desire to turn their romance into an idealised moment, worthy of art, and not a base sexual exchange. However, one of the most striking moments in the film's blurring of life and art occurs during the post-performance party after Lemaître has appeared as Othello, where Lacenaire is confronted by the Count. Knowing that Garance, the Count's mistress, is kissing Baptiste on the balcony, Lacenaire pulls aside the curtain to reveal the scene outside; in opening the curtain, there is thus an explicit reference to theatre. Lacenaire certainly relishes the situation for all the meaning and drama it creates.

We can see, then, that *Les Enfants du paradis* shares key similarities with Carné's work of the 1930s, but that it also departs from it in a number of ways. Dudley Andrew discusses these differences, arguing that the film exhibits a greater degree of self-consciousness about its use of established conventions, claiming that by the war poetic realism had become 'codified and citable' (1995: 321). For him the difference is essentially that the prewar films were immediate and naive, whereas *Les Enfants du paradis* (along with Carné's next film, *Les Portes de la nuit*) is sentimental and distant. For instance, the film's framing device, showing curtains rising and falling, is distinct from techniques used in *Le Jour se lève*, which are concerned with entering the mind of the protagonist. Instead of this intimacy, *Les Enfants du paradis*, through its stylisation and scale seeks to please the audience in other ways, as Andrew (1995: 328) argues: 'From this standpoint *Les Enfants du paradis* is at once the apotheosis of poetic realism and a betrayal, through contrivance and theatricality, of its innocence and vulnerability. It asks first for admiration from its audience rather than for unthinking involvement in the world portrayed.'

Of course, many French films of the Occupation adopted a more 'distant' view of life as a way of evading the immediate social context. It was for this reason that the costume film, which had been a popular genre in the 1930s, became even more significant at this time. This is another important way of considering *Les Enfants du paradis*, which has been described as the French *Gone With the Wind* (Victor Fleming, 1939) (see McCann, 2006: 58). Indeed, as Vincendeau (2004: 143) points out: 'The best-known war-time French costume film is of course *Les Enfants du paradis* (1945), which is usually cited as the culmination of Poetic Realism but is also, indeed primarily, a spectacular costume film.' Vincendeau also argues that, because of French cinema's theatrical intertext, spectacle was one of its defining features in the 1930s and beyond. In this respect, *Les Enfants du paradis* is a continuation of a broader tradition at this time, but also an apotheosis of it, because of the sheer scale and complexity of the spectacle. Of crucial importance here are the film's sets and costumes, which were discussed at length in the period's fan magazines and in promotional materials. For example one of the film's press books includes pictures of the sets in the process of being constructed and a discussion of how they were made. Similarly, an article by Jacques Lombardy (1944: 6–7) entitled 'Il a fallu reconstruire Paris pour ... *Les Enfants du paradis*' ('Paris had to be reconstructed for ... *Les Enfants du paradis*') emphasises the scale of these reconstructions. The spectacular dimension of the film is also crucially stressed through Prévert's dialogue, a contribution that has been examined by, amongst others, Jill Forbes (1997: 36–41) and Michel Chion (2008: 42–47). Both writers emphasise the significance of Prévert's 'poetic' dialogue – his play on words, particularly with sayings, and the deployment of his populist lexicon – which was undoubtedly a significant pleasure for audiences at the time, and in this respect was continuing the 1930s tradition. However, one of the film's most important spectacular elements is its use of performance, particularly as it is a film *about* performance, ensuring that various instances of acting are brought to the fore throughout the film. Because the characters blur the line between life and theatre, by putting on performances embedded in everyday life, the actors engage in what James Naremore (1988: 68–82) refers to as 'performance-within-performance'. This creates mini-spectacles in the narrative as a whole and serves to showcase the acting of the film's extremely talented cast – Arletty, Barrault, Brasseur and Herrand in particular.

Typical of the costume film, in *Les Enfants du paradis* such spectacle is brought towards creating a nostalgic view of the past, and, typical of Carné–Prévert, such nostalgia is based upon populism. Whereas many costume films, such as *La Duchesse de Langeais* (Jacques de Baroncelli, 1941) and *Le Capitaine Fracasse* (Abel Gance, 1942), focus on the higher echelons of society, *Les Enfants du paradis* is more interested in ordinary lives. As in other Carné films, the masses are presented as full of vitality and with a strong sense of community and desire for freedom. This is stressed through the depictions of the four main protagonists, all representatives of the ordinary people of Paris: as performers, Lemaître and Baptiste show their vitality through their passion, imagination and creativity; Garance, who comes from a popular *faubourg* of Paris called Ménilmontant, is depicted as a witty, free-spirited embodiment of the people, enhanced by the fact that it is Arletty in this role, who as we have seen possesses these characteristics in *Hôtel du Nord* and *Le Jour se lève* (though here she is also more ethereal, a point to which I'll return); Lacenaire, too, is a passionate individual, evident through his articulate use of words, his wish to write plays at the beginning of the film and his attentiveness to the artistic possibilities of everyday life (such as when he reveals to the Count that Garance and Baptiste are kissing on the balcony outside). Aside from these central characters, the many other ordinary people we see emphasise similar qualities, something that is particularly evident when they are in the theatre. The shots of them, sitting together in joyful disorder, some with their legs hanging over the balcony, captures a strong sense of togetherness, as well as of their liveliness and emotional sincerity – they are moved by Baptiste's sad performances. The film's vision of spectatorship, based on a passionate, communal engagement with the performance, could be called utopian. Indeed, for Andrew (1995: 324), one of the main longings that the film registers is the nostalgia for a 'better form of representation' – melodrama that scales such artistic heights, while appealing to a mass audience. Of course, one of the main ways that the vitality of the people is stressed is through the depiction of its opposite: the Count. Whereas the masses are lively and passionate, he is staid and cold, such qualities being conveyed through Louis Salou's reserved theatrical acting, and through the way he is filmed. A particularly striking example of this occurs when he has a conversation with Garance in her room. As they talk, she sits facing her mirror, her back towards the direction he is in; he sits in an alcove, his back facing her direction. The image stands as a complete opposite to the passionate engagement of the other characters and the *paradis* in the theatre. This past world, then, is presented as a time of freedom for ordinary people, abundance (conveyed through the spectacle), love and community, and, as a melodrama, it is a world of emotional intensity and moral certainty – it is not hard to see the appeal of such qualities in the harsh, austere and suspicious period immediately after the war.

As well as the film's poetic realist aesthetics, then, its identity as a costume film is extremely important. In addition to generating the film's pleasures and 'artistry', both elements are significant for their contribution to its ideological messages and to the way the film relates to the period's political turmoil. Indeed, as with *Les Visiteurs du soir* there has been significant debate about the film's politics, another reason why it has been discussed at such length. As with *Les Visiteurs du soir*, there are a few key ways of thinking about this relationship, and, again, even though the film was released after the Liberation of Paris, much of this is driven by the question of where *Les Enfants du paradis* can be situated within the politics of collaboration and resistance that characterised the time of its making.

In this respect, the first point to consider is the film's production background, which for some provides evidence of Carné's apathy towards the occupying forces. It is important to stress again that, in the context of wartime France, simply making films, or indeed having any professional activity, *was* controversial. In addition, Carné cast some actors who in postwar trials were considered to have collaborated with the enemy. For instance, Robert Le Vigan, who publicly expressed fascist views, was initially cast in the role of Jéricho and even appears in one of the film's press books. However, when it became apparent that the Allies were to liberate France, Le Vigan fled with the fascist writer Louis-Ferdinand Céline, who was his friend. He was replaced by Pierre Renoir (Jean's brother), who appears in the finished version. In addition, Arletty was put under house arrest for eighteen months at the end of the war because of her relationship with a German officer, which lasted for most of the Occupation, following which her career never really recovered. In her defence, she famously stated: 'Mon cœur est français, mon cul est international!' ('My heart is French, my arse is international!'). At the same time, aspects of the film's production history support Carné's claim that he was making the film as an act of resistance. In particular, he argues that, when he realised that France was soon to be liberated, he slowed down the completion of his film, so that it would be the first to be released at the end of the Occupation.

In trying to understand further the film's position within this context, scholars have turned to an analysis of the film itself. In this respect *Les Enfants du paradis*, like *Les Visiteurs du soir* before it, has been subject to allegorical readings, facilitated by its aura of poetic realism, as a form that deals with abstractions and idealisations, and as a costume film, a genre set in the past and thus inviting symbolic connections with the present. Again, though, the film supports wildly different readings. On the one hand it is seen as promoting messages of resistance, particularly through the narrative centering on the Count's 'protection' of Garance. When Garance, a carefree Parisian woman is (wrongly) accused by the police of involvement in a crime, she has to ask the Count for his help. This leads to her spending a number of years as his mistress, giving up the freedom that we have seen her relishing in the first part of the film. In this scenario, the Count has been interpreted as representing the Germans, or Vichy France, and Garance as the heart of the French people; when Lacenaire takes a stand against the count, killing him at the end of the film, this can also be read as an allegory of resistance. In addition, Jéricho, the rag and bone man, an unpleasant character and someone who gives information to the police, may express a critique of informers. However, his name of Hebrew origin, his dark features, and his embodiment of negative Jewish stereotypes, such as untrustworthiness, have suggested to some that there is an anti-Semitic element in the film. In this respect, at the very least, the film fits squarely within the period's ambiguous 'cinema of paradox'.

Stronger, yet also ambivalent, signs of 'resistance' are found in the film's nationalism, which stems from its celebration of two historical French performers: Baptiste Deburau and Frédérick Lemaître. This narrative, highlighting France's ability to create artistic genius, fits into the broader tradition in the cinema of the period of biopics about writers and artists, or films based on their work. Moreover, *Les Enfants du paradis*, with its emphasis on 'quality' and scale, is itself a continuation of the nation's celebrated artistic history. As Andrew (1995: 328) explains, the film 'asks first for admiration from its audience'. In this respect, Carné and Prévert can be seen as part of the nation's strong artistic lineage, as can the performers whose acting is showcased in the film. James Agee stated that before Barrault artistic genius had not been sufficiently portrayed on screen, a point Andrew (1995: 326) elaborates upon: 'José Ferrer is merely a signifier for Toulouse-Lautrec in *Moulin Rouge* (1952); Harry Baur is a ludicrous shadow of Beethoven in Gance's 1936 biographical film; but Jean-Louis Barrault stuns us in exactly the way Baptiste Deburau stunned the audiences of the Funambules a century ago until we are led to wonder if those audiences would not have preferred Barrault.' Thus, the film is nationalistic not only through a celebration of *past* artistic figures but also through its showcasing of *current* gifted individuals.

However, as with *Les Visiteurs du soir*, the film does most to resist the occupiers and the Vichy ideology through its representations of gender. Firstly, though, it should be noted that the character of Garance is a conduit for a range of reactionary attitudes towards femininity. While she possesses her own identity, she is at the same time defined by the way a variety of men perceive her, and project their fantasies upon her. In this respect, she is in keeping with the women from Carné's earlier films, such as Annabella in *Hôtel du Nord*. Lemaître, Don Juan-like (Sellier, 1997: 62), views women in terms of sexual conquest, evident from his liaison with Madame Hermine (Jane Marken), the owner of the guesthouse where Baptiste resides, who sleeps with him and is then discarded in a manner that is supposed to emphasise her foolishness (as an 'older' woman) for getting involved with him in the first place. Garance also mobilises this aspect of Lemaître's identity. While he enjoys her wit, which is to his taste as a talkative and humorous character, he is essentially interested in her erotic powers. This aspect of her personality is also stressed at the beginning of the film when we see her as 'the naked truth': as a street attraction, she poses naked in a well while men look at her. The episode evokes a moment in *Le Jour se lève* in which François, finding Clara naked in her apartment washing herself, says, 'On dirait la vérité qui sort du puits' ('You look like truth climbing out of a well'), itself based on a familiar French saying: 'La vérité est au fond d'un puits' ('Truth is found at the bottom of a well'). Indeed, one contemporary article on Arletty entitled 'Arletty, ou la vérité toute nue' ('Arletty, or the naked truth') (Pol, 1944: 8–9) emphasised this erotic dimension to her persona, with a number of pictures showing her in seductive poses: opening the top of her dress in *Les Enfants du paradis* as she is about to get undressed, and sitting down, showing her legs, in *Les Visiteurs du soir* and *Le Jour se lève*, as well as an image of the nude scene from *Le Jour se lève* that was cut for censorship reasons. In *Les Enfants du paradis*, Lemaître's philandering is, to some extent, celebrated. While he is shown to be something of a buffoon, with his vanity stretching to ludicrous extremes, he also possesses great style, charisma, and wit, particularly as he is played with excellence and charm by Pierre Brasseur.

Another perspective on gender comes from the Count, who views women in terms of property and ownership, and to some extent robs Garance of her freedom. While the Count is clearly viewed critically by the film for this, and his death at the hands of Lacenaire is presented as justice, Garance is ultimately resigned to her loss of freedom, acting in a self-sacrificial way, which reinforces dominant female stereotypes. Even Baptiste advances a conservative view of femininity, through his tendency, in line with other poetic realist protagonists, to put women on a pedestal, to view them as transcendent and ethereal beings. This is dramatised quite literally in a play-within-the-film, in which Garance portrays a statue on a pedestal, while Baptiste and Lemaître's characters struggle for her affections, thus mirroring wider events in the film's narrative. Not coincidentally, this scene is one of the most frequently reproduced pictures from the film – for instance adorning the cover of Jill Forbes's BFI film classics book.

Yet, in other ways, like in *Les Visiteurs du soir*, the representation of gender in *Les Enfants du paradis* disrupts traditional attitudes. In keeping with Carné's 1930s films and changes in the broader social sphere, there is a challenge to representations of 'fathers'. Negative images of older males include Jéricho and the owner of the Théâtre des Funambules, as well as Baptiste's actual father, who provides the clearest indication of the shift in attitudes to mature male figures, which Burch and Sellier link to the broader weakening of patriarchy brought about by France's military defeat. Baptiste's father begins the film by ridiculing his son in front of a large crowd of people, stating that he is worthless and without acting ability. But soon it is he who looks ridiculous as it transpires that Baptiste is an acting genius. The father's role diminishes as the film progresses, with him later taking directions and instructions from his son, his power almost completely gone. In this respect, what is also striking about the film is the centrality of the female character, Garance. While she is a canvas for male fantasies (and a fictional creation, while the male characters are based on historical figures), her central role is also significant, particularly as she is shown to possess many positive qualities. In the first half of the film, she is strong-willed and free, challenging Baptiste's romanticised view of passive femininity, particularly when she attempts to seduce him in her room at Madame Hermine's. This demonstrates her sexual agency, with her being unashamed and guiltless in embracing this side of her nature. In the second half, when she is the Count's mistress, she further demonstrates positive values by not being corrupted by the wealth around her; she longs to return to her earlier carefree days. Most importantly, Garance's strength is conveyed through the force of Arletty's assertive performance. It is significant that Garance is celebrated at the expense of Nathalie as this elevates the sexual woman over the married, maternal woman, whose intense love for Baptiste presents femininity – despite Casarès's normal charisma as a performer – in terms of restriction, confinement and suffocation; the very antithesis of the transcendence Baptiste hopes to attain with Garance. In representing marriage in this way, Carné, as a gay director, is challenging one of the strongest institutions supporting heterosexual monogamy. By extension, he is also challenging Vichy's ideas of family – after all, its slogan was '*Travail, Famille, Patrie*' ('Work, family, fatherland').

Central to the film's disruption of gender is the role of Baptiste, whom Sellier refers to as the 'homme doux'. We have seen Cuny embody a similar male persona in *Les Visiteurs du soir*, and indeed, the two performers at the time were compared in an article, 'Les artistes les plus discutés' ('The most discussed artists') (G. B., 1944). In this respect, there is continuity in the representation of masculinity in Carné's Occupation films. Baptiste's embodiment of this role is apparent through his delicate appearance, his passionate desire for romance, and the nature of his miming, which centres upon his vulnerability and fragility, particularly as he wears white makeup on his face for his performances. Off stage too, he exhibits similar qualities, with him wandering around holding a flower in the early parts of the film, dreaming of Garance.

Such disruptions to traditional notions of gender suggest that *Les Enfants du paradis* and *Les Visiteurs du soir* provide a fuller exploration of Carné's homosexuality than the films of the 1930s. Both Baptiste and Garance embody a gay sensibility through their challenge to conventional attitudes – Baptiste possesses sensitivity and Garance strength and assertiveness. But the film goes even further, in providing explicit representations of male homosexuality with Lacenaire and Avril. Lacenaire, the historical figure, was gay, which is alluded to at a number of points in the film, particularly through his dandyish appearance – he wears shirts with frills and a long dark coat, carries a cane, and has carefully curled hair and a neatly trimmed moustache – and apparent lack of physical or romantic interest in Garance. While he admires her intelligence, it is clear that he does not seek to form a couple with her in the way the other male characters do. In addition, there are hints of homosexuality in his relationship with his sidekick, Avril, who offsets his tough guy image by wearing a flower behind his ear. Moreover, a gay subtext is evident at points in the film's iconography, particularly in the Turkish bath scene near the end of the film, depicting several semi-naked men lounging by the pool. Turk (1989: 326) describes the scene as homoerotic, pinpointing Carné's use of imagery from Jean Auguste Dominique Ingres's painting *The Turkish Bath*, but with the bathing women swapped for men. This argument is given weight by the film's numerous other allusions to Ingres, such as when we see Garance lounging semi-naked on Baptiste's bed (referencing *La Grande Odalisque*), and when she mentions in a conversation to the police a little later that she has modelled for 'Monsieur Ingres'.

In part these disruptions to gender relate to the broader changes discussed, as already mentioned, by Burch and Sellier. At the same time, they represent another instance of Carné's unconventional approach to gender, and it is notable that the key instances of the 'homme doux' appear in *his* films (indeed, Burch and Sellier's (1996: 155) exploration of this phenomenon begins with a discussion of

Carné). Because *Les Enfants du paradis* conflicts so strikingly with Vichy and Nazi hetero-normative views of gender we can see the importance of its dissonant representations, which constitutes one of the main ways that the film may be thought of as resisting the ideology of both Vichy and Nazi Germany.

We can see, then, some key reasons behind the extraordinary nature and status of *Les Enfants du paradis*. Central to this, as I have argued, is that the film balances the demands of art and entertainment. This issue is indeed the core subject of *Les Enfants du paradis* in which melodrama is shown as both a popular and an elevated form of entertainment, performed by geniuses for an adoring mass audience. In addition, as the culmination of poetic realism the film advances a prestigious and critically revered type of cinema while still appealing to the public; as a costume film, it offers its spectators intense nostalgia and lavish spectacle, which also emphasises the skill of Carné – his creation of polish, precision and scale – and of his performers. However, while aspects of the film may be seen as resisting the dominant Vichy ideology, particularly the representation of gender, its success would not prevent Carné from being embroiled in controversy at the Liberation. On 25 August 1944 Paris was liberated by the Allies and on 9 March 1945 *Les Enfants du paradis* was released to huge acclaim. It would prove to be Carné's greatest achievement, but from now on his career would be a bumpy ride.

The aftermath

Les Portes de la nuit

The postwar period was marked by attempts to 'purify' the nation (known as the *épuration*), and punish those responsible for collaborating with the Nazis. Senior political figures in the Vichy regime were tried, and a number were executed. Although Maréchal Phillipe Pétain, leader of Vichy France, escaped execution, with judges taking into account his services to France in the First World War, he died soon afterwards in prison. Women who had had relationships with the occupiers were targeted, with many having their heads forcibly shaved, a development that signified patriarchy's aggressive desire to reassert its authority, and to put blame for recent events on women – a process dramatised in Alain Resnais's *Hiroshima mon amour*

(1959). Such developments also had an impact on the film industry, with creative personnel being targeted by postwar authorities. Many filmmakers and actors were severely criticised for working under the Nazis, including Pierre Fresnay, Sacha Guitry, Henri Decoin, and Henri-Georges Clouzot. Robert Le Vigan was sentenced to ten years' hard labour for his public support of the occupiers and in extreme cases senior figures were executed, such as the director Jean Mamy and the critic Robert Brasillach.

These events affected Carné, a key target of the *épuration*. Because he had signed with Continental, albeit briefly, and had continued to work during the Occupation, he was seen by many as guilty of collaboration. Although he wasn't banned from the industry, he was given a public censure, which badly affected his reputation. The decline of his status was evident when he made his first film after the war, *Les Portes de la nuit*, a huge critical failure. Jean Fayard (1946), for example, referred to the film as 'une histoire insipide, générale-ment incompréhensible, et d'une prodigieuse prétention' ('an insipid story, generally incomprehensible, and prodigiously pretentious'). However, with 2.6 million spectators[4] the film is certainly not the flop it is generally thought to be – an example of critical reception being confused with popular taste. In addition, *Les Portes de la nuit* is a key text about Carné's relationship with the postwar cinematic and social context and in fact a rare screen document about postwar Paris.

To some extent *Les Portes de la nuit* contains important continu-ities with Carné's earlier filmmaking. Most importantly, it was written by Prévert, though it would be their last film together, on account of the film's reception as well as the emergence of disagreements between them. Taking place in the space of twenty-four hours in a war-ravaged Paris, the film follows Jean Diego (Yves Montand), a resistance fighter, who has an intense and romantic, albeit brief, affair with Malou (Nathalie Nattier). Other characters include Raymond Lécuyer (Raymond Bussières), Diego's friend from the resistance; Guy Sénéchal (Serge Reggiani), Malou's brother and an informer and collaborator during the war; Monsieur Sénéchal (Saturnin Farbre), Guy and Malou's father and also an informer; Georges (Pierre Brasseur), Malou's husband and a munitions industrialist who has profited from the war; and a homeless man called Destin (Jean Vilar), a mysterious

---

4 Box-office information for Carné's postwar work has been taken from Simon Simsi's *Ciné-Passions* (2000).

character and personification of fate. Although Diego experiences a brief moment of transcendence and escape from postwar hardships in his relationship with Malou, the film ends with Georges, motivated by jealousy, shooting and killing her.

As this synopsis may suggest, central to the film is its use of poetic realist features. While some of Carné's later films would contain similar elements, this was the last of his works to truly belong to this type of film. There is a strong sense of doom, pessimism and fate as well as a worldview bound up with poetic realism's Manicheism. This is tailor-made for the postwar context, with the resistance characters representing 'good' and the various informers and profiteers 'bad'. Whereas the films of the Occupation turned to the past, *Les Portes de la nuit* is a return to the present, making its articulation of the tension between the 'poetic' and the 'realist' more in keeping with the films of the 1930s. In addition to the references to real events, such as rationing and food shortages,[5] the film includes various working-class settings, such as the neighbourhood café, the canal, and the Barbès-Rochechouart métro station. These settings are transformed in characteristic ways: they are recreated by studio sets, filled with mist and steam, and the streets are dark and rain-swept. One scene taking place in a sculpture yard encapsulates the duality of poetic realism's *mise en scène*, with the setting being a plausible space for action to take place, but with the statues also creating the feeling of time standing still, as the lovers first meet. The film also includes a working-class hero, this time played by Montand, and a glamorous woman, Nathalie Nattier, who again stands for the possibility of romantic transcendence. All of this ensures that the poetic realist 'atmosphere' in *Les Portes de la nuit* remains intact, an atmosphere signalled to the spectator from the very 'poetic' title of the film.

At the same time, the film signals new departures in a number of ways. For Andrew (1995), it is – as with *Les Enfants du paradis* – a reflection upon the earlier films, drawing knowingly upon the conventions of poetic realism. One of the elements that best illustrates this is the character of Destin (the French word for 'destiny'). Whereas there is always a hint of fate governing the lives of characters in poetic realism, through Destin this is made much more explicit: not only

---

5 Turk (1989: 357) highlights other 'topical allusions': 'These include the August 19 insurrection, Drancy Prison and the *épuration*, the "Chant des Partisans," blackouts, black markets, the famine, and the last metro.'

does he claim to *be* fate, he also makes predictions about the future which turn out to be true. In addition, as Turk writes (1989: 360), the film's knowingness is evident through the numerous references to Carné's prewar work, such as the 'chiaroscuro' of *Le Quai des brumes* or the street singer of *Jenny*.

One notable difference from Carné's earlier work is in his choice of stars. *Les Portes de la nuit* was supposed to star Marlene Dietrich and Jean Gabin, who after spending time together in Hollywood during the war, were now a couple. Had they made the film together, Dietrich's glamorous image would have fitted well within Carné's representations of women. At the same time, Gabin's immediate postwar attempts to resurrect his prewar persona were generally unsuccessful as Vincendeau notes (2000, 74). In the end the couple didn't make the film, citing that its subject matter – dealing with collaborators – was too controversial (see Turk, 1989: 354). To some extent, Dietrich's replacement, Nattier, works well as a poetic realist heroine: she is young, glamorous, acts in a nuanced, understated way, and is photographed and lit in a manner similar to prewar stars like Morgan and Annabella, thus heightening her photogenic qualities. At the same time, she lacked the piquancy and prestige of these earlier stars, and her career went into decline. *Les Portes de la nuit*, however, launched the career of Yves Montand, who became one of the top stars of French cinema from the 1950s onwards, up to the acclaimed *Jean de florette* (Claude Berri, 1986) and *Manon des sources* (Claude Berri, 1986). As Jill Forbes (1993: 8) argues, regardless of the criticism the film received, which was considerable, Carné should be praised for his discovery of Montand, which stresses once more his talent as a discoverer of stars. Montand, who began as a music-hall singer, provides a different vision of the poetic realist protagonist to Gabin's earlier roles. Despite his own modest origins, Montand did not embody the strong working-class identity, or the immediacy and authenticity central to Gabin's persona, creating instead the 'distance' we have encountered in *Les Enfants du paradis*. However, while *Les Enfants du paradis* was hugely successful, *Les Portes de la nuit* was a critical failure. Why was this?

In part this stemmed from the demonisation of Carné at the time. In the context of the *épuration*, in which Carné was accused of collaboration, the film's condemnation of collaborators was considered by some to be hypocritical. In addition, he was publicly criticised for his 'tyranical' on-set manner and for his costly aesthetic whims, such as his decision to recreate the Barbès-Rochechouart métro station in the studio. The elaborate set was discussed at length in the film's press book and articles on the film, in much the same way as the sets of *Les Enfants du paradis* and *Hôtel du Nord* had been celebrated. However, when the film was released such extravagance was considered to be inappropriate.

In truth, however, the film was attacked because of the bleakness of Carné's representation of the immediate postwar world. Its treatment of this context is one of its most interesting features, partly because other films at the time concentrated on glorifying the resistance, and partly because of how this treatment is refracted through the aesthetics of poetic realism. Together Carné and Prévert provide an unflinchingly harsh portrayal of France in the postwar period, dealing with a range of controversial issues. The film begins with a caption stating that the action is set during the cold winter following the Liberation. We witness the shortages that people have to endure: they queue for wood; others on the métro look hungry and dishevelled. To some extent the film reveals hints of a community, through exchanges in the apartment block between Quinquina (Julien Carette) and Lécuyer, and the prominence of the singer at the station, which evokes the prewar period – 1930s films often included street singers as an index of community (for example, at the beginning of *Sous les toits de Paris*). However, the film is far removed from *Hôtel du Nord*, for instance, which portrays the inhabitants of the hotel as a large, extended family. Instead, *Les Portes de la nuit* ultimately shows the beginning of the deterioration of the community – the France we are presented with is based upon various forms of division. We witness a significant gap between rich and poor, with Monsieur Sénéchal living in a large, well decorated apartment, with a big fire burning, while other characters are impoverished. Moreover, by separating the characters into resistance fighters and collaborators, *Les Portes de la nuit* stresses another way the nation is divided: between the guilty and the not guilty.

The fact that the period's social issues are explored through the aesthetics of poetic realism inevitably means that the film advances a pessimistic assessment of the current state of France. Romantic love, as in the earlier films, fails to offer an escape, and, instead, the film draws towards a negative, fatalistic ending. It has been suggested that audiences did not want to confront this vision of France, and, indeed, the cinema of the time avoided focusing on collaboration. The majority of films that dealt with the war in the immediate postwar period dealt instead with the heroics of the resistance, evident in such films as *La Bataille du rail* (René Clément, 1946). However, the film's reception cannot be explained only through the fact that it explores the grimness of postwar France. As Andrew (1995: 325) argues, such a perspective is too 'reflectionist': 'Can it be this simple? Can we calculate the success rate of films according to the degree to which the topics they treat are in public favor?' For him (1995: 326) the problem with *Les Portes de la nuit* is that it falls between the immediacy of prewar poetic realism and the 'finesse', the stylistic perfection, of *Les Enfants du paradis*. Others have claimed that poetic realism was not appropriate for the postwar context, such as Susan Hayward (1993: 165), who states: 'The whole notion of poetic realism just did not sit comfortably with the new times of jazz and modernity'. Thus, while Carné's nostalgic worldview had facilitated his popularity during the war, it was now something of an impediment. Turk (1989: 361) adds that the problem was also that poetic realism had been superseded by new forms of realism, such as Italian neorealism, and in France the work of René Clément, whose *La Bataille du rail* used location shooting and amateur actors.

There is yet another dimension to this, which is that Carné's poetic realist vision presented gender in a way that conflicted with the postwar cinematic context. Burch and Sellier (1996) discuss the backlash against women in the postwar years, during which they were used as scapegoats for the nation's problems, and identify a rise in negative female stereotypes. Of particular importance, they note how the period's resistance films would often downplay women's role at this time, or worse would present them as duplicitous and evil in contrast to the male heroes. *Les Portes de la nuit* offers a quite different vision of femininity, through the character of Milou. Throughout the film she is searching for her lost innocence, a loss that is signified in Carné–Prévert's populist universe through her wealthier appearance: whereas the prewar heroines were modest and understated in their dress, signifying their purity, Milou has elaborately coiffeured hair and wears a large fur coat and jewellery. In her melancholy, she also appears to bear guilt, which could be read as an allegory of the postwar attack against women for 'horizontal collaboration' (sleeping with the enemy). In addition, as she spent the war away from France, this could be seen as Carné attacking people who were away, such as Renoir (who by contrast was critical of people like Carné who stayed and worked in occupied France). Milou is also presented as guilty through her association with a number of the film's negative characters: she has been married to a war profiteer (Georges), and is related to two informers, her brother Guy and her father Monsieur Sénéchal. However, as Turk (1989: 357) argues, Milou represents 'absolute goodness': she wants to escape from her husband and is in the thralls of 'pure love' with Diego; she is also encoded visually as pure, through her pale face, blonde hair and glamorous treatment, involving the use of soft lighting. Here then, Carné and Prévert continue to mould gender through the aesthetics of poetic realism, inspired by melodrama, in which the woman (as part of the young idealistic couple) signifies 'good', in contrast to an array of men who represent 'evil'. Consequently, *Les Portes de la nuit* not only deals with the taboo issue of collaboration, it also places the blame on men, rather than women.

Because of the controversial reception of *Les Portes de la nuit* the Carné story from this point on is conventionally seen as involving a steep and depressing decline. There is certainly some truth in this, as he would never attain the strong position in the film industry that he had experienced during the Occupation. However, in the chapters that follow I will depart from this narrative by discussing ways in which his postwar work has more value than many have claimed. I would like to begin this by stressing some of the important aspects of *Les Portes de la nuit* that were not celebrated at the time. First of all it should be pointed out that Carné's forthright confrontation of difficult issues relating to the war was very much ahead of its time. It would be a long time before films, such as *Le Chagrin et la pitié* (Marcel Ophüls, 1969), confronted head-on the issue of collaboration during the war. In part Carné's visionary approach may be seen to derive from his attitude to gender within his poetic realist aesthetics. Nevertheless it is also typical that Carné was ahead of his time in not subscribing to the macho misogyny found in other films of the period, such as the resistance films. The centrality of politics to *Les Portes de la nuit* is significant in that Carné didn't often engage in such issues, or had been seen as evading them – for instance, during the Popular Front. In this respect, the film can be seen as Carné's 'defence', a reply to the criticism he received during the *épuration*. By tackling these issues in such a direct and controversial way, Carné is showing that he *is* concerned about France's activities during the war; that these issues *do* matter to him.

In keeping with Ehrlich's notion of the 'cinema of paradox', the war was a mixed period for Carné. On the one hand, he reached the height of his success, emerging as the most prestigious figure of the Occupation, in part because the period was ideal for his type of cinema. The emphasis on polished, finely crafted films, set in closed contexts, suited his approach to filmmaking. The turmoil of the Occupation also enabled him to experiment: by making films that were set in places far removed from contemporary life, he could safely explore his unconventional attitudes to gender, while also challenging the Vichy ideology. The Occupation also suited Carné's cinema because it allowed him to explore his interest in a nostalgic, populist vision of France. Moreover, the popular genres in vogue at the time facilitated his creation of films that were at once recognised as 'art' *and* 'entertainment'. On the other hand, the Occupation marked the beginning of the end for Carné. During the war he had been in sync with the dominant film culture, but in the postwar period he began to drift away from the centre of the industry. There would be ups, with popular films such as *La Marie du port*, but also downs, particularly *Juliette ou la clef des songes* – it is this next phase in Carné's cinema that the following chapter will explore.

References

Andrew, D. (1995), *Mists of Regret: Culture and Sensibility in Classic French Film*, Princeton; Chichester, Princeton University Press.

Bazin, A. (1983), 'The disincarnation of Carné', in M. L. Bandy, ed., *Rediscovering French Film*, New York, Museum of Modern Art, pp. 131–5.

Burch, N., and G. Sellier (1996), *La drôle de guerre des sexes du cinéma français, 1930–1956*, Paris, Nathan.

Carné, M. (1996), *Ma vie à belles dents*, Paris, L'Archipel.

Chion, M. (2008), *Le Complexe de Cyrano: La langue parlée dans les films français*, Paris: Éditions Cahiers du Cinéma.

Daix, D. (1942), 'Les films de cette semaine', *Ciné-mondial*, 69, 18 December, p. 7.

Darke, C. (1993), '*Les Enfants du paradis*', *Sight and Sound*, 3:9, pp. 55–6.

Ehrlich, E. (1985), *Cinema of Paradox: French Filmmaking under the German Occupation*, New York; Guildford, Columbia University Press.

Fayard, J. (1946), 'Avec 100 millions et 30 locomotives, Carné et Prévert n'ont fait des *Portes de la nuit* qu'un film triste et prétentieux', *Résistance-Paris Matin*, 11 December.

Forbes, J. (1993), 'Surreal eye in the city', *The Guardian*, 20 August, pp. 8–9.

Forbes, J. (1997), *Les Enfants du paradis*, London, British Film Institute.

G. B. (1944), 'Les artistes les plus discutés', *Ciné-mondial*, 149–50, 21 and 28 June, p. 9.

Hayward, S. (1993), *French National Cinema*, London; New York, Routledge.

Heuze, P. (1943), 'Autour du meilleur film de l'année', *Ciné-mondial*, 112, 22 October, p. 4.

Jackson, J. (2001), *France: The Dark Years, 1940–1944*, Oxford, Oxford University Press.

Jeancolas, J.-P. (2000), 'Beneath the despair, the show goes on: Marcel Carné's *Les Enfants du paradis* (1943–45)', in S. Hayward and G. Vincendeau, eds, *French Film: Texts and Contexts*, 2nd edn, London, Routledge, pp. 78–88.

Jehander (1942), '*Les Visiteurs du soir*', *Ciné-mondial*, 67, 4 December, pp. 6–7.

Lombardy, J. (1944), 'Il a fallu reconstruire Paris pour ... *Les Enfants du paradis*', *Ciné-mondial*, 151–2, 4 and 11 August, pp. 6–7.

McCann, B. (2006), '*Les Enfants du paradis*', in P. Powrie, ed., *The Cinema of France*, London, Wallflower.

Naremore, J. (1988), *Acting in the Cinema*, Berkeley; London, University of California Press.

Pol, A. (1944), 'Arletty ou la vérité toute nue', *Ciné-mondial*, 137–8, 28 April and 5 May, pp. 8–9.

Pol, A. (1944a), 'Les créateurs', *Ciné-mondial*, 149–50, 21 and 28 June, pp. 5–6.

Reader, K. (2001), 'Mon cul est intersexuel? Arletty's performance of gender', in A. Hughes and J. S. Williams, eds, *Gender and French Cinema*, Oxford, Berg, pp. 63–76.

Renald, J. (1942), 'Un metteur en scène qui voit grand', *Ciné-mondial*, 53, 28 August, p. 3.

Sadoul, G. (1953), *French Film*, London, The Falcon Press.

Sellier, G. (1992), *Les Enfants du paradis*, Paris, Nathan.

Sellier, G. (1997), '*Les Enfants du paradis* dans le cinéma de l'Occupation', *1895*, 22 (July), pp. 55–66.

Simsi, S. (2000), *Ciné-Passions: 7ᵉ art et industrie de 1945 à 2000*, Paris, Editions Dixit.

Turk, E. B. (1989), *Child of Paradise: Marcel Carné and the Golden Age of French Cinema*, Cambridge, Mass.; London, Harvard University Press.

Vincendeau, G. (2000), *Stars and Stardom in French Cinema*, London, Continuum.

Vincendeau, G. (2004), 'Forms 1930–1960: The art of spectacle', in M. Temple and M. Witt, eds, *The French Cinema Book*, London, British Film Institute, pp. 137–52.

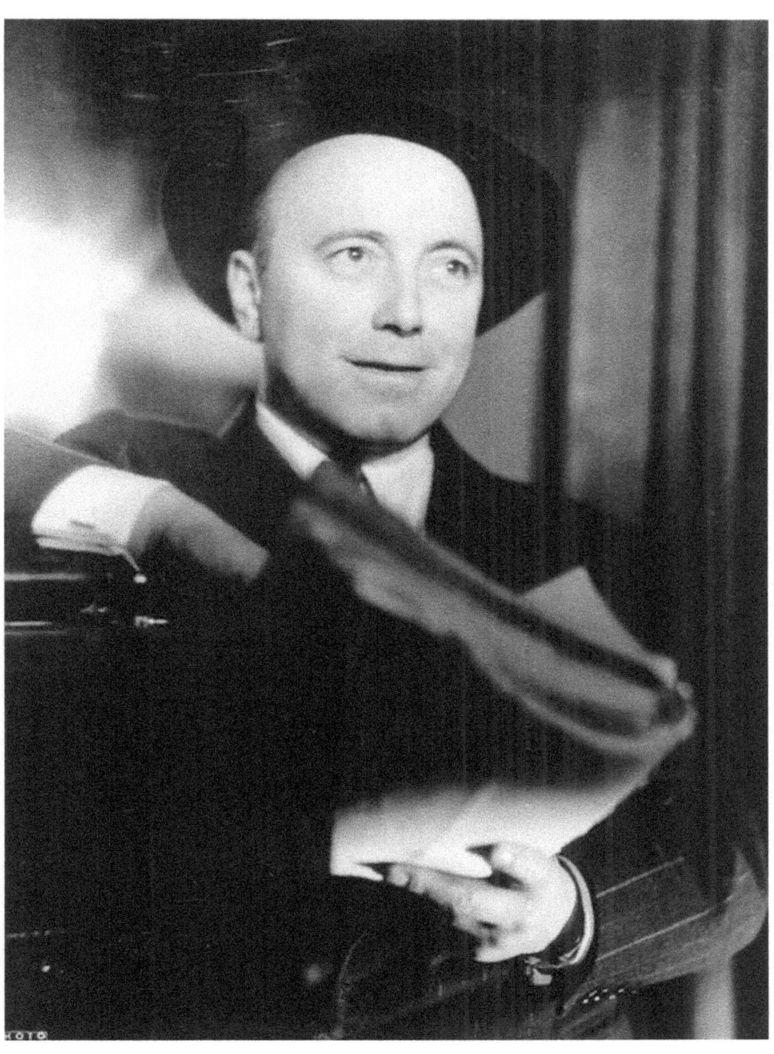

1 Marcel Carné.

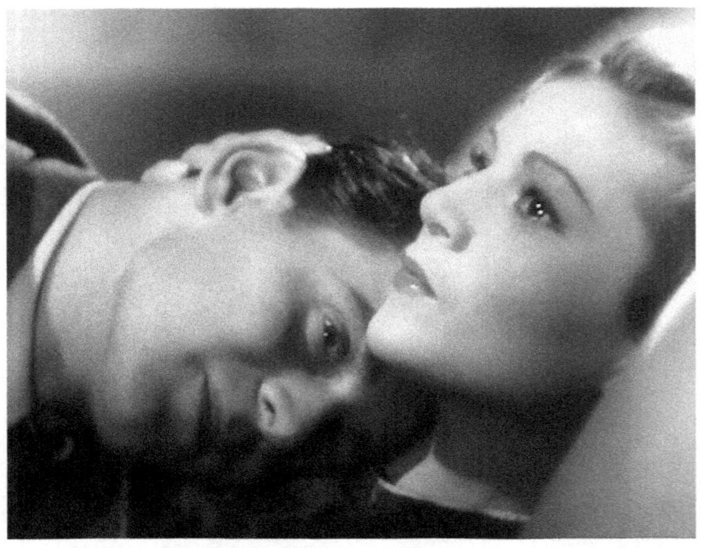

2 A fatalistic couple: Jean-Pierre Aumont and Annabella in *Hôtel du Nord* (1938).

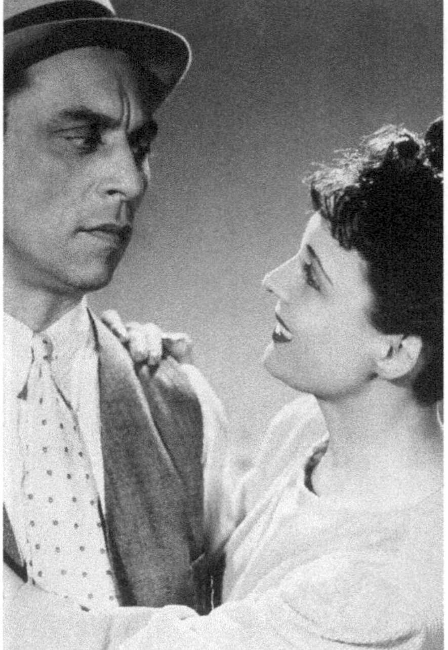

3 War of the sexes: Louis Jouvet and Arletty in a publicity still for *Hôtel du Nord* (1938).

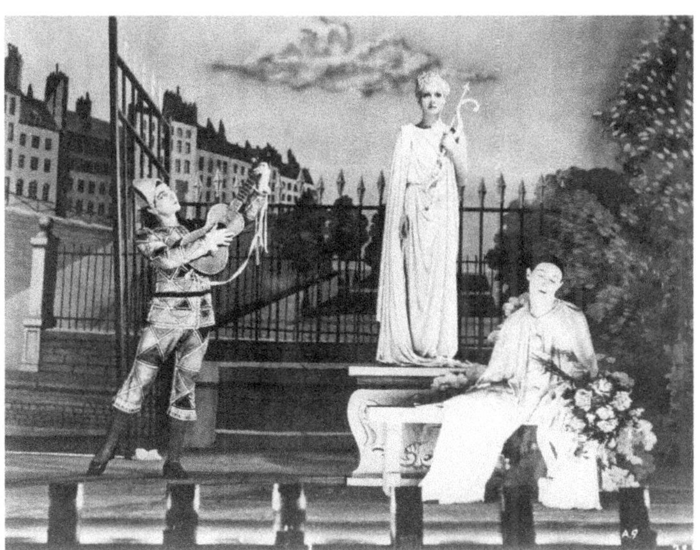

4 Woman on a pedestal: Pierre Brasseur, Arletty, and Jean-Louis Barrault in *Les Enfants du paradis* (1945).

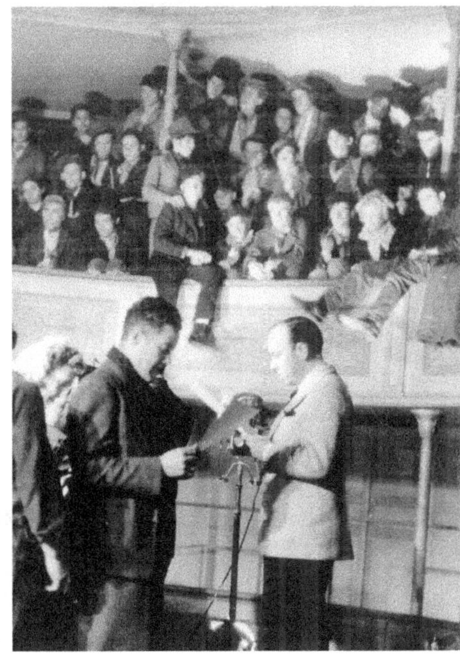

5 The director at work: Carné on the set of *Les Enfants du paradis* (1945).

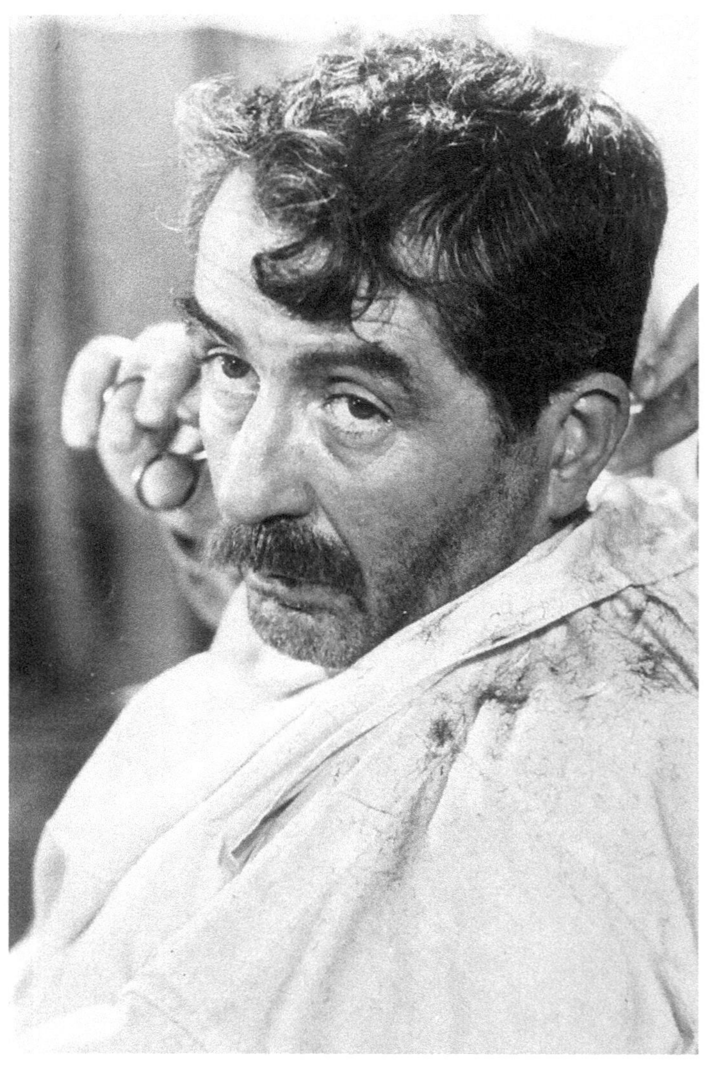

6 A Carné regular: Julien Carette in a scene from *La Marie du port* (1950).

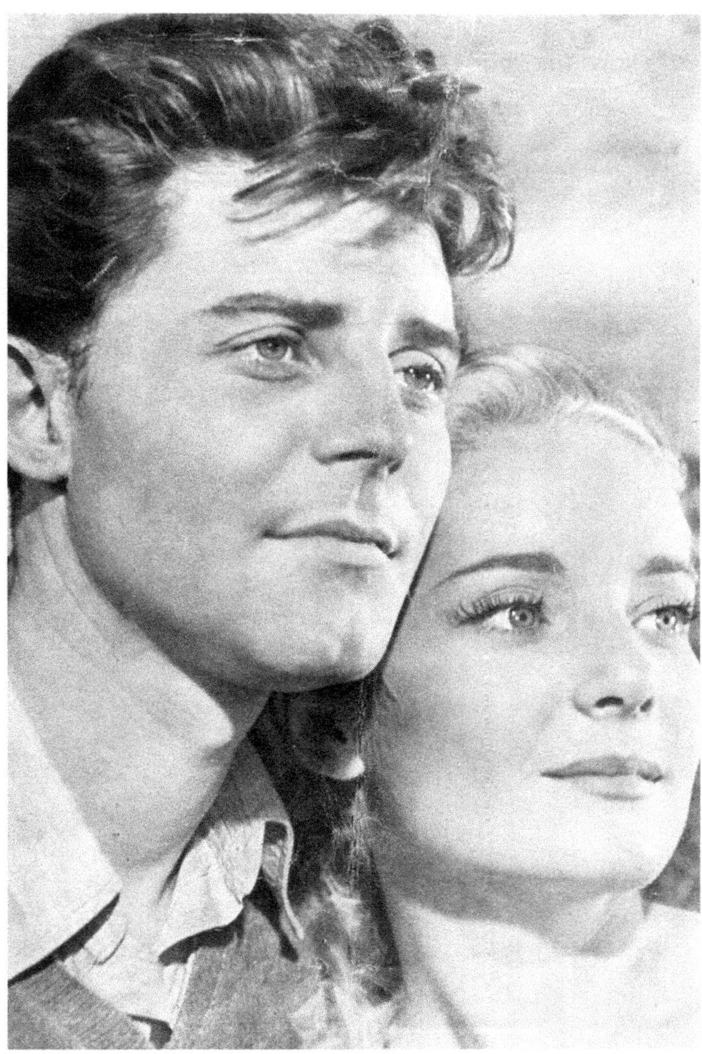

7 Matinee idol: Gérard Philipe with Suzanne Cloutier in a publicity still for *Juliette ou la clef des songes* (1951).

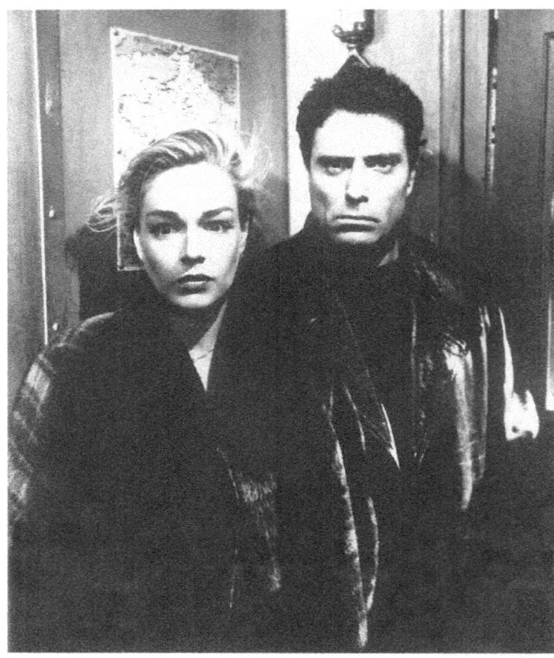

8 Doomed lovers: Simone Signoret and Raf Vallone in a publicity still for *Thérèse Raquin* (1953).

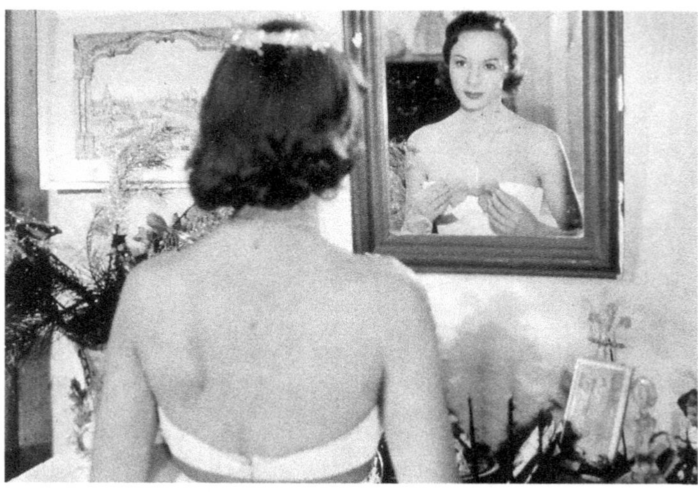

9 Fairy tale femininity: Françoise Arnoul in *Le Pays d'où je viens* (1956).

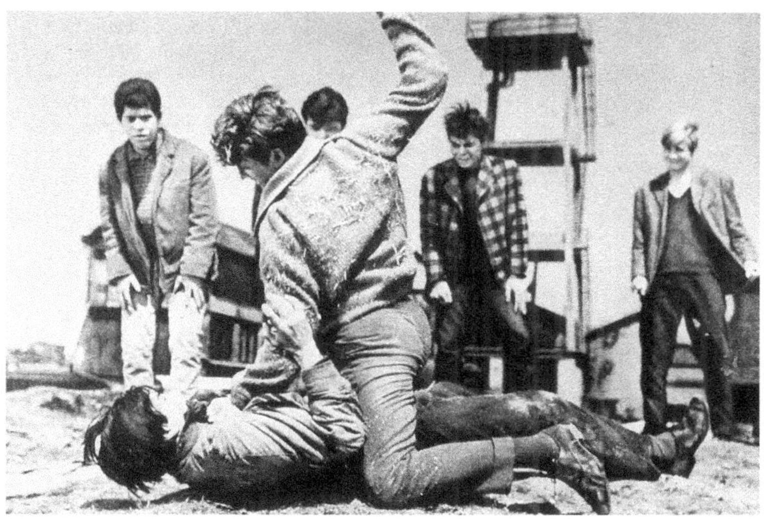

10 Youth delinquency: *Terrain vague* (1960).

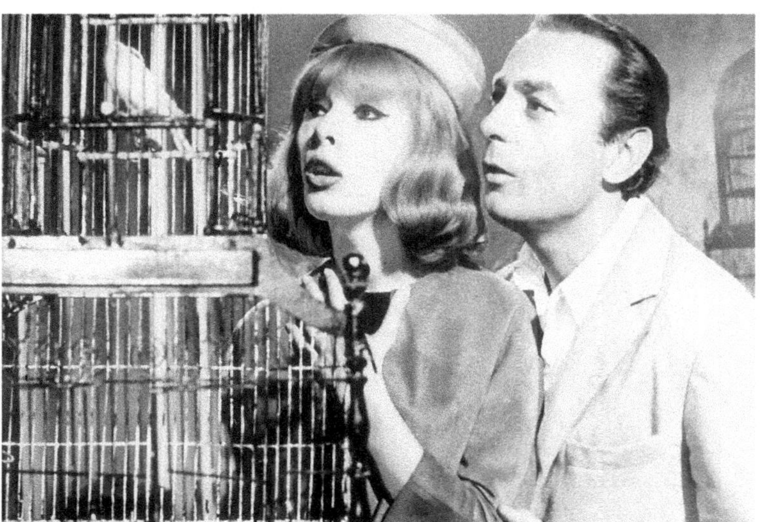

11 A caged bird as a symbol of entrapment: Dany Saval and Roland Lesaffre in *Du mouron pour les petits oiseaux* (1963).

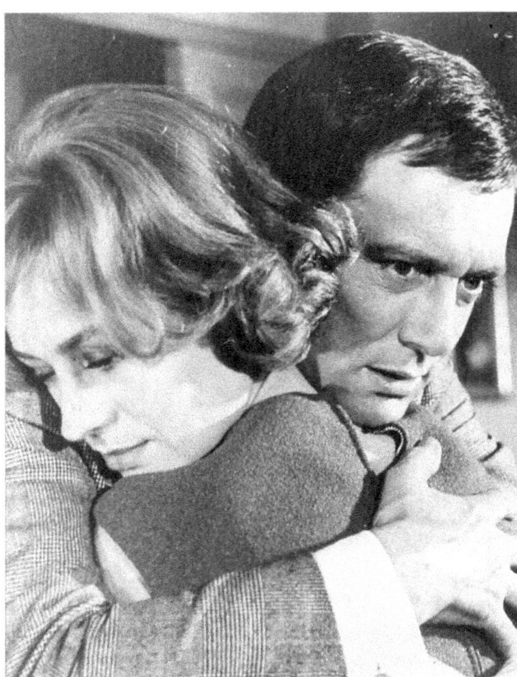

12 Romantic love: Annie Girardot and Maurice Ronet in *Trois Chambres à Manhattan* (1965).

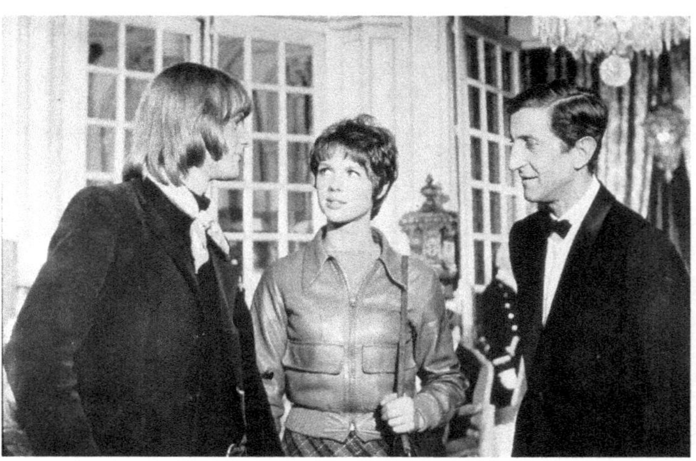

13 1960s youth culture: Yves Beneyton and Haydée Politoff with Maurice Garrel in *Les Jeunes Loups* (1968).

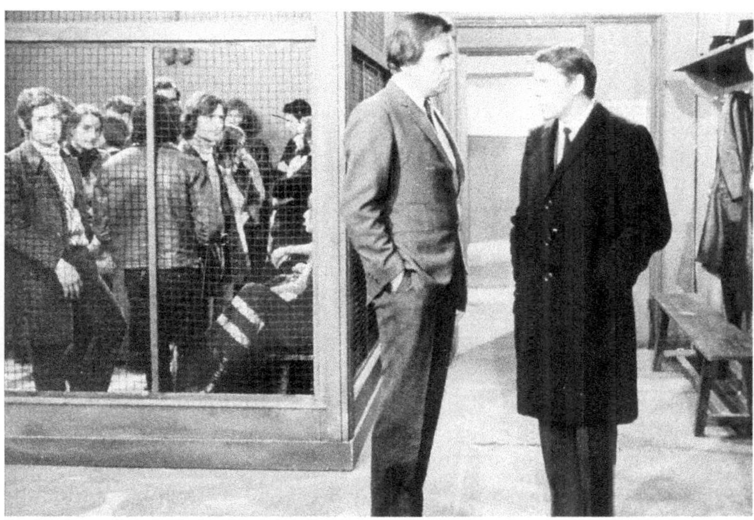

14 Challenging police corruption: Michel Lonsdale and Jacques Brel in *Les Assassins de l'ordre* (1971).

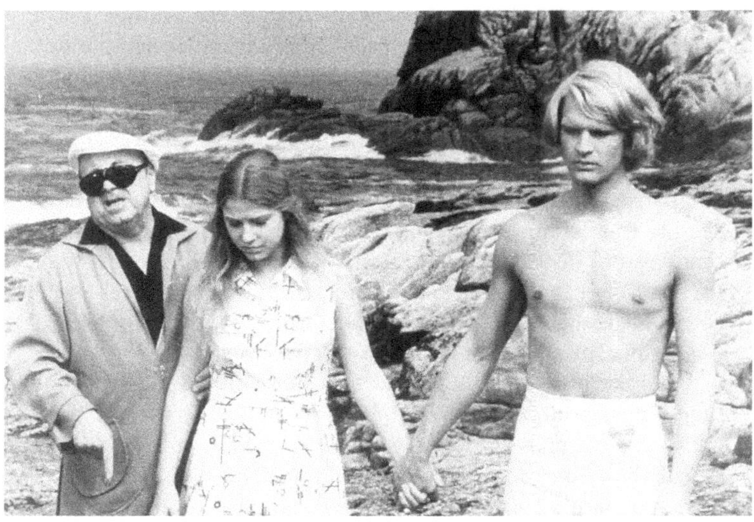

15 The end of a long career: Carné during the filming of *La Merveilleuse Visite* (1974), with Gilles Kohler and Deborah Berger.

4

Postwar cinema and the tradition of quality

Marcel Carné's films of the 1950s have received significantly less scholarly attention than his earlier work. In large part this stems from the profound hostility shown to these films by critics from the *Cahiers du Cinéma*. While Turk (1989) provides useful discussion of Carné's postwar films, he does not consider them in the same depth as the earlier work. In part this is symptomatic of a more general neglect of postwar popular French cinema; only in recent years have scholars begun to challenge the negative evaluation of this period. Indeed, more recently, scholars such as Richard Dyer (2000) and Susan Hayward (2003 and 2004) have written on some of Carné's postwar films. In this chapter I would like to continue this re-examination of this work, which I consider to be important for the following reasons.

Firstly, this period is notable for the fact that Carné was now working without Prévert. The importance of this has been noted by other writers, with Turk in particular providing a detailed discussion of this issue. His chapter on Carné's postwar work, 'Carné sans Prévert' ('Carné without Prévert'), highlights the centrality of Prévert's absence to understanding these films. In this chapter I shall contribute to this debate about whether Carné's work without Prévert was significantly different from his work with him.

I will also place emphasis on Carné's continuing popularity at this time, which is surprisingly downplayed by most writers. The *Cahiers* critics, for example, driven by a desire to expose Carné as 'out of touch', show little concern for the popularity of his films. Turk (1989) points out that *La Marie du port*, *Thérèse Raquin*, and *Les Tricheurs* were popular, though he gives little space to discussing them. By contrast, Vincendeau (1997) argues that Carné's continuing popularity in the postwar years is significant. Indeed, while his critical success wanes around this time, he achieved a number of box-office successes; his films were discussed at length in popular film fan magazines, and the large number of articles focusing on him shows that within the French film industry he was still something of a celebrated personality. In addition, another index of his films' place within the period's popular cinema is that they continue to include France's biggest stars. During this period he worked with Jean Gabin, Gérard Philipe, Simone Signoret, Gilbert Bécaud, and Arletty (though, following the postwar controversy surrounding her involvement with a Nazi officer, she was no longer prominent). The fact that Carné was working with such A-list stars indicates he was still a key player in popular French cinema. Examining the popularity of his work is thus central to understanding his significance in postwar French cinema and in particular the hugely popular, but critically despised, tradition of quality.

The tradition of quality became dominant in the postwar period, though it was already emerging during the Occupation; as a spectacular costume film *Les Enfants du paradis* was an important precursor to this type of cinema. As its name suggests, the tradition of quality was a cinema of 'quality': these middlebrow films were often based on prestigious French literature and exhibited high production values; the sets and camerawork are impeccable, and the accomplished actors were often taken from 'respectable' theatre, such as the Comédie-Française. Until recently, these films have been viewed in largely negative terms, with the *Cahiers* critics disparagingly referring to them as the 'cinéma de papa', implying that it was old-fashioned and out of date. They were particularly critical of the emphasis in these films on the script, with Truffaut in January 1954 making a famous attack in 'Une certaine tendance du cinéma français' ('A certain tendency in French cinema') (2009) on Jean Aurenche and Pierre Bost, screenwriters responsible for many classics of the tradition of quality, such as *Douce* (Claude Autant-Lara, 1943), *La Symphonie pastorale* (Jean Delannoy, 1946), *Le Diable au corps* (Claude Autant-Lara, 1947), and *Jeux interdits* (René Clément, 1952). For Truffaut, the anti-bourgeois and overly literary emphasis of their work conflicted with his more romantic and cinephilic view of film. In Film Studies attitudes to this period are changing, and recent years have witnessed a renewed interest in this cinema. It is now acknowledged that the tradition of quality played an important role in defining French national film production in the postwar years, that it was central to the period's popular cinema, and that in certain respects it contains progressive political positions, particularly through its emphasis on female-centred films and discourses. Carné's place within the tradition of quality is important to this revisionist history. In many ways he was an ideal contributor to this type of cinema. As we have seen he was a master craftsman, who tended to work on studio sets, placed great importance upon achieving a polished finish to his films and adopted a careful and controlled style. He also advocated a collaborative approach to filmmaking, meaning that he fitted well within the tradition of quality's emphasis on scriptwriters, and he was keen on using major stars, many of whom came from theatrical backgrounds. In exploring these issues, I will highlight ways in which Carné's filmmaking continued to explore the themes and style of his earlier work, while also stressing the shifts that occurred, particularly towards a 'psychological realist' aesthetic, an important style emerging at this time.

A final important consideration for this chapter will be to examine Carné's relationship with the context of postwar France, a period that witnessed huge social and political changes. In her book on this period, *Fast Cars, Clean Bodies*, Kristin Ross (1995) examines how a range of cultural forms related to dominant issues emerging at this time. As the nation surrendered its colonies, it went through a period of rapid modernisation. The years between 1945 and 1975 are referred to as 'les trente glorieuses' ('the glorious thirty') on account of the economic boom that occurred. This brought about an increased 'embourgeoisement' of the nation, along with a growing Americanisation, evident in a range of cultural products, including films. These changes had an impact on all areas of French society, not least on notions of gender. The cinema of the years between 1945 and 1955 (the main period this chapter is concerned with) has been discussed by Noël Burch and Geneviève Sellier, who explore how masculinity reasserted its power following the nation's 'emasculation' during the war – resulting in an often misogynistic vision of femininity. Less has been written about Carné's relationship to this context, though Vincendeau (1997) makes a number of crucial points, arguing that his films of the period give insight into changes in France, such as its increasingly bourgeois character, the deterioration of communities, and shifts in gender and sexuality, areas that I will consider in this chapter.

Incarnation and disincarnation

Carné's immediate postwar work was defined by a series of false starts, with him trying, unsuccessfully, to get a number of projects off the ground. Although he had started and abandoned a number of films in the 1930s and during the war, there is an increase in such failed attempts at this time. The most intriguing of these projects was *La Fleur de l'âge*, which Carné and Prévert had already tried and failed to make in 1936 as *L'Île des enfants perdus*. Although Carné shot some scenes, the film ran into financial trouble and was abandoned. Like Carné's other work *Fleur de l'âge* would have involved big stars. As discussed in Chapter 2, the film was initially going to star Danielle Darrieux; the postwar version would have included Arletty, in her return to the cinema, Martine Carol, one of the biggest stars of the period, and Anouk Aimée, in one of her first roles. Aimée, who was referred to in one article on the film's production as 'la révélation féminine du film' ('the female revelation of the film') (Anon., 1947: 7), would go on to become a prominent star, appearing in such films as *La dolce vita* (Federico Fellini, 1960), *8½* (Federico Fellini, 1963), and *Un homme et une femme* (Claude Lelouch, 1966). This again stresses Carné's ability to spot fresh talent; as we have seen, he was responsible for launching the careers – or at least accelerating the rise – of a number of stars.

The fate of *La Fleur de l'âge*, and Carné's other false starts, shows that his position in the industry was becoming increasingly weak. It also marks the end of the Carné-Prévert partnership, in part linked to, according to some sources, an increasingly difficult working relationship (see Turk, 1989: 362). That said, Carné's next film, *La Marie du port*, included some contribution from Prévert, though the extent of this is disputed. Whereas Prévert has claimed that his involvement was minimal, Carné has stated that he had a significant role in the writing of the film. Either way, Prévert is not credited for his contribution.

La Marie du port

Carné now badly needed a success. He still had ambition, in particular to make *Juliette ou la clef des songes*, a large-scale film he had been hoping to make for a number of years (he attempted but failed to make it in 1942). The producer Sacha Gordine told him that he would fund the risky project if Carné first made a popular success. With this in mind, in 1949 Carné set about filming *La Marie du port*, a 1938 novel by Georges Simenon, the author most famous for writing the Maigret stories. The narrative follows the relationship between a middle-aged man called Henri Chatelard (Jean Gabin) and a young ambitious woman called Marie (Nicole Courcel). At the film's beginning Chatelard, who is in a couple with Odile (Blanchette Brunoy), falls for her younger sister, Marie, who works in a seafront bar. Marie, who is determined to advance socially, loses interest in her boyfriend, Marcel (Claude Romain), a hairdresser's assistant, and becomes interested in the wealthy and successful Chatelard. The film ends with them starting a relationship, with him attaining the younger woman, and her achieving the social elevation she desires.

The film possesses clear continuities with Carné's earlier films, most notably his use of his familiar *équipe*. In addition to Prévert's (albeit contested) contribution, Carné used Trauner and Kosma, and was also going to use Shüfftan, though this plan did not come to fruition. The film also drew on familiar actors, such as Jean Gabin and Carette (in the role of Thomas Viau, Marcel's father). Indeed, one *Cinémonde* article announced the Carné–Gabin reunion with the following title: 'Le cinéma français retrouve son équipe no. 1: Marcel Carné–Jean Gabin' ('The French cinema rediscovers its no. 1 team: Marcel Carné–Jean Gabin') (Chazal, 1949: 3). Nevertheless, on the whole, the film represents a significant departure for Carné. Indeed, central to the film's public identity was that it was *not* like his recent work. In particular, whereas the promotional materials for his recent films had stressed their use of huge sets, with *La Marie du port* simplicity was emphasised. The difference from the 'excesses' of *Les Portes de la nuit* is noted in a few places, such as in one article that took a Carné quotation as its title: 'J'ai voulu faire un film simple, vivant, c'est pourquoi j'ai tourné *La Marie du port*' ('I wanted to make a simple, lively film, that's why I shot *La Marie du port*') (Pecheral, 1949: 12–13). The film's marketing also set about refuting Carné's bad publicity and his apparently tyrannical manner on set. As part of the same feature, short pieces written by the film's cast defended the director. Carette, for example, stated that, although making a film for Carné is like going into battle, if he is pleased after viewing the evening rushes, 'On est content et prêt à recommencer le lendemain avec joie' ('I am happy and ready to joyfully start again tomorrow') (Carette, 1949: 12). *La Marie du port*, then, was being marketed as a

Carné film, while attempting to remove negative connotations associated with him.

One of the most striking aspects of the film's aesthetics is its adoption of a different type of realism, distinct from the poetic realism of the 1930s and 1940s. Vincendeau (2004: 150) argues that there were two main ways in which poetic realism developed in the postwar years: the period witnessed the emergence of police films (*policiers*) and noir psychological realism – *La Marie du port* falls into the latter category. Whereas Carné's earlier work placed great emphasis on the use of studio sets, lit in an Expressionistic way, *La Marie du port* is filmed much more on location, with a greater number of daytime scenes. This should be qualified by mentioning his use of a studio recreation of the harbour where Marie meets her boyfriend at a number of points during the evening. However, on the whole, the film's exterior shots are filmed outdoors, with scenes taking place in the harbour and the roads joining Port-en-Bessin and Cherbourg in Normandy, where the film's action is set. The effect is to remove the sense of 'magic' filling everyday reality, in the way it does in poetic realism. This shift also extends to the film's treatment of romance. Whereas the earlier films centred on idealised romantic scenarios, a central element of the Carné–Prévert inflection of poetic realism, this is not the case in *La Marie du port*: the relationship between Chatelard and Marie is not idealised. To some extent, Marie shares qualities with the heroines of the 1930s: she is young and beautiful and is filmed and lit in a way that heightens her photogenic appearance. She is also played by a young rising star, Nicole Courcel, who would go on to have significant success in the years that followed. However, her character is not interested in romance, but in upward mobility and financial security, which she hopes to attain through her relationship with Chatelard.

Carné's use of Gabin also relates to changes in his filmmaking, as well as in Gabin's persona. Up until this point Gabin's postwar films, such as *Martin Roumagnac* (Georges Lacombe, 1946) and *Au-delà des grilles* (René Clément, 1948), had attempted to perpetuate his prewar image. However, as Vincendeau (2000: 74) explains, 'It seemed that Gabin's "myth" did not gel any more.' In *La Marie du port* he departs from this prewar identity, a move that would be crystallised in *Touchez pas au Grisbi* (Jacques Becker, 1954), in which he plays a gang leader, a 'Godfather' figure. *La Marie du port* thus marks his progression towards playing older men. Most notably, he has grey hair, which was commented upon by André Bazin in the title of his review of the film, a title that also indicates that Gabin was reinventing himself with this role: 'Dans *La Marie du port* de Marcel Carné, un Gabin à cheveux gris va créer un nouveau personnage' ('In Marcel Carné's *La Marie du port*, a grey haired Gabin will create a new character') (Bazin, 1949). Apparently Gabin insisted that his advancing age should be allowed to show through in the film, something that Carné was also keen on. Bazin too was complimentary about this, particularly as it represents a significant contribution to the film's realism.

As well as participating in shifts in the period's aesthetics, *La Marie du port* is also symptomatic of broader social change, and in particular the country's rapid modernisation. *La Marie du port* is the first Carné film to dramatise a tension between this sudden change and the more traditional elements found in his earlier work. Indeed, in the scenes set in Port-en-Bessin, in particular, there is still a sense of community. This is evident from the funeral at the beginning of the film, which shows the whole village coming together, following the death of Marie's and Odette's father. The seafront bar is also presented as a communal space, all the more so as the *patronne* of the bar, Madame Josselin, is played by Jane Marken, recalling her role as Madame Lecouvreur, the owner of the Hôtel du Nord. Despite these reminders of Carné's representations of the community in the 1930s, *La Marie du port* shows the beginnings of the decline of community. This is particularly clear from the scenes set in Cherbourg, which is presented as more modern and bourgeois. In contrast to the seafront bar in Port-en-Bessin, Chatelard has a clean, bright, white, up-to-date restaurant in Cherbourg, with a cinema attached to it – at one point the two locations are explicitly juxtaposed, primarily to emphasise Marie's desire for social elevation, but also to articulate a tension between two visions of France: the old and the new. In this respect, one of the film's key features is Chatelard's car. Linking the film's two spaces – Port-en-Bessin and Cherbourg – the car, as a symbol of modernity, viewed with great fascination at the time (Ross, 1995), plays a significant role in the breakup of the community through its creation of greater mobility. Whereas Carné's films of the 1930s present a largely unfavourable vision of modernity, preferring instead to concentrate on nostalgic populism, *La Marie du port* offers a more positive vision of the modern world. Although the film opens with Chatelard changing the car's tyre by the side of the road, thus stressing its limitations, gradually the car, along with other signifiers of the modern, is presented in a more favourable way: we see it from a variety of angles, glistening in the sun, speeding along the country roads. Mirroring the attitudes of many people in France at this time, Marie is certainly fascinated by it. This is evident when she tells Marcel she is leaving with Chatelard for Paris, *in his car*, suggesting that the automobile is a significant part of her desire for him.

These changes are linked in particular with the film's characters and stars. As Vincendeau has explained, the shifts in Gabin's postwar persona from the working-class hero to the Godfather figure echo 'wider changes in French culture and society' (2000: 74), related to France's increased affluence and bourgeois nature. While his 1930s films present him as a proletarian hero, engaged in an Oedipal struggle with an older male, such as Zabel in *Le Quai des brumes*, or Valentin in *Le Jour se lève*, in *La Marie du port* he plays a successful cinema and restaurant owner, a figure of power in the community. Because Gabin achieved huge popularity in the postwar years for this change in his persona, and because its transformation was linked to broader changes in France at this time, we can see that his role in the film contributes to a positive representation of the modernisation of France.

Nicole Courcel also contributes to the film's affirmation of change. Marie's desire to escape from her life of tradition in Port-en-Bessin, corresponds with Courcel's extra-filmic persona, established in Jacques Becker's *Rendez-vous de Paris* (1949), in which she plays a modern young woman, dancing to jazz in Paris's underground bars (known as *caves*). This role positioned her within the period's movement towards greater youth and female independence, something that would develop during the decade, particularly through the stardom of Brigitte Bardot, and then later with Carné's *Les Tricheurs*. Whereas the heroines of Carné's earlier films are motivated by love and romance (with the possible exception of Françoise in *Le Jour se lève*), Marie is much more interested in the pleasures of the modern world. Although she wants to leave Marcel at the beginning of the film, as he is 'just' a hairdresser's assistant, he manages to keep her for a bit longer by giving her some perfume, highlighting her desire for such consumer products. This scene takes place at night on the harbour, evoking Marcel Pagnol's 1930s classic *Marius* (Alexander Korda, 1931), though in contrast to that film it is significant that here it is the woman who wants to escape the constraints of the traditional community. However, while she sticks with her boyfriend for a little longer, she soon gravitates towards the wealthy Chatelard.

Surprisingly, if we take into account Carné's earlier celebrations of romantic love, the woman's break with tradition and search for greater power is not presented in a completely negative way. To some extent she is depicted as shallow, calculating and cold and at many points in the film her face is expressionless and impenetrable. During one conversation Chatelard gently taps her head with his knuckle, asking: 'Qu'est ce qu'il y a dans cette petite tête là?' ('What's going on in that little head of yours?'). In this respect she is one of Simenon's typically two-dimensional women, who, as Becker (2006: 11) writes, 'serve merely as catalysts to provoke the reactions of the males'. On the other hand, the film registers a degree of sympathy and understanding for Marie, and to a certain extent we are granted a female perspective. Her first scene, following her father's funeral, shows her role in the family, where she is waiting upon men who sternly order her around. From the beginning of the film, then, she is shown to have a good reason for wanting to leave. The film finishes with Chatelard giving her a key to his property, meaning she has attained her goal: literally it is the key to his restaurant, symbolically it is the key to the new world she wants to enter. As they walk together by the sea she is shown in close-up, capturing her beauty as the wind blows through her hair, which is combined with triumphant music. This then provides a positive view of the modern: her victory is celebrated, suggesting that her goal is a valid one. This also arguably promotes a progressive view within the film with regards to gender – the woman is able to benefit from the modern and escape her traditional home life.

In addition, to some extent Chatelard, the older male, is presented as weak. He now needs to be wealthy to attract a woman, and, more significantly, at one point his girlfriend, Odette, cheats on him, with Marcel, a much younger man, which shows him losing some of his authority (even though he cheats on her). At the same time, he symbolises a reassertion of male power, evident through Gabin's confident performance style. Previously his understatement had been used to show his working-class authenticity; now it captures his sense of control as someone with money and power. This is also evident from his relationship with Marie. Early on we see that Chatelard is a womaniser, establishing him as a predatory figure. However, Marie is also predatory and spends time plotting how to 'capture' him. This is evident when it is revealed to her that Marcel is at the Chatelard household (where he is recovering from injuries sustained after jumping in front of Chatelard's car). We see her smiling to herself as she forges her plan; the situation gives her the opportunity to go to Chatelard's house to continue seducing him. In the end both characters are victorious. She attains the social elevation she seeks; he gets the attractive woman less than half his age. Here, then, the film continues the Oedipal narratives of the 1930s, but with Gabin switching from his previous role as the son who challenges a father figure. Now *he* is the older male who has the relationship with the young woman, a trend that would continue in many of his subsequent films.

We can see, then, that *La Marie du port* is distinct from Carné's earlier work, not only in terms of aesthetics, with a shift towards psychological realism and location shooting, but also in terms of its politics. Carné's attentiveness to the new social context is indicative of his exceptional observational skills, a strength that was behind the bleak realism of his earlier poetic realism. This is in spite of the fact that André Bazin in his 1951 article, 'Carné et la désincarnation' (1983: 132), hinted that Carné was now out of touch: 'His prewar success was linked to a harmony, but times have changed and the myths now required are no longer the same'. Although Bazin may be correct that Carné doesn't deal with the period's 'myths', he does respond to dominant discourses circulating in the postwar years, with him representing, for example, the increasingly bourgeois nature of France, an element of the film that can explain much of its appeal. In doing so, and in contrast to his work in the 1930s, Carné registers sympathy for the modern; we will see more examples of this in the films that followed. The shifts in *La Marie du port* also highlight the necessary changes that Carné had to make in order to move from the extravagances of *Les Portes de la nuit* towards a more commercially viable cinema. By and large he was successful with this, with the film being a critical and commercial success (it attracted 2.7 million spectators). Indeed, one of the main indicators that the film had performed well was that Sacha Gordine kept to his word and helped Carné to make *Juliette ou la clef des songes*.

Juliette ou la clef des songes

Whereas *La Marie du port* represents Carné's attempts at reintegrating himself in the film industry, *Juliette ou la clef des songes* was a much more personal project, one he had been working on for quite some time. Based on a play by Georges Neveux, it was initially conceived as an idea for a film during the war. It was to be a collaboration with Jean Cocteau, the top creator of the period's cinéma fantastique, and was to star Jean Marais, a huge figure in French cinema during the Occupation and the immediate postwar years. For the 1950s version Carné collaborated instead with Neveux and Jacques Viot (who had also worked on the Occupation version).

The story centres on Michel (Gérard Philipe), who at the beginning of the film is lying in a cell in prison. We later learn he has been put there for stealing money from his employer in order to impress Juliette (Suzanne Cloutier), a customer at the shop where he works. As he closes his eyes, a light shines on his face from across the room, which it is revealed comes from a door leading out to a country path. Leaving his cell through the door, he finds himself in a magical land, called Oblivion, where time doesn't exist and people don't have memories. In this world he sets about looking for Juliette, who he believes is there. However, we learn that she is also being pursued by the 'Personage' (Jean-Roger Caussimon), a Bluebeard-like character, who seeks to marry her. Just when Michel appears to have 'won' her, he is woken up in his cell by the prison alarm. Back in the real world, his employer, who it is revealed is identical in appearance to the Personage (and also played by Caussimon) drops charges against him but gives him the sack. Following his release from prison, Michel sneaks into Juliette's apartment, where she tells him that things would not have worked out between them because he is too poor. He tells her that it doesn't matter anyway because he's already found another woman, one who is maybe even prettier than her. He runs off into the night, with her pursuing him. The film finishes with Michel entering a door with a sign on it that says, 'Entrée Interdite. Danger' ('Entry Forbidden. Danger'), which leads him back to the land of Juliette.

As this was one of the first films Carné made entirely without Prévert, it helps us to consider the vexed question of whether his work with Prévert is significantly different from his work without him. André Bazin argues that in terms of subject matter there are in fact many continuities between *Juliette ou la clef des songes* and the earlier films. He refers, in particular, to such themes as 'happiness through escape from reality and unhappiness through memory' (1983: 132), the film's Manicheism, which is present in the contrast between the evil Personage and the idealised Juliette, and fate, an element that is represented through 'Yves Robert and his accordion' (1983: 134) – the one character in Oblivion, aside from Michel, who has memories. To this we can also add the film's populism: Michel is a poor shop assistant who cannot marry the richer Juliette, a typical populist narrative, which conflates his romanticism with his modest financial situation. For Bazin, the fundamental difference between *Juliette ou la clef des songes* and Carné's earlier work is that the themes are dealt with in a more idealised, less realist way. As with *Les Visiteurs du soir*, which is in many respects a similar film, *Juliette ou la clef des songes* functions on the level of allegory and abstraction.

Whereas *La Marie du port* was a hit, *Juliette ou la clef des songes* was met with great hostility. It was selected as one of the French entries for the Cannes Film Festival, but was given an extremely negative reception. Carné (1996: 254) recounts that he and Philipe were ignored in the foyer of the cinema after the film's premiere, and Bazin notes that the film's promotion in Paris 'had to be based on the myth of judicial error, even of conspiracy' (Bazin, 1983: 131). Indeed, the film also failed at the box-office, something Bazin sought to explain. Firstly he argues that disappointment at Carné's new releases is in part related to the expectations generated by his earlier successes: 'His films are judged not only by what they are, but more or less implicitly by what they have ceased to be' (1983: 132). For Bazin the prewar films, *Le Quai des brumes* and *Le Jour se lève* in particular, represented a coming together of many key elements: personnel, style, themes, and, importantly, a specific historical context – for him it is the resonance the films had with the 'myths' of the period that is of special importance. His comments help us understand the failure of *Juliette ou la clef des songes*, which was not responding to the period's questions in the same way as his earlier work, and, in contrast to *La Marie du port*, doesn't deal overtly with the immediate social context or contemporary themes, in particular the postwar modernisation of France.

However, Turk opts for a different approach to this issue, suggesting that it is Bazin's bias towards realism that is at stake. Whereas Bazin is sceptical about *Juliette ou la clef des songes*'s absence of realism, Turk sees this and its increased symbolism as something to be valued, for, according to him, it is these elements that reveal the film to be one of Carné's most intensely personal projects. Turk's central idea is that *Juliette ou la clef des songes* has little concern for social context, but *does* explore, to a significant degree, Carné's identity and, in particular, his psychology. It is presumably for this reason – the personal nature of the film – that he gives more space to *Juliette ou la clef des songes* than he does to *La Marie du port*, even though the earlier film was a box-office success. Using a psychoanalytic approach Turk draws out some fascinating interpretations of *Juliette ou la clef des songes*, which reveal, in particular, ways in which the film relates to Carné's sexuality. Here his discussion centres upon Michel's desire, evident from his pursuit of Juliette, but also, his masochism, signified by the fact that his dream keeps creating obstacles to prevent his successful attainment of her. Because of this, his dream dramatises a 'retreat from a situation laden with anxiety: adult heterosexuality' (1989: 371). Turk concludes by arguing that the film was unpopular with critics because it was *too* personal, that Carné laid bare 'his most primitive obsessions' (1989: 376).

In addition to Bazin's discussion, which implies that *Juliette ou la clef des songes* failed because it was divorced from its social context, and Turk's, which focuses on the film's psychological dimension, another key issue to consider is the film's position within the broader cinematic context of the tradition of quality. On the surface the film appears to be part of this trend. It was directed by Carné, a key 'quality' director who brought important elements of this type of cinema to the film. Some of these are hinted at by Bazin, who refers to its 'grandeur' and 'sumptuous' quality (1983: 135). The film is indeed extremely accomplished in its *mise en scène*, owing to its wealth of costumes and stunning visual spectacle, which even involved the recreation of a forest in a studio. In addition, the film's performances add to its aura of 'quality'. Suzanne Cloutier and Jean-Roger Caussimon both bring theatrical acting to the film, but Gérard Philipe is most significant in this respect. He was an important figure in the tradition of quality who had started his career in the theatre before moving into film, appearing in the late 1940s and 1950s in a string of major tradition of quality hits, including *L'Idiot* (Georges Lampin, 1946), *Le Diable au corps* (Claude Autant-Lara, 1947), and *Une si jolie petite plage* (Yves Allégret, 1949). As Vincendeau (2000: 6) points out, because of his background in the legitimate stage, his presence brought to his films 'the cultural legitimacy and refined tones of classic plays'.

Such acting was used to shape his portrayal of alienated, romantic heroes, as noted by Andrew (1995: 330): 'When Gérard Philipe appeared as the Gabin of the postwar years in such films as *Le Diable au corps* and *Une si jolie petite plage*, he was acclaimed for the intelligence of his performances, for the minute correctness with which he portrayed characters like François, alienated to the point of suicide, but forthright and honest.' This is certainly evident in *Juliette ou la clef des songes*, in which he is tortured by Juliette's unattainable quality, which drives him further into his own interior world – a conclusion that shares similarities with *Le Jour se lève*. Michel's anguish is particularly evident in these final scenes, as he runs away from Juliette. Here we see Philipe's skill in conveying his tortured state, which is indeed distinct from Gabin's authentic combination of nuance and explosive aggression.

However, in other respects, *Juliette ou la clef des songes* is not in keeping with the mainstream of the tradition of quality. Its idealism was not typical of broader trends at this time. which placed more emphasis on a cynical view of the world, rendered through psychological realism, or spectacular costume films, as opposed to the Surrealism of *Juliette ou la clef des songes*. Although Philipe's character has great cynicism towards real (as opposed to imaginary) women, evident from his return at the film's conclusion to the dream world and rejection of (the real) Juliette, this is ultimately because of his profound idealism and the continuation of his idealisation. With such abstraction the film appeared, as Bazin argues, to be somewhat out of date, a point reiterated by Alan Williams (1992: 283–4): 'In 1951 it was a terrible anachronism ... Life was no longer a dream, for most critics and film spectators, or at least not so self-proclaimedly one. The Tradition of Quality continued with cinema fantasy – stars turned into fetishes acting in wish-fulfilling decors and stories – but abandoned the fantastic.' Turk's point that two other fantasy films did well at Cannes that year, *Miracolo a Milano* (Vittorio De Sica, 1951) and *Los Olvidados* (Luis Buñuel, 1950), would seem to refute this. Nevertheless, notions of 'quality' *French* cinema at this time were governed by different ideas, ideas that Carné's film flirted with, but ultimately did not sufficiently deliver. Once more then, Carné's career in the cinema was under threat; he was in desperate need of another hit.

Tales of doomed passion

Carné's next two films – *Thérèse Raquin* and *L'Air de Paris* – were much safer projects than *Juliette ou la clef des songes*. They pursued some of the successful elements of his recent work, such as the realist mode of filmmaking he had adopted in *La Marie du port* and featured top stars: Simone Signoret in *Thérèse Raquin* and Jean Gabin in *L'Air de Paris* with Arletty in a smaller role. Though not instances of poetic realism, both return to some of its familiar elements: darkness, 'atmosphere', and an emphasis on romance that is constrained, trapped and, ultimately, doomed. While these films, then, can be seen as something of a 'return', both contain important elements of change. As we shall see, *Thérèse Raquin* and *L'Air de Paris* are evidence not only of transformations in Carné's filmmaking but also shifts in the film industry and, importantly, in French society, as the 1950s progressed.

Thérèse Raquin

The first of these films was *Thérèse Raquin*, based on the novel by Émile Zola (1867). Turk suggests that Carné's motivation for pursuing this project stemmed from his competitiveness with Renoir, who had beaten him to making an adaptation of *La Bête humaine* in the late 1930s, and Feyder, who had made a version of *Thérèse Raquin* in 1928, a film now lost, but considered by many who saw it to be his masterpiece (Abel, 1984: 134–6). In contrast to Feyder's version, Carné updated Zola's novel, with the action taking place in Lyon in contemporary France. The story centres on the character of Thérèse (Simone Signoret) who lives with her dull and sickly husband Camille (Jacques Duby) and her hostile mother-in-law, Madame Raquin (Sylvie), who is very protective of her son. Thérèse's passionless life involves working in their shop and sitting in on games nights held in their apartment. This changes when she meets Laurent (Raf Vallone), an Italian immigrant lorry driver, with whom she begins an affair. Laurent tries to persuade Thérèse to leave Camille; she attempts to do this, but, out of pity, agrees to go away for a short holiday with Camille to Paris, with him believing they can work things out. However, Laurent also boards Thérèse and Camille's train, and in a confrontation and scuffle, ends up throwing Camille from the moving vehicle, killing him – the news of this gives his mother a stroke, leaving her paralysed for the remainder of the film. Initially it seems as though the lovers will get away with this crime, with the investigators, not knowing that Laurent was on board, concluding that Camille fell from the train by accident. However, a sailor (Roland Lesaffre), who saw Thérèse leaving her carriage, blackmails them. It is agreed that they will pay him a sum Thérèse has received in compensation from the train company for Camille's death, in order to keep him quiet. Before going to collect the money he writes a letter to the police explaining what happened, which he instructs the cleaner (Maria-Pia Casilio) of the hotel he is staying in to deliver if he has not returned by three o'clock. He is given the money by Thérèse and Laurent, but as he leaves the shop he gets hit by a lorry. As he dies he whispers to the couple, 'La lettre!' ('The letter!'), which they realise spells their doom.

The prime issue that has concerned writers on the film is its status as an adaptation of Zola, a point explored by Turk (1989) and Hayward (2003). For each the main focus is that Carné's film is vastly different from the Zola original; indeed, for Hayward it is almost a complete reversal of the novel. This is something that was noted by critics when the film was released; a number of them tackled Carné for not being faithful to the original work. Nevertheless, Carné and Charles Spaak's adaptation brings about a version of *Thérèse Raquin* that is original and fascinating in many ways.

Central to adaptations of Zola is the issue of how his naturalism is treated – Zola's writing sought an objective, almost scientific discussion of the lives of his protagonists. Turk (1989: 376), drawing upon the work of Leo Braudy (1969), explains that there are two main tendencies in filmic adaptations of Zola: there are those that seek to emulate his naturalism, with such filmmakers aiming to efface signs of their own input and point of view; others are more concerned with problematising such naturalism, to show that the author's viewpoint will always be present. Carné and Spaak's *Thérèse Raquin* is, for Turk, an example of the latter. As we shall see, Carné gives the film his distinctive authorial signature. However, the film's differences from Zola's original are not just the product of Carné and Spaak's work; they are also related to its stars and the way the film engages with genre. But before considering this, it is necessary to ask, how does Carné's version differ from Zola's?

The first concern is Carné's attitude to character motivation. As part of his 'scientific' approach, Zola would create characters who are clearly influenced by a combination of environmental and physiological factors, which would have a deterministic effect on their lives. In *Thérèse Raquin*, for example, Thérèse and Laurent's unpleasantness is presented as the result of their squalid environment and Thérèse's 'miscegenated' body – she has some African blood in her. This dimension of Zola's work is treated differently by Carné, who shows characters propelled by *particular* circumstances rather than broader biological and social realities. While the film retains the original novel's fatalism, this is instead made concrete through the sailor, a role entirely created by Carné for the film. By blackmailing Thérèse and Laurent he explicitly controls their destinies.

Another important difference with Zola's work is that Thérèse and Laurent are presented much more favourably in Carné's film. Whereas for Zola Thérèse is animalistic and physically unattractive, with her 'white, dry, thin-nosed and thin-lipped' face and a 'skinny and wiry' body (Hayward, 2003: 7), for Carné she is beautiful and compassionate. Of course, this is in large part because she is played by the young Signoret, one of the most beautiful stars of the period. Similarly, Laurent is presented in a better light than in the novel. To some extent, he is shown in a negative way because he is excessively passionate and emotional, which has disastrous consequences when he throws Camille from the train. At the same time, as a working-class man, with romantic sensibilities, he is also, in keeping within the Carné universe, portrayed sympathetically. In the novel Thérèse and Laurent plot a murder, and are driven by animalistic, sexual and bloodthirsty, not to mention financial, desires. By contrast, in Carné's film the murder is not premeditated; it is the result of Laurent losing his temper on the spur of the moment. It is a crime of passion, motivated by a desire for freedom and love, not money. In addition, the early scenes, which present Thérèse as a victim of her husband and mother-in-law, both of whom adopt a highly unpleasant and demanding attitude towards her, encourage us to feel sympathy for her plight.

These changes to Zola's novel obviously reveal a significant amount about Carné's authorship and wish to use the story to explore his own agenda. *Thérèse Raquin* is another example of Carné working without Prévert (instead he scripted it with Charles Spaak) as well as without other members of his *équipe*, such as Trauner who was now working in America and Kosma who was composing for Prévert and Renoir. But again the film highlights, in spite of such absences, the continuity of key Carné themes, as well as elements reminiscent of his earlier poetic realism. For instance, the film explores the central Carné theme of entrapment, even using a character (the sailor) to embody fate – as he does in a number of his films, such as *Les Portes de la nuit*. As Hayward (2003: 6) observes, the decor in the Raquin household also plays an important role in creating a sense of suffocation, with the abundance of furniture and soft furnishings serving to 'literally pinion Thérèse into her place of submission'. Another way in which entrapment is frequently conveyed in Carné's cinema is through a shot of someone looking through a window, its frames and horizontal slats serving to constrain and contain the character. In an image similar to the one from *Le Quai des brumes* showing Jean and Nelly at Panama's, we see Thérèse and Laurent at one point looking from a window, capturing their entrapment but also their unity as a doomed couple.

However, *Thérèse Raquin* is a long way from 1930s poetic realism. On the one hand the film's romance is, as Carné himself stated (cited in Turk, 1989: 378), more idealised than in the original Zola novel, because we sympathise with the protagonists' passionate desire to be together. At the same time, the romance is not as idealised as in earlier Carné films, particularly as the sets do not possess the same symbolic and transcendent resonance. Another reason is the more physical aspect of the couple's sexual desire for each other, added to which Signoret does not possess the ethereal quality the earlier stars possessed. Of course, Signoret is very attractive but, in contrast to these stars, she is a much more grounded part of her environment. Indeed, Hayward (2004: 33–4) sees this as one of the main ways that Signoret injects independence into her roles: 'she embodies a strong sense of the everyday, of being a part of the "real" world. The rough, even wounded and seemingly untrained edge of her voice reinforces this, inviting audiences to identify with her apparent ordinariness.' This comes to a significant degree from her physique, as a strong and curvaceous woman, but also from her performance style: whereas the ethereal women of the 1930s entered the cinema directly, Signoret began her career on stage, deploying in plays, and then in the cinema, finely crafted performances that facilitated her portrayal of 'real women', which is confirmed by her later role in the British realist film *Room at the Top* (Jack Clayton, 1959).

Rather than being part of poetic realism, then, *Thérèse Raquin* belongs instead to the 'noir' realism of the postwar period, a key strand of the tradition of quality. This French 'film noir' nevertheless has been seen as an offshoot of poetic realism, a point discussed by Vincendeau, who states:

> We were still in the popular *faubourgs* of the city on the whole, but the main difference was that, unlike Poetic Realist films like *Le Quai des brumes*, *Le Jour se lève* and *Hôtel du Nord*, love no longer had any redeeming power. Bazin saw the change as a movement away from the 'poetic' towards the 'realist', and as a loss of spirituality, towards a cinema in which 'the *mise en scène* no longer tries to create through the expressionism of lights and décor a transcendent metaphysics of disaster which pre-exists the script' (Bazin 1983: 22). Without necessarily following Bazin down the spiritual route, it is the case that the increased cynicism of the films' contents is echoed by their more polished yet gloomier and in some cases sordid set designs. (Vincendeau, 2004: 150)

Thérèse Raquin is very much in keeping with this definition. While the film does not possess the same suggestion of transcendence as Carné's earlier films, it maintains a strong sense of realism. This is evident from the focus upon ordinary, populist spaces, as in Carné's earlier work, such as the lorry depot, the cafés, the hotel, and the many exterior shots of streets. Unlike the earlier films, which were filmed in the studio to enable Carné to have control over such spaces, which could then be transformed through complex lighting arrangements, the streets in *Thérèse Raquin* were filmed on location, as in *La Marie du port*. Because of this, certain shots are particularly striking, such as a long take of around forty-five seconds with static camera showing Thérèse ascending an embankment next to the railway track in order to identify Camille's body. In keeping with this form of realism, *Thérèse Raquin* has the very polished appearance Vincendeau refers to, something that was noted at the time by Bazin (1953) in his review of the film: '*Thérèse Raquin* n'est, certes, pas le meilleur film de Marcel Carné, mais c'est peut-être celui où la maîtrise du metteur en scène atteint sa perfection la plus dépouillée.'[1] Indeed, while the original novel contains some grimy scenes, Carné's film is clean and ordered, evident from the camerawork, the high-key lighting, which contributes to the noir aesthetic, and the *mise en scène*, as well as from Simone Signoret's performance, which is precise and studied,

---

1 '*Thérèse Raquin* is certainly not Marcel Carné's best film, but it's perhaps the one in which the director's mastery reaches its most pared down perfection.'

with her bringing psychological complexity to the role. In 'Carné et la désincarnation', Bazin (1983) had argued that Carné's films were moving towards greater idealisation and abstraction. However, his observation was premature; this was a trend that would more or less come to an end with *Juliette ou la clef des songes*, aside from *La Merveilleuse Visite* (1974), later in his career. Instead, the defining feature of Carné's aesthetics from *Thérèse Raquin* onwards is his realism.

This heightening of realism has wider significance for the film. As with *La Marie du port*, it gives great insight into France during an important transitional period. In part, and most obviously, this is because of another significant change Carné made to Zola's novel: he set the action in the present, and in Lyon, rather than in Paris during the late nineteenth century. While we can see continuity with the 1930s, through the film's populism, discussed above, we also get a sense of the changes occurring at this time. As Vincendeau (1997: 15) argues, in *Thérèse Raquin* there are signs of the breakdown of community, with the large communal gatherings of the earlier films being replaced by a small games night, a much more insular affair, attended only by Camille, his mother, and a few friends.

Another change is that while in Laurent there is a working-class male at the centre of the film, he is in many respects quite different from the working-class male of the 1930s, Jean Gabin. Most importantly, whereas Gabin stood for the ordinary *Frenchman*. Vallone was Italian. To some extent this is related to the fact that the film was a Franco-Italian co-production – other Italian performers include Maria-Pia Casilio, in the role of Georgette, the cleaner at the sailor's hotel. At the same time, the film deals overtly with immigration, a prominent issue at the time, even if the treatment of this topic is somewhat ambiguous. For example, in the scuffle between Laurent and Camille on the train, Camille says: 'Vous êtes les mêmes. On vous accepte chez nous, on vous nourrit. Et vous en profitez pour faire vos saletés.'[2] With this Laurent throws him from the train. As he looks out of the carriage's open door, contemplating what he has just done, we can see a map of France next to him on the wall, emphasising his outsider status. On the one hand, the scene presents Laurent in a sympathetic way, with him rescuing Thérèse, particularly as we know that Camille plans on locking her up at his aunt's house when they

2 'You're all the same. We take you in, we feed you. And you take advantage of it to do your dirty tricks.'

arrive in Paris. On the other, as a murderer, he is presented as not in control of his emotions, killing Camille in a moment of anger. This can be seen to confirm Camille's bias, while also playing into the stereotype of the overly passionate Italian.

But while there is a somewhat ambiguous and potentially problematic depiction of the film's main foreign character, the representation of gender is, with necessary qualifications, much more progressive. This is the case in two main ways: the film provides a positive vision of femininity and advances a gay subtext.

In terms of the representation of femininity, Thérèse is to begin with an extremely passive character. She is trapped in her disempowered and degrading position in the Raquin household, and appears to do little to resist such oppression. Other characters have a huge amount of power over her, initially Camille and her mother-in-law, but later Laurent too who to a certain extent also bosses her around, such as when he assertively tells her she must leave Camille. However, on the whole the film provides a progressive view of femininity, something of a rarity in French postwar noir. Burch and Sellier (1996), for instance, show that the representation of women in films of the period was generally misogynistic. To some extent the film avoids this because of Signoret, whose persona, as Hayward (2004: 33) has argued, centres upon her independence: 'Despite the limitations of these roles, in which she nearly always ends up losing everything, she consistently embodied the role of a woman with a mind of her own.' She puts this down to key aspects of Signoret's acting, which work against conservative subject matter, particularly her assertiveness, her ability to convey a wealth of meaning without or with little speech, and her capacity to create a sense that she is an everyday presence, and thus a 'real' woman. In addition, the film itself explores in an overt way the position of women in society. For instance, the treatment of Thérèse's situation highlights the injustice of her confinement. Not only are we encouraged to sympathise with her, owing to the hostility of her husband and mother-in-law; the film also emphasises the fact that this oppression is legally defined through Camille stating that by law she has to do what he says because she is his wife. This then is referring to the very real oppression of women at the time – while French women had been (belatedly) given the vote in 1946 they were still certainly not treated as equals. The film's female discourses are also supported by the fact that the story is told from Thérèse's point of view. The two men, one representing male weakness and mediocrity (Camille), the other male strength, escape and passion (Laurent), each perform a function with regards to *her* narrative, dramatising the tension between her life at the beginning of the film and the life she desires. In addition, Hayward (2003: 9) makes the important point that the film dramatises Thérèse's acquisition of a voice. Although she is quiet for the majority of the film, there is a key moment at which she delivers a lengthy monologue, about the harsh treatment she has received, to her paralysed mother-in-law.

Patriarchy is challenged further through the film's gay subtext, which centres upon the sailor character, played by Roland Lesaffre, who would go on to appear in all of Carné's remaining films (aside from *Le Pays d'où je viens* (1956) and *La Bible*) and would become Carné's closest companion and supporter. Lesaffre was abandoned as a child and during the war, still just a schoolboy, joined the resistance, before enlisting in 1943 in the French Marines by faking his date of birth. Having become friendly with Jean Gabin, a fellow soldier, he decided upon leaving the Marines to visit his old friend, who was currently working on *La Marie du Port*. It was here that Carné spotted him and soon after cast him in *Juliette ou la clef des songes* in the small role of an unlucky legionnaire, in the dream world, whose palm reading reveals his miserable *past* (the characters have no memories). By making his character in *Thérèse Raquin* a sailor, the film alludes to the period's controversial battles in Indochina, while also drawing upon Lesaffre's real-life identity and experiences.

One reason the film is open to gay readings is because of the importance given to the sailor, who doesn't even appear in the original novel. As well as including him for his narrative function, it is likely that Carné wrote this role for Lesaffre to facilitate the exploration of gay themes. A strong reason for believing this is that even though he appears only in the last twenty-five minutes of the film he is in a disproportionately large number of shots (Hayward, 2004: 93). In addition, the film draws upon prominent elements of gay iconography, as pointed out by Dyer (2000: 130), who writes: 'In *Thérèse Raquin* a year earlier, Carné's treatment of Lesaffre, in an important but secondary role invented for the film, is less body-baring [than in *L'Air de Paris*] but, in one telling sequence, much more gay iconographic: a striped sailor top is torn to reveal a nipple and a bicep flexed to hold a hand mirror, imagery that could come straight from Cocteau's *Le Livre blanc* (republished with said imagery in 1949) or much 1950s gay pornography.' In many respects, the sailor is presented as the film's most attractive form of masculinity, which is understandable given Carné's homosexuality. For one thing, although he blackmails the protagonist, he is actually quite a sympathetic character, who is presented as unlucky rather than bad (rather like the Legionnaire in *Juliette ou la clef des songes*). As he takes the blackmail money, which he apologises for, he states that he has always been unlucky. Bazin (1953) remarked that such sympathetic elements meant that he departed from Carné's standard Manicheism. Also, whereas Camille is too weak and Laurent is too strong and aggressive, Lesaffre is the character who, like Gabin in the 1930s, combines masculine and feminine qualities. As a sailor, with large biceps, he is presented as strong, and with the accent on his appearance – his objectification *and* his narcissism, evident from his mirror – as well as his ultimate failure, he is simultaneously presented as passive and vulnerable. Consequently, complexity is given to the sailor, despite his marginal role: with such emphasis on Lesaffre in terms of shots, the eroticisation of his presentation and performance, and his role as the blackmailer of the film's protagonists, he plays an *homme fatal*, stressing further the film's gay dimension. As we shall see, he would be used in a similar way in Carné's next film, *L'Air de Paris*.

Within the context of the tradition of quality, then, *Thérèse Raquin* is an interesting film to consider. It boasts impressive cinematography, as well as excellent stars and performances, which were complimented by Bazin (1953). It also gives us insight into the social context of France at the time – comparing the film with Carné's work of the 1930s reveals ways in which France had changed. Moreover, we can see that Carné's adaptation advances progressive ideas. This is particularly important considering the unflattering view of femininity offered by the original novel and by many films of this period, as explored by Burch and Sellier (1996). Indeed, while the tradition of quality has been criticised, one of its positive features was that a number of its films, such as *Thérèse Raquin*, were woman-centred, enabling in some cases emancipating female discourses.

Despite some criticism of how the film adapted Zola, *Thérèse Raquin* was generally received quite positively and, whereas *Juliette ou la clef des songes* had failed at the Cannes film festival, *Thérèse Raquin* was much more successful with critics, winning a Silver Lion at Venice.

The film was also popular with audiences, attracting 2.4 million spectators. This was an important success for Carné, particularly as it had been achieved without his regular collaborators. Whereas Prévert was doing little work in the cinema at this time, Carné was showing that he could still make popular, critically respected films.

L'Air de Paris

Carné's next film, *L'Air de Paris*, follows André Ménard (Roland Lesaffre), a young and poor rail worker who one day meets Victor Le Garrec (Jean Gabin), a boxing gym owner, who sees potential in the young man. Victor persuades him to train at his gym, and eventually, because of his poverty, André moves in to Victor's house, much to the annoyance and jealousy of Victor's wife Blanche (Arletty). One evening, while out in Paris, André meets a glamorous woman called Corinne (Marie Daems), and they begin a relationship. However, André's late nights with Corinne begin to threaten his development as a boxer and he is told by Victor that he must choose between her and his career. He chooses her, but upon arriving at her apartment discovers that she has left Paris to make sure she doesn't threaten his career as a boxer. The film finishes with the two men reconciling and walking away together. In addition to the film being quite successful with critics and at the box-office, it is of paramount interest to Carné scholarship today. It highlights the continuation of his approach to realism in the postwar period, and it is the Carné film that deals most overtly with the director's homosexuality – generating much recent critical interest, with work by Richard Dyer (2000) and Alexander Dhoest (2003).

As with *Thérèse Raquin*, Carné pursues a realist approach. The film includes a number of 'ordinary' settings, such as the side of some railway tracks where André works at the beginning of the film, the gym, various Parisian streets, and the boxing arena where people go to watch matches. Here the image of fans cheering from the balcony above the ring evokes the image of the *paradis* in *Les Enfants du paradis*. Indeed, by centring on the milieu of boxing, the film contains a strong populist dimension, particularly as it is placed in contrast to the high-class Parisian life represented by Corinne. While Corinne's lifestyle is viewed with fascination, through the images of her wearing expensive clothing and the rich decor in her apartment, the film's loyalty is to working-class Paris; ultimately, Corinne's life is presented as a prison, which has robbed her of her authenticity and freedom. By contrast, boxing in the film embodies positive aspects of working-class life – as Carné states, his interest in the sport stemmed from its populist qualities:

> Ce qui m'intéressait, en plus de l'atmosphère particulière du milieu, c'était d'évoquer l'existence courageuse des jeunes ouvriers qui, à peine achevé le travail souvent pénible de la journée, se précipitent dans une salle d'entraînement pour 'mettre les gants' et combattre de tout leur cœur, dans le seul espoir de monter un jour sur un ring.[3]
> (Carné, 1996: 267)

Thus for Carné boxing emphasises working-class labour, authenticity, and aspiration. In this respect, it fits in with the idea articulated by Baptiste in *Les Enfants du paradis* that the ordinary people of Paris have small lives, but their dreams are big. In addition, whereas Paris's high-class world is presented as artificial, particularly through Corinne's cynicism towards it, the world of boxing is about sincerity, in part owing to the earnestness of a boxer's passion but also through the straightforwardness of the sport. Moreover, the film's emphasis on authentic and ordinary people is stressed by the fact that Gabin and Arletty take central roles. The couple they form is a particularly significant one, and, as Vincendeau puts it (1997: 16), they can be seen as a projection of what would have happened had François chosen Clara instead of Françoise in *Le Jour se lève*. Although Gabin had been playing a number of bourgeois characters around this time, for instance in *La Marie du port*, his postwar persona stressed that underneath his newly acquired wealth he was still an ordinary, working-class Frenchman, qualities that are conveyed in *L'Air de Paris* through, in particular, his Parisian accent, his physique, and his understated acting style.

The film's tension between populist Paris and an affluent and glamorous milieu reveals the sense of change that was occurring in France at the time, as with most of the other films mentioned in this chapter. Again, whereas the films of the 1930s presented strong images of community, in *L'Air de Paris* we see the beginning of its

---

3 'What interested me, as well as the particular atmosphere of the milieu, was to evoke the courageous existence of the young workers who, having hardly completed the often painful day's work, head straight for the gym "to put on the gloves" and to fight with all their heart, in the sole hope of one day climbing into the ring.'

breakdown. Although we see some communal spaces, such as the boxing arena, Paris is presented as more cosmopolitan. While *Hôtel du Nord* contains one immigrant, an orphan from the Spanish civil war, *L'Air de Paris* shows many Italians living in Paris, such as one of the boxers, his supporters in the crowd, and Victor and Blanche's neighbours. Again, this may partly be related to *L'Air de Paris* being a Franco-Italian co-production, but the film also includes a black youth who trains at the gym and a scene in an Arab café below where André initially lives, all of which illustrates demographic changes in France at the time. In addition, the film presents a move away from the nostalgia of the working-class *quartiers* through its depiction of a modernising Paris. This is largely represented through Corinne, who wears modern, glamorous clothes, such as fur coats. Yet, the film still testifies to the persistence of Carné's populism. The final image shows Gabin and Lesaffre walking, not driving, away from Corinne's apartment, Gabin walking his distinctive, heavy-footed walk that somehow manages to convey a sense of authenticity.

Indeed, this milieu is imbued, as in other Carné films, with a suggestion of something 'higher'. The title itself refers to the 'air' of Paris, evoking its atmosphere and a feeling of possibility, which is also captured in shots of the city, especially those depicting the area around the Île Saint Louis. However, one of the main ways this atmosphere is created is through the film's doomed romance, a narrative signalled to potential viewers through one article entitled 'Dans *L'Air de Paris* un miroir a brisé les reflets d'un impossible amour ...' ('In *L'Air de Paris* a mirror has broken the reflections of an impossible love ...') (Anon., 1954a: 16). To some extent Corinne, with her beauty and glamour, represents the transcendence found in Carné's earlier films. At the same time, she is, like Thérèse/Signoret, a move away from the heroines of the 1930s. Whereas they signified innocence and purity, these are qualities she feels she has lost and which she hopes – probably in vain – to re-attain. Moreover, in *L'Air de Paris*, transcendence is located elsewhere. In a move hinted at in *Thérèse Raquin*, it is now a male – Lesaffre – who embodies this quality. In order to understand this it is necessary to consider *L'Air de Paris*'s gay readings, which have dominated recent considerations of the film.

While the 'impossible love' mentioned in the *Cinémonde* article is ostensibly referring to the relationship between André and Corinne, in light of recent readings of the film, one may be inclined to think otherwise: as critics have observed, the film potentially contains more than one impossible love. A number of writers have seen it as possessing a strong gay subtext, with the relationship between André and Victor moving beyond straightforward friendship. The issue is briefly discussed by Turk, though a more thorough investigation is provided by Dyer (2000) and, more recently, Dhoest (2003). Underpinning these interrogations is the question of to what extent homosexual meanings can be read into the film when on the surface it deals with the heterosexual relationship between André and Corinne. Indeed, all three writers acknowledge that reviews from the period don't mention any homosexual dimension to the film (aside from a couple of ambiguous references identified by Dyer (2000: 138)). Yet, analysis of the film and its context uncovers a clear gay subtext. Turk identifies this, though he is extremely careful in his discussion, wary of the dangers of reading 'too much' into the film. Dyer and Dhoest are also tentative, while ensuring that they identify the film's salient gay qualities. So, what constitutes this gay subtext? And how is homosexuality represented?

There are three main elements to the film's gay identity. Firstly, a couple of the more minor characters are presented as overtly gay. These are the designer, Jean-Marc (Jean Parédès), whose homosexuality is signified through his 'mincing' performance and comments on André's attractiveness, and Chantal (Simone Paris), who it is strongly suggested, through her jealous attitude to André and Corinne (with whom she lives), has lesbian affections towards her friend. The homosexuality of Jean-Marc is conveyed further through the fact that he is played by Parédès, who frequently played camp characters in his films, with other key examples including *Plaisirs de Paris* (Ralph Baum, 1952) and a later Carné film, *Du mouron pour les petits oiseaux*.

Secondly, and less overtly, there is the gay subtext between André and Victor. This is implied to a significant degree through the jealousy with which Blanche views their relationship. She wants her and Victor to sell the gym and move away to the sea, rather like Raymonde wants to escape Paris with Edmond in *Hôtel du Nord*, but he is adamant that he will remain there to oversee André's training. A number of hints suggest the bond between the two males does indeed consist of something more than just friendship. In one exchange Victor tells André he has a nice smile; later, as Victor leaves André's room, André looks lovingly after him. Boxing also allows the two characters to get very close to each other, which creates moments of intimacy, such as when Victor massages André, who is wearing nothing but briefs. Another key image from the film, which as a production photograph was circulated widely in promotional materials, shows Victor with his hand partially down André's boxing shorts, midway through a fight as he rests between rounds (the image appeared, for example, in a *Cinémonde* article on the film (Anon., 1954: 17)). He is clearly massaging his stomach to help his boxing performance, but it can also be seen as a hint at a more erotic physical bond between the characters. The implication that this is a gay relationship is suggested further when Victor becomes jealous of André's relationship with Corinne. While the two characters are on the surface heterosexual, the film skilfully allows us to read the relationship in another, 'queer', way.

Thirdly, the film can be seen to possess a gay subtext through the way Lesaffre is presented, particularly how his appearance – his face (especially his smile, mentioned above) and his body – is celebrated. Boxing of course provides many 'excuses' for him to be shown in various states of undress. Aside from the scenes of boxing, in which his arm muscles are bare and bulging, we see him taking a shower at one point, and, when Victor massages him, he is wearing only briefs. Although these scenes make sense within a boxing film, Carné uses these opportunities to show Lesaffre's body, which is muscular and well defined, thus positioning him as object of the gaze. Such scenes are motivated, but are also part of Carné's gay 'gaze' at his protagonist and star.

Beyond considering the extent to which the film contains a gay subtext, we can ask, *how* does Carné present homosexuality? Interestingly, the film, like Carné's other work, is ideologically conflicted. While it is important that Carné deals with this topic, in a *de facto* homophobic context, the film is also limited in particular respects. Dyer (2002:149), who emphasises the uneasy relationship between the film's gay content and the context of Paris, states: '*L'Air de Paris*, a film so startlingly overt for its time, nonetheless portrays homosexuality as a love that does not even know its name, or place.' In addition, in places the film actually exhibits some quite homophobic attitudes. This is evident from a consideration of Jean-Marc and Chantal, the two overtly gay characters, who are both presented as unattractive in different ways. Jean Parédès's extremely camp performance places him as a figure of fun, and Chantal is presented negatively because she comes between André and Corinne when they return to her apartment to make love. For Dyer (2000: 131) such negative representations are part of a 'strategy of the closet'; he argues that Carné inserted homophobic elements into the film as a way of avoiding accusations that the film has a gay subtext. In part this was because Carné didn't want to draw attention to the film's homosexual content because audiences were culturally unprepared to accept such narratives. In addition, the strategy of the closet was aimed at keeping Gabin on his side, as the star was aware of the fact that Victor and André's relationship could be interpreted as gay, which he was not pleased with, apparently stating: 'No way, I don't want to look like a queer' (cited in Dyer, 2000: 129).

In light of Carné's use of Parédès in a later film comedy, *Du mouron pour les petits oiseaux*, it is likely that Carné's attitude towards Jean-Marc is also one of homophobia, or more precisely, hostility towards camp notions of homosexuality. Carné himself was not camp, and was generally less overt in expressing his sexuality than a small group of openly gay French filmmakers of the time, as Vincendeau (1997: 15) writes: 'he was also gay and – though not "out" in the modern sense, or in the sense that Cocteau and Genet were – this fact was known.' We can also discern hostility towards camp in *Du mouron pour les petits oiseaux*, in which Parédès plays the very similar role of Monsieur de Fleurville. In this, the homophobia attached to Parédès is more caricatural. Again, he is very camp, and performs with the same 'mincing' quality. Sporting a neatly trimmed moustache, at one point he wears a smoking jacket and cravat, and at another a white suit, while holding a cane. His character, who is not a leading role, but who receives more screen time than Jean-Marc in *L'Air de Paris*, spends the entire film trying to lure young postmen to his apartment, even posting letters to himself. This culminates in one of these postmen giving him a black eye in what is supposed to be a humorous moment in the film. This use of comedy and the dramatisation of humiliating violence towards a gay character betrays a homophobic sensibility in a film that doesn't have the more liberating gay subtext of *L'Air de Paris*. This, then, suggests that while in the earlier film Jean-Marc fulfils the role of 'closeting' Carné, he also articulates problematic attitudes towards a certain group of gay men.

If we consider ideas explored in Carné's previous films, we can see that such an attitude towards camp not only draws upon a common stereotype of the time, it is also entirely consistent with Carné's broader worldview. His films on the whole celebrate authenticity and sublimated sexuality, concepts that are in contrast to the theatricality, role-playing and physical nature of camp. Indeed, *L'Air de Paris* presents us with a different form of homosexuality one that is much more in keeping with Carné's ideals. According to Dyer (2000: 134), the presentation of Lesaffre conforms to a broader trend in gay culture, centred on the use of angel iconography. This is evident through his appearance, owing to his blonde hair, light features and excellent physique, as well as the way he is lit, with the use of halo effects enhancing his angelic quality. He is even referred to by Corinne at one point as 'mon ange' ('my angel'). Moreover, Dyer points out that Carné uses angel iconography in a more explicit way in one of his later films, *La Merveilleuse Visite*, which has a strong gay subtext, as we shall see, and in which Gilles Kohler, who is at the centre of the film's gay erotic interest, actually plays an angel. What this also shows is a continuation of Carné's idealisation from earlier films, in which Michèle Morgan, Annabella, and Jacqueline Laurent were all used to represent pure and ethereal beings. However, the key, and obvious change, is that whereas in the 1930s Carné and Prévert used young women to present such transcendent qualities, in *L'Air de Paris* it is a man who takes this role (*La Merveilleuse Visite* would be another example of this). Whereas Jean-Marc makes sexually suggestive comments about André, Carné views Lesaffre in a more elevated, idealised way. Indeed, it is significant that the postman Monsieur de Fleurville preys upon in *Du mouron pour les petits oiseaux* has similar characteristics to Lesaffre and Gilles Kohler, as the actor is young and has blonde hair; the difference is that Carné idealises such beauty, rather than 'vulgarising' it through what he presents as Jean-Marc and Monsieur de Fleurville's camp lustiness. As Dyer (2000: 136) argues, with Carné celebrating a heavenly, sublimated and celibate notion of homosexuality, rather than a more physical and sexual form, the use of angel iconography is 'the fantasy resolution of a conflict between lust and morality endured by generations of gay men'.

L'Air de Paris was quite well received. Although it experienced some criticism, such as Bazin's assertion (1954) that it is 'déséquilibrée, désorientée' ('out of balance, disorientating'), it won the newly established 'Prix Populistes du Cinéma' in 1954, which recognised Carné's important contribution to this key strand of French film, and attracted just over two million viewers. As a rare example of gay French cinema of the 1950s and the work that provides the clearest expression of Carné's sexual identity, it is a crucial and revealing film in the director's filmography, and moreover one in which he is able to channel personal views about non-normative sexuality in a mainstream genre film.

During the 1950s Carné's position in the French film industry weakened. While he was still a celebrated director, discussed at length in film journals and magazines, he was no longer the prestigious figure he had been. Whereas between 1936 and 1946 he made eight films, a number of which were huge popular and critical triumphs, between 1947 and 1957, he made only five (*Le Pays d'où je viens* will be considered in the next chapter), which met with mixed reactions. Nevertheless, the films he made at this time represent an interesting stage in his career. As we have seen, a number of them were successful at the box-office, especially *La Marie du port* and *Thérèse Raquin*. By using top stars and dominant genres, particularly the period's psychological realism, while drawing on elements of his familiar style and many of his recurring themes, the success of these films showed there was still an audience for his work. Indeed, the continuities between his postwar films and his earlier work also demonstrate that the subject matter explored in his films was not just the product of Prévert's involvement, challenging the notion that Carné was a mere 'metteur en images'.

The films are also fascinating for the view they provide of France in the 1950s. On the one hand they retain Carné's populism, particularly in *L'Air de Paris*, and thus show his continuing central role in the populist trend at the heart of French cinema between the 1930s and 1950s. On the other, the importance of this work also stems from the insight it provides into changes in France as it went through a period of rapid modernisation. Carné's films mirror the nation's increased wealth, Americanisation, and cosmopolitanism.

These features emphasise not only the importance and consistent popularity of the critically disdained tradition of quality, but also, in particular, the significant contribution Carné made to this type of cinema. In part the neglect of Carné's postwar films is related to the box-office and critical failures that he encountered occasionally (though, as we have seen, these were balanced by some great successes), but it is also a product of developments in the historiography of Carné's work (outlined in Chapter 1). One of the reasons for the tradition of quality being neglected is that hostility was shown towards it by dominant cinephile journals and in particular the *Cahiers du Cinéma*. As Carné was one of the main victims of these attacks, they came to define his career and legacy for a number of years. For this reason it is essential to any reassessment of Carné to consider this relationship in more detail. This I will do in the next chapter, by focusing on the films Carné made at the end of the 1950s and in the early 1960s, just as the French new wave was arriving.

References

Abel, R. (1984), *French Cinema: The First Wave, 1915–1929*, Princeton; Guildford, Princeton University Press.

Andrew, D. (1995), *Mists of Regret: Culture and Sensibility in Classic French Film*, Princeton; Chichester, Princeton University Press.

Anon. (1947), 'Premières photos du nouveau film de Marcel Carné', *Cinémonde*, 669, 27 May, p. 7.

Anon. (1954), '*L'Air de Paris* souffle en bourrasque au central sporting-club', *Cinémonde*, 1029, 23 April, pp. 16–17.

Anon. (1954a), 'Dans *L'Air de Paris* un miroir a brisé les reflets d'un impossible amour ...', *Cinémonde*, 1033, 21 May, p. 16.

Bazin, A. (1949), 'Dans *La Marie du port* de Marcel Carné, un Gabin a cheveux gris va créer un nouveau personnage', *Le Parisien Libéré*, 17 August.

Bazin, A. (1953), '*Thérèse Raquin*', *Le Parisien Libéré*, 10 November.

Bazin, A. (1954), '*L'Air de Paris*, du grand air à la romance', *Le Parisien Libéré*, 30 September.

Bazin, A. (1983), 'The disincarnation of Carné', in M. L. Bandy, ed., *Rediscovering French Film*, New York, Museum of Modern Art, pp. 131–5.

Becker, L. F. (2006), *Georges Simenon: 'Maigrets' and the 'Romans Durs'*, London, Haus.

Braudy, L. (1969), 'Zola on film: the ambiguities of naturalism', *Yale French Studies*, 42, pp. 68–88.

Burch, N., and G. Sellier (1996), *La drôle de guerre des sexes du cinéma français, 1930–1956*, Paris, Nathan.

Carette, J. (1949), 'Carné, c'est Napoléon', *Cinémonde*, special Christmas issue, December, p. 12.

Carné, M. (1996), *Ma vie à belles dents*, Paris, L'Archipel.

Chazal, R. (1949), 'Le cinéma français retrouve son équipe no. 1 Marcel Carné – Jean Gabin', *Cinémonde*, 785, 22 August, p. 3.

Dhoest, A. (2003), 'How queer is *L'Air de Paris*? – Marcel Carné and queer authorship', *Scope: An Online Journal of Film and TV Studies*, May, online at www.scope.nottingham.ac.uk/article.php?issue=may2003&id=258§ion=article&q=dhoest (25 October 2010).

Dyer, R. (2000), 'No place for homosexuality: Marcel Carné's *L'Air de Paris*', in S. Hayward and G. Vincendeau, eds, *French Film: Texts and Contexts*, 2nd edn, London, Routledge, pp. 127–41.

Dyer, R. (2002), '*L'Air de Paris*: no place for homosexuality', in *The Culture of Queers*, London, Routledge, pp. 137–51.

Hayward, S. (2003), 'Literary adaptations of the 1950s: *Thérèse Raquin* (1953) and *Les Diaboliques* (1955)', *Studies in French Cinema*, 3:1, pp. 5–14.

Hayward, S. (2004), *Simone Signoret: The Star as Cultural Sign*, New York; London, Continuum.

Pecheral, S. (1949), 'J'ai voulu faire un film simple, vivant, c'est pourquoi j'ai tourné *La Marie du port*', *Cinémonde*, special Christmas issue, December, pp. 12–13.

Ross, K. (1995), *Fast Cars, Clean Bodies: Decolonization and the Reordering of French Culture*, Cambridge, Mass.; London, MIT Press.

Truffaut, F. (2009), 'A certain tendency in French cinema', in P. Graham, ed., with G. Vincendeau, *The French New Wave: Critical Landmarks*, London, British Film Institute / Palgrave Macmillan, pp. 39–63.

Turk, E. B. (1989), *Child of Paradise: Marcel Carné and the Golden Age of French Cinema*, Cambridge, Mass.; London, Harvard University Press.

Vincendeau, G. (1997), 'Paradise regained', *Sight and Sound*, 7:7, pp. 12–16.

Vincendeau, G. (2000), *Stars and Stardom in French Cinema*, London, Continuum.

Vincendeau, G. (2004), 'Forms 1930–1960: The art of spectacle', in M. Temple and M. Witt, eds, *The French Cinema Book*, London, British Film Institute, pp. 137–52.

Williams, A. (1992), *Republic of Images: A History of French Filmmaking*, Cambridge, Mass.; London, Harvard University Press.

5

The French new wave

This chapter focuses on another important stage in Carné's career by examining his relationship with a key moment in French film history – indeed, probably its most famous moment – the French new wave. In the last chapter and in Chapter 1 I began to discuss the significance of this meeting, between one of France's great classical directors and the filmmakers of the new wave. While 'Most *Cahiers du Cinéma* writers treated Marcel Carné quite fairly', as Turk (1989: 391) points out, others, especially François Truffaut, attacked Carné's work, and this had an adverse affect on the remainder of his career. This hostile relationship can in part be explored through the critical skirmishes that pitted Carné against certain *Cahiers* critics, but it can also be understood through an examination of the films Carné made at the time, particularly as there are, surprisingly, many connections between them and the context and films of the new wave – more than the latter movement was willing to admit.

There is critical dispute about when the new wave began, with recent work exploring the significance of important 'precursors' to the movement in the early to mid-1950s, including directors Alexandre Astruc, Roger Vadim, and Jacques Doniol-Valcroze and stars such as Brigitte Bardot and Jeanne Moreau. Leaving these debates aside, the 'core' new wave films are generally accepted to be two films by Claude Chabrol, *Le Beau Serge* (1958) and *Les Cousins* (1959), François Truffaut's *Les Quatre Cents Coups* (1959), Alain Resnais's *Hiroshima mon amour* (1959), and Jean-Luc Godard's *À Bout de souffle* (1960). Arriving to much publicity and acclaim, the new wave contributed to some profound changes in French cinema, its films differing from the tradition of quality in several important ways. A number of films advanced modernist self-reflexive strategies, others centred on an unpolished, improvised aesthetic, manifest through the use of handheld cameras and filming on location. While many of the famous filmmakers of the new wave began their careers as journalists for the *Cahiers du Cinéma*, including Chabrol, Godard, Jacques Rivette, Eric Rohmer, and Truffaut, there were others, such as the so-called 'Left Bank Group' consisting of Chris Marker, Alain Resnais, and Agnès Varda, filmmakers who similarly worked on the margins of the industry, but engaged in more avant-garde and/or political cinema.

In a number of respects Carné shares similarities with the new wave filmmakers. As we have seen, at the beginning of his career he was celebrated as a young and rebellious critic-turned-director. In addition, poetic realism was the last major critical and popular movement in France before the new wave. One of Carné's defining films from this era, *Le Quai des brumes*, was even considered a precursor to Godard's *À Bout de souffle* in an article from 1960 by Georges Sadoul (2009). The new wave critics, however, were not inclined to perceive similarities between themselves and Carné. On the contrary, Truffaut in particular launched a vicious attack on him. In part such contempt clearly comes from his involvement in the tradition of quality, which, in contrast to the new wave with its spontaneous, improvised look, was concerned with the creation of a polished aesthetic. As one of French cinema's master craftsmen, Carné was an obvious target for their critical hostility. The *Cahiers* critics were also hostile to Carné because of their doubts about the extent to which he could claim authorship for his films. Because of his advocacy of collaborative filmmaking and his partnership with Jacques Prévert, they were convinced he was not an 'auteur' – the term they coined for a film artist who uses a distinct approach to style and form to explore a personal vision. Encapsulating this criticism, Truffaut wrote:

> [Carné] has never known how to evaluate a scenario [and] has never known how to choose a subject. For a long time others performed these tasks for him, and for years we have been offered films created by Jacques Prévert and rendered in images by Marcel Carné. Henceforth Carné is condemned to be 'taken in' by the first screenwriter to come along. (Truffaut cited in Turk, 1989: 391)

Beyond issues of authorship and aesthetics other factors undoubtedly account for a degree of the animosity between Carné and the new wave critics, in particular politics. While Carné's films tend not to be overtly political, his left-wing sympathies are evident in his realism and populist celebration of 'ordinary' people, while the *Cahiers* critics were not concerned with such issues. Martin O'Shaughnessy (2000: 34) pinpoints how their critical discussions of Renoir tended to remove the political dimension of his films, and Geneviève Sellier (2008) has demonstrated the apolitical nature of much new wave cinema as well as the right-wing implications of their celebration of middle-class male characters. Here Truffaut's (2009) attack against the so-called 'anti-bourgeois' content of tradition of quality films is revealing, and in clear opposition to Carné's outlook – his populist cinema would frequently cast the bourgeoisie in a negative light.

More generally the *Cahiers* critics were self-consciously part of the new, modern France. Kristin Ross (1995) argues that in the postwar years France's sudden obsession with cleanliness, as evident through a sharp rise in the purchasing of commodities such as washing machines and soap, stemmed from a national desire to be cleansed of negative aspects of recent history. In discussing this work, Guy Austin (2003, 44) states: 'The origins of this "deep psychological need [...] to be *clean*" can be located in a resolve to purify and modernise France after the trauma of the Second World War (the German Occupation, collaboration by the Vichy state, civil war of a kind).' This is another significant aspect of the animosity towards Carné since he was strongly associated with these recent events, from which the *Cahiers* critics' generation were keen to distance themselves.

We have seen how Carné's representations of gender are central to his films' politics. In this respect too there are significant differences between him and the *Cahiers* critics. This needs to be understood against the backdrop of broader changes in France at this time, particularly the youth culture that emerged in the 1950s. The term 'new wave' was initially used to describe the generation of people who became teenagers in the 1950s, a group who received increased exposure in the period's culture. This is evident through the rise to prominence of the youth-oriented films of Roger Vadim, new stars such as Brigitte Bardot, and the writing of novelists such as Françoise Sagan, who, at the age of nineteen, published *Bonjour tristesse* (1954), the story of a hedonistic seventeen-year-old woman. To some extent, this movement offered possibilities for the creation of more emancipated female identities. Sagan, for example, wrote about the contemporary context from the point of view of female characters and through narratives about young women who desire the same pleasures and freedoms as the men. By contrast, as Sellier has argued, the new wave was more concerned with dramatising a male experience of these events. Their auteur films closely follow the point of view of a male protagonist, who is essentially an alter-ego for the director (Sellier, 2008: 100).

It is possible to detect similarities in attitudes to gender between Carné and the new wave. As Sellier (2008: 100) argues, a recurring character type in new wave cinema is the sensitive, vulnerable, male, a form of masculinity that is comparable to many men in Carné's cinema. However, there are divergences when it comes to the representation of women. Although new wave women possess modern traits, they are also viewed conservatively, with Sellier (2008: 81) arguing that women in Chabrol's films are 'derisive', in Truffaut's 'menacing', and in Godard's 'infantilized'. While Carné's films also contain regressive notions of femininity, particularly the ethereal women of poetic realism, he often explores female subjectivity, as in *Thérèse Raquin* and, to a lesser extent, *La Marie du port*. Moreover, Carné's own sexuality, and its expression in his cinema, also conflicts with the new wave. On this subject, Turk (1989: 393) perceptively notes the presence of homophobic language and attitudes in a number of the *Cahiers* articles and reviews, pointing out, for instance, that Henri Agel refers at one point to Carné's cinema as 'inverti' ('inverted'), a French term for 'homosexual'. Truffaut's discussions of Carné also include potentially homophobic overtones, as Turk (1989: 393) argues: 'the tenor of Agel's 1959 critique makes one wonder if sexual orientation was a half-hidden item on the agenda of Truffaut's early attack program'.

Carné responded strongly to the criticism he received from the *Cahiers* critics. As we know, he was an assertive character; not the type of person to take such criticism lightly. One of his main attacks was in a 1965 interview published in *Le Figaro Littéraire*, in which he stated: 'It is very simple. We experienced a period in which a new director was born each morning ... And, out of two hundred of these "creators", how many survived? Three or four. Once emerged from their autobiographical stammerings, the others could only demonstrate their incapacity to build a story. They could exhibit only their congenital impotence!' (Carné cited in Turk, 1989: 393–4). We can see, then, that Carné's relationship with the French new wave consisted of very public mutual animosity. However, this gives only a partial understanding of Carné's relationship with the new wave era. Around this time he also made a number of films, which can help us understand his position better. It is to these films I now turn.

Towards the French new wave

Le Pays d'où je viens

Carné's next film, *Le Pays d'où je viens*, was released in 1956. While this was still a couple of years before the new wave, it was during this period that the new youth culture, which would influence the film movement, was becoming prominent. Carné did not conceive of and develop *Le Pays d'où je viens*; he was asked to make it once the package had already been finalised, including the film's concept and main actors. He was attracted to the project because it was to be shot in Technicolor – up until this point Carné had used only black and white – and because he was keen to work with Gilbert Bécaud, who had been hired as the film's lead. Bécaud was a star of the music-hall, primarily a singer, and *Le Pays d'où je viens* was to be his first, much hyped, feature film. Carné had worked with other singing stars such as Montand and, as a fan of the music-hall, was keen to repeat the experience (Turk, 1989: 397). Articles appeared in *Cinémonde* discussing Bécaud's debut and how Carné was a good choice for guiding the debutant into the film industry, as a director famous for 'discovering' or 'making' stars. One *Cinémonde* (Anon., 1956: 11) article was even entitled 'L'élève Gilbert Bécaud fait ses classes de cinéma avec le professeur Carné' ('The student Gilbert Bécaud takes his cinema classes with Professor Carné'). The film also stars other performers of note, such as Françoise Arnoul, who had recently appeared in Jean Renoir's *French Cancan* (1954), and Pierre Brasseur's son, Claude Brasseur, who was making his first major appearance (the opportunity to work with Claude Brasseur was another significant part of the film's appeal for Carné). With these stars, the colour photography, and Carné at the helm, the film had a lot going for it, and, while it was strongly criticised by Truffaut (1956), it actually performed very well at the box-office, selling almost three million tickets. It thus deserves more attention than it has so far received.

Set in the Alps during Christmas, the story follows a young man called Éric Perceval (Bécaud) on the run from his rich uncle, who is annoyed by his nephew's free-spirited and profligate behaviour. Pursued by two of his uncle's henchmen, Éric enters a small town, where a comedy of misrecognition ensues: it transpires that he is the exact double of one of the town's inhabitants, a classical pianist named Julien Barrère (also played by Bécaud). However, while the two characters look and sound the same, their personalities are quite distinct: Éric is confident and energetic; Julien is timid and apathetic. Such confusion is heightened when Éric, unbeknown to Julien, decides to help his doppelgänger to attract a young woman called Marinette (Arnoul). The story follows various mishaps and instances of misrecognition, before Éric leaves the town, evading his uncle, and Julien and Marinette form a romantic couple.

One of the most immediately striking features of the film is how light-hearted and cheerful it is, placing it in sharp contrast to most of the Carné films considered so far. While he usually deals with fatalism, melancholia, and loneliness, *Le Pays d'où je viens* is a happy film, shot in Technicolor, focusing on a small town during the Christmas period – the streets are covered in snow, there is an abundance of Christmas decorations, and a use of bright colours. With comedy and regular musical numbers, mostly sung by Bécaud, the film sustains this light-hearted spirit throughout. Nevertheless, despite this, it contains clear continuities with Carné's earlier work, such as the themes of romantic love and innocence, both of which are conveyed through the Christmas context.

In terms of gender, the film demonstrates a number of continuities and differences from Carné's earlier work. Françoise Arnoul's persona at this time centred upon an image of sexy and compliant femininity, of which there are hints in *Le Pays d'où je viens*, particularly when she has, in a recurring joke, her skirt accidentally pulled away, revealing her underwear. At the same time, she plays a romantic and 'pure' character, evident from the way she cares for her orphaned brother and sister and visualised through the scenes of her dressed like a fairytale princess in a white gown with a tinsel halo on her head. Aside from her vocal and assertive criticism of Julien, whom she considers to be too passive and bumbling, she is, then, a largely submissive vision of femininity. Taken together Bécaud's characters serve to celebrate Éric's virile form of masculinity – his confidence, control, and physical strength – over the weaker and timid Julien. While female idealisation is a familiar element from Carné's early cinema, such a celebration of male virility and attack against male weakness is less common, and is undoubtedly related to the fact that Carné joined the project at a late stage.

Le Pays d'où je viens in many ways still belongs to the tradition of quality, particularly through its style, which is classical throughout. At the same time, it contains notably up-to-date elements, especially through its treatment of youth. Bécaud, who was popular with a youth audience, makes an important contribution to this: while Julien signifies the past through his talent at performing classical music, Éric represents modern attitudes through his contemporary music and his frantic mobility and energy, trademark features of Bécaud's performance style, a man whose nickname was 'Monsieur 100,000 volts'. This is particularly significant when we consider the lethargic way in which many of Carné's characters move, such as Gabin in *Le Quai des brumes*. In addition, of particular importance in terms of the film's representation of youth culture is the character of Roland (Brasseur), a member of a young gang, who wear fashionable clothing and listen to rock and roll on their transistor radio. An instance of the disruptiveness of this group occurs at the beginning of the film when Roland, in the venue where Julien is playing the piano, turns the radio on, interrupting the performance with loud popular music. On the other hand the gang is discredited, particularly owing to the way Roland is continually duped by the doppelgänger scenario: he beats up Julien with two friends, but, when he tries to do this again shortly after, he and his gang are beaten up by Éric (who they believed was Julien). In this respect they perform an essentially comic function in the film.

This emphasis on youth is important for a few reasons. Although such content was part of the scenario before Carné took his position as director, representing youth culture would be one of the last significant additions to his filmmaking identity, and one that would continue in a number of his subsequent films. Of course, he'd always been interested in youth – it is used to signify innocence in a number of his early films, and *Les Enfants du paradis* is in certain respects a film about getting old, about losing youth, something Prévert and he were in the process of experiencing. While *Le Pays d'où je viens* is by no means a new wave precursor, it is symptomatic of an increased interest in the wider culture in issues relating to youth. This would become an important element in the creation of the new wave, and would be explored by Carné in more detail in his next two films, *Les Tricheurs* and *Terrain vague* (1960).

The new wave of youth culture

Les Tricheurs

Carné's *Les Tricheurs*, released in 1958, was a huge success as far as the public was concerned. It was the fifth most popular film of the year with 4.9 million spectators, won the 1958 Grand Prix du Cinéma and was named in a referendum by *Cinémonde* and *Le Figaro* as 'the best French film of the year'. It also received huge amounts of marketing exposure: a whole issue of *L'Express* was devoted to it and it was discussed at length in the period's fan magazines. Such popularity is highly significant within the context of Carné's career, particularly as many had written him off by this time. *Les Tricheurs* is also interesting because of its relationship with the cinema of the new wave: while Carné was rejected by the 'Young Turks' of the new wave as hopelessly out of date, here was a film by him about the young generation that reached a huge audience.

The story, based on a screenplay by Jacques Sigurd, centres on the lives of a number of youths living in the Saint-Germain-des-Prés area of Paris, told as a flashback from the point of view of one of them, Bob Letellier (Jacques Charrier). Bob befriends Alain (Laurent Terzieff), a bisexual dropout from the Sorbonne, who regularly attends large parties along with other young people. At one of these, Bob meets and falls in love with a young woman called Mic (Pascale Petit), who also loves him. However, they keep their distance from each other because in this group of friends love and sentimentality are rejected as unnecessary constraints. At the end of the film the main characters, including Bob and Mic, who have fallen out with each other, attend a party at Clo's (Andréa Parisy) parents' country house. When Mic publicly announces that she loves Bob, and he turns her down, she drives off into the night. Bob realising his error – he does love her – drives after her. However, in the chase that ensues, Mic crashes her car, and later dies in hospital.

In histories of the French new wave, *Les Tricheurs* has, until recently, received little discussion. When writers do mention it, most, out of reverence for the new wave, adopt the same attitude as the *Cahiers* critics, criticising Carné for his 'outdated' approach. In this respect, *Les Tricheurs* can be placed alongside other films such as Henri-Georges Clouzot's *La Vérité* (1960) and Claude Autant-Lara's *En cas de malheur* (1958): all three explored the new wave of youth culture but were made by established tradition of quality directors working in a classical idiom. Even recently, David Thompson (2009: 24) wrote: 'Today, *La Vérité* just avoids looking like the work of one of the old guard keen to ride the success of the *nouvelle vague* by getting down and dirty with promiscuous Parisian youth (as Marcel Carné and Claude Autant-Lara did, with embarrassing results).' Such an evaluation is problematic on several counts, quite apart from its derivative nature. Firstly, *Les Tricheurs* was released *before* the new wave, so can't have been 'riding' its success. Moreover, Thompson's assessment neglects the many ways in which Carné's film, and these others, hold potential interest as documents from, and on, the period. Recent work on the new wave that has taken a more historical approach, considering the movement from a broader cultural perspective, has tended to give *Les Tricheurs* greater importance. It is mentioned by Ross (1995), Neupert (2002) and Sellier (2008), and in a book by Jean-Lou Alexandre called *Les Cousins des tricheurs* (2005) it is brought right to the fore, through comparisons with Chabrol's *Les Cousins*. Such interest, which refreshingly departs from the earlier prejudice against Carné, stems from the film's exploration of youth culture. *Les Tricheurs* was actually one of the first films to be referred to as belonging to a 'new wave', as highlighted in 1962 by Robert Benayoun, a critic at *Positif* (a more political, rival publication to *Cahiers du Cinéma*) writing in his usual vitriolic style:

> Let me put it bluntly: the catchphrase 'Nouvelle Vague', which arose as everyone knows from an investigation into youth by Françoise Giroud which appeared in *L'Express*, was first applied by that same weekly to a film by Marcel Carné called *Les Tricheurs (The Cheaters)*. The film was extraordinarily vulgar, redolent of the immediate postwar period. It was nevertheless well received, and the catchphrase made a hit. (Benayoun, 2009: 165)

Although 'Nouvelle Vague' would come to stand for a different type of film, it is still significant that *Les Tricheurs* was the first work to be described in this way as it hints at some of the similarities between Carné's film and the cinema that would go on to define the movement.

In addition to *Les Tricheurs*'s treatment of youth, which I will expand upon shortly, the film was cheaply made and it used youthful rising performers rather than established stars. Although some new wave actors attained stardom, most notably, Jean-Paul Belmondo and Jeanne Moreau, many of the films would use non-professional performers. Almost all the actors in *Les Tricheurs* were unknown before the film was released – the main exception being Roland Lesaffre who has a relatively small role as Mic's brother. This represents a major transformation in Carné's cinema; as we have seen, his films would usually include the period's biggest stars. Importantly, one of the 'unknowns' cast in *Les Tricheurs* was Jean-Paul Belmondo, who would go on to be the star of *À bout de souffle* – Godard in fact spotted him in *Les Tricheurs* (Neupert, 2002: 210). While his role is not huge, he displays elements of the persona that would develop in the years that followed, such as when we see him have a fight at a party – in the following years such skirmishes would crystallise into his 'angry young man' persona.

Carné has stated that *Les Tricheurs* was an important film in enabling the new wave to emerge, claiming that by proving a hugely successful film – one of the highest grossing of the year – could be made on a small budget, this encouraged the production of similarly low-budget films, such as those of the new wave (cited in Turk, 1989: 401). Turk points out that even Truffaut commented on how the new wave benefited from *Les Tricheurs*. Despite this Carné received virulent criticism for the film as is indicated by the above Benayoun quotation. A number of sources refer to it as opportunistic, as Williams (1992: 288) explains: 'Carné was widely seen as pandering uncritically – and unsuccessfully – to the young' (it is not clear what Williams means by 'unsuccessful' here, given the popular triumph of the film). *Les Tricheurs* is indeed a departure for Carné, most strikingly through the overt treatment of sex and sexual promiscuity that makes the film distinct from the sublimated romanticism of his earlier work. Nevertheless, in other respects there are clear continuities. According to Turk (1989: 404), Carné in the film adopts a position of 'prurience and guilt-ridden voyeurism' with regards to the youths he depicts, which suggests his distance from his subjects. Yet there is another way of seeing *Les Tricheurs*, as a film that reveals his fascination with this world: by living outside of society's rules and conventions, these characters are in certain respects similar to the marginalised heroes found in Carné's other work – for example, the protagonists of poetic realism, or his many doomed lovers. Arguably the film's fascination with 'outcasts' can also be read in relation to Carné's homosexuality.

Mainly, though, Carné's film has been criticised for being 'out of date', particularly in comparison with the new wave. Following its release, Carné was described in the title of the review by *Positif* as 'Croulant!' (Crumbling!) (cited in Vincendeau, 1997: 15). In large part this is related to his style. The films of the new wave tend to use an improvised, spontaneous aesthetic and/or adopt a modernist deconstruction of conventional film language. By contrast, Carné's 'classical' techniques were seen as outdated and as a clear continuation of the tradition of quality. In addition, Carné was seen as out of touch with the youths he represents and, more importantly, as critical of their behaviour. Indeed, Turk's insight, stressing Carné's 'voyeurism', emphasises distance between Carné and the group, which is in contrast to the autobiographical intimacy established between director and protagonist in many of the new wave films. In *Les Tricheurs* we are to some extent aligned with the position of Bob, initially an outsider to the group, with the story presented as *his* flashback. However, by adopting a more omniscient perspective, we are also placed at a distance from the events depicted.

The key difference between Carné and the youths is that they are presented as enjoying the repression of sentiment, whereas his cinema is concerned with the importance of emotional expression. As we later see, great destruction is caused by characters not following their feelings; it leads, for example, to the fatal car crash that kills Mic. The youths' cynical attitude towards emotional expressivity is evident during a scene in which various characters go to watch a double bill of a Rudolph Valentino film followed by a James Dean film. Here we see a cinema full of youths, all laughing hysterically at the Valentino film, at its melodramatic acting and emotional intensity. Although we don't see their reaction to James Dean, it would presumably be more to their taste: his youthful, rebellious and cool persona characterises their own attitudes, and at one point Mic states that she would be happy to die the same way as Dean. While new wave cinema is famous for its cinephilic references to other films, in *Les Tricheurs* we witness a moment in which youths express hostility towards an historically important star, and one who is significant in relation to Carné. Not only does Valentino embody the sensitivity at the heart of his cinema, he also, as a gay icon, represents an expression of Carné's sexuality. The youths' behaviour, then, emphasises a distance between them and Carné.

For Turk, this distanced treatment of youth is reactionary, with the film adopting a highly moralistic attitude towards its subjects – while some of the attitudes of the young protagonists are revolutionary, such as their rejection of heterosexual monogamy, these acts are, for Turk, undermined by the film's catastrophic conclusion. In addition, Neupert (2002: 16) refers to the film as a 'cautionary' tale. While these are certainly important observations, *Les Tricheurs* is more complex in its attitude to the young. This is hinted at by Turk in his discussion of the film's ending, which to some extent places blame on the older generation. Following the surgeon's unsuccessful attempt to save Mic's life, he asks: 'Qu'est ce qu'ils ont ces gosses bon dieu? Qu'est ce qu'ils ont?' ('What's the matter with these youngsters for God's sake? What's the matter with them?'). Roger (Lesaffre), Mic's brother, replies: 'Cinquante ans de pagaille derrière eux, sans doute en avant. Pour les jeunes c'est dur' ('Fifty years of mess behind them, without doubt fifty more ahead. It's hard for the young'). With this the youths are to some extent excused of their behaviour. In addition, as Vincendeau (1997: 16) argues, the middle-aged doctor, a symbol of the status quo, is shown to be ineffectual when he is unable to save Mic's life, which hints further that the source of the youth 'problem' is actually the older generation.

Les Tricheurs also contains elements that represent a progressive attitude to the changing times. An important aspect of this stems from the film's realism, which shapes on screen the details of the modern world, and as such held much fascination for viewers of the time. Turk (1989: 401) sees thematic similarities between the film and the new wave – the emphasis on modern youth culture – as being a 'coincidence', stating: '*Les Tricheurs*'s foreshadowing of certain New Wave preoccupations is a matter of coincidence, not revised aesthetics.' Yet, Carné's engagement with such issues is related to his ability to spot important cultural developments as they are happening; as I have argued in previous chapters, he was highly attentive to changes in the broader social contexts in which he worked. *Les Tricheurs* is replete with details of the modern world, including cars, scooters, juke boxes, pinball machines, modern clothing (such as Alain's black leather jacket), and makeup. As part of this, we also witness in a highly visceral way the pleasures that are part of the modern world, particularly during the numerous scenes that take place at crowded parties, which include punch bowls, energetic, and at times acrobatic, dance moves, and contemporary jazz music by, amongst others, Ray Brown, Fats Domino, Stan Getz, Dizzy Gillespie, and Coleman Hawkins. The same can be said about the film's treatment of the white Jaguar that Mic buys, with cars being one of the most potent symbols for the modernisation of France. When we first see it, it descends from above on an elevator in the garage, its whiteness and elevated position making it stand out as an exceptional and transcendent object. Even in the moments before Mic's death, cars and the excitement they provide are celebrated. As Bob and Mic drive through the countryside, there is a dramatic percussion-based musical soundtrack and quick cutting showing us the cars from various angles. While the car and its speed ultimately kills Mic, the exhilaration of the scene, as an index of the excitement of the modern world, should not be discounted. Indeed, the parties and the car scenes are both brought to the fore in the film's trailer, suggesting their importance in terms of how the film was being marketed to people and the pleasures it was expected to generate.

Importantly, the modern is also celebrated because of how it is shown to liberate people. For instance, *Les Tricheurs* includes several explicitly modern women, who are in control of their relationships, go to parties, and engage in sexual relations before marriage. What's more, these women are attractive, intelligent, and glamorous, dressing in the latest fashions and applying cosmetic products as they sit in Saint-Germain-des-Prés cafés. Clo is also interesting as a rich, sexually free, character who organises parties for her friends, but who also, on becoming pregnant, refuses to have an abortion as her mother urges. The film's bisexual character, Alain, also stresses the notion of freedom, with him living very much from hand to mouth as a Sorbonne dropout. It is established at the beginning of the film that he is a source of fascination for Bob, and as such is presented as a source of fascination for the audience too. Even though the narrative ends in destruction, the emphasis on these elements is possibly what would linger in the minds of the audience.

The film's main female character Mic is particularly interesting in providing a female view of the changing social context. She aspires to greater freedom, evident initially from her adoption of the masculine name Mic rather than Michele, and, more overtly, from her desire to go to parties and buy a car – the ultimate symbol of freedom at this time. To some extent she is treated in a conservative way, with the film emphasising her 'natural' need for the love of a man – the implication being that, if she had formed a romantic couple with Bob, her death could have been averted. Also, her demise can be viewed as comeuppance for her transgressions and adoption of a modern lifestyle. However, more positively, the film places the issue of women's emancipation at the fore. Sellier (2008: 15) writes: '[*Les Tricheurs*] gives the viewer a privileged access to the point of view of the young woman, ... whose malaise evokes the difficulties faced by young women of the new generation in constructing their identity outside of the traditional norms of femininity.' In this respect Mic is similar to characters found in the work of writers who explored female-centred narratives about the modern world, such as Françoise Sagan. Indeed, Sagan's *Bonjour tristesse* also concludes with a woman dying in a car accident, committing suicide by driving over a cliff. The film's similarities with such popular literature are very important. As Sellier argues, it was through this type of literature and the popular cinema of directors such as Vadim that more progressive female discourses could be located, with representations of emancipated femininity having significant appeal at this time. By contrast, the new wave filmmakers were disparaging towards this culture, both because it was aimed at a mass female audience and because it threatened the position of middle-class males as the creators of art. In this respect, Carné's film, as an exploration of the female experience of the period, offers something that the new wave does not, which also gives added insight into why his film was criticised – he was perpetuating the discourses associated with Sagan and mass female culture that the new wave filmmakers were keen to dismiss.

Towards the end of his discussion of *Les Tricheurs*, Turk (1989: 405) states: '*Les Tricheurs*'s box-office success makes clear that the film spoke to desires and needs of the French public, old and young alike. But the movie's notoriety was ephemeral and parochial.' While Turk is dismissive of such 'ephemeral' qualities, the film's popularity is of great interest because of what it tells us about the wider context. Rather than being 'old-fashioned' and 'out of touch', *Les Tricheurs* found widespread appeal because of its ambivalent vision of modern France, emphasising the pleasures, excitement, and liberating potential of the modern world, particularly for women, but also its fears and dangers.

Terrain vague

Whereas *Les Tricheurs* explores the lives of wealthy youths in central Paris, *Terrain vague*, Carné's next film, is set in the *banlieue* (suburbs) of Paris, specifically the Porte de Sainte-Ouen. It focuses on a gang of underprivileged teenagers led by a girl called Dan (Danièle Gaubert), and including, amongst others, three boys: Babar (Jean-Louis Bras), Lucky (Maurice Cafarelli) and Le Râleur (Dominique Dieudonné). They meet in their den, constructed in a ruined building on their housing estate, and engage in mischievous, but essentially juvenile activities – their headquarters contains various 'trophies', objects they have stolen. This equilibrium is disrupted when Marcel (Constantin Andrieu) arrives, a slightly older young man who has just escaped from a juvenile detention centre. He encourages them to engage in more serious crimes and in doing so takes the leadership of the gang. Following this, they prepare to rob a petrol station, but the plan is a failure; Babar gets blamed and is pursued by the remaining members. Meanwhile Lucky and Dan, who have left the gang, start a relationship, unbeknown to Babar who is in love with Dan. The film concludes with him finding out, which leads him to commit suicide by jumping from one of the ruined buildings.

Terrain vague, like *Les Tricheurs*, deals with many of the central issues of new wave cinema, specifically youth, modernity, and Americanisation. However, it is significant that Carné focuses on working-class characters, rather than the bourgeois males found in most new wave films. As Sellier points out, the movement, which was largely made up of young middle-class men, was not interested in social issues and when representing the working class would often do so in a highly disparaging way. This is particularly evident in *Les Bonnes Femmes* (1960) by Claude Chabrol, which provides a contemptuous portrayal of a group of shop girls. By presenting them as living meaningless and shallow lives, made up of long uninteresting days in the shop where they work and various flings with exploitative men, the film combines the sexism and class snobbishness that is evident in many other films of the movement. By contrast, *Terrain vague* is a social problem film, exploring the issues relating to youth and the *banlieue*. This is significant not only in terms of positioning Carné outside the new wave; it is also an important example of Carné channelling his left-wing ideas into a more overtly political, though ultimately ideologically conflicted, film.

Terrain vague is attentive to the details of the modern world. A number of scenes take place in a pinball machine café, which is presented as a haven from the harsh reality of the housing estate, and cars are again part of the iconography, particularly when one is taken for the petrol station robbery. The robbery scene emphasises the inequalities of modern France, in which some people are benefiting from the nation's economic boom while others are being left behind. Daunting images of Americanisation are provided by the petrol station's large Esso sign, which looms behind Lucky as he works at the pumps. By associating Esso with a story of social breakdown and juvenile delinquency, the film appears to be implicating the Americanisation it stands for – it certainly doesn't provide the solution to the film's social problems. This is in contrast to the ending of *Les Parapluies de Cherbourg* (Jacques Demy, 1964), which also uses an Esso petrol station, though in a more positive way. In the final scenes, we learn that the main character, Guy (Nino Castelnuovo), has invested his money in the station, and is living a life of domestic bliss: his family is inside, preparing for Christmas, while the snow falls outside, lending the Esso station a magical quality. This is symptomatic of a welcoming attitude towards the Americanisation of France found in many new wave movies. By contrast, Carné's film shows less optimism towards the modern world. To consider this further it is useful to turn to the film's representation of Paris.

As we have seen, Carné's films frequently enact a love affair with Paris, while also dramatising the lonelier, darker side of life in the city – a paradox we also find in *Terrain vague*. Discussion of Parisian *banlieue* cinema has increased in recent years, with key work by Ginette Vincendeau (2005) and Carrie Tarr (2005). While most analysis has focused on recent films, such as *La Haine* (Mathieu Kassovitz, 1995), Vincendeau points out that there are also early examples of *banlieue* cinema, such as Carné's *Nogent, Eldorado du dimanche*, which, we will recall, represents the suburbs as a paradise, and *Le Jour se lève*, which conveys a strong populist, anti-modern message. Vincendeau has also found positive portrayals of the *banlieue* in films such as Agnès Varda's *Le Bonheur* (1965).[1] On the other hand she (2005: 18) discusses the various negative portrayals of the *banlieue* in the 1960s, particularly *Alphaville* (1965) in which Godard's protagonist, Lemmie Caution

1 Talk at the British Film Institute, 'A historical overview of women's filmmaking in France', 11 May 2010.

(Eddie Constantine), refers to the HLM, which stands for *habitation à loyer modéré* (low-rent housing), as *hôpital de longue maladie* (hospital for long illness), thus capturing the grimness of the buildings, as does his view of prostitution as a condition of modern *banlieue* living in *Deux ou trois choses que je sais d'elle* (1967).

Carné's film has unfairly been left out of such discussions of *banlieue* cinema, yet it deserves to be included in such debates as an important text. In *Terrain vague*, as in other films, the *banlieue* is an index of France's modernisation, most vividly with the modern buildings that arose in the postwar period:

> The economic boom and rapid expansion of Paris during the 'trente glorieuses' (1945–1975), especially under President Charles De Gaulle (1958–1969), demanded a massive building programme to house both immigrants and French workers, who flocked to the city from the land. (Vincendeau, 2005: 17)

To some extent the representation of the *banlieue* in *Terrain vague* possesses a positive dimension because it is amongst the rubble of the housing estate that the young characters have their den, which is presented as a utopian space. However, in general the *banlieue* is shown in a negative light. Carné draws expertly upon his realist style to capture the harshness of the environment, depicting the area as a vast wasteland (the meaning of the title 'terrain vague'), with rubble and wrecked buildings surrounding the newly constructed blocks of flats – such scenes also make the film reminiscent of Italian neorealist films, such as *Bicycle Thieves* (Vittorio De Sica, 1948). This is enhanced by the film's noir quality: at the beginning, as the gang approach their den, they move through ruined buildings and in and out of large, looming shadows. In addition, the interiors contribute to this representation. For instance, as the opening titles are shown, we watch as a woman climbs the stairs to her apartment. This is filmed in one long take, the camera rising up the stairwell, showing her tiredness as she ascends the seemingly never-ending staircase. While the *banlieue* is frequently used in contemporary films to convey the subordination and economic hardships of France's immigrant population, in *Terrain vague* – made much earlier than most '*banlieue* films' – Carné is interested in using this environment to capture the plight of the nation's marginalised youths. Ultimately, Carné's film brings to the fore the housing problems that became a major issue, thereby meshing with a growing trend in such cinema, and marking a distance from his own view of the *banlieue* several decades earlier.

In Carné's film the *banlieue* is also a manifestation of the 'waste land' that is the youths' lives. There are a few scenes where the liberation of these characters is stressed, particularly during the scene showing the group at the fair. As Turk (1989: 407) points out, the shots of them on rides capture a sense of exhilaration not normally found in Carné's films. However, this representation shifts, with the meaning of the gang changing as the leadership moves from Dan to Marcel, and then to Le Râleur: with Dan in control, the gang is rebellious but essentially childish; with Marcel it becomes criminal (the planned robbery of the petrol station); with Le Râleur it becomes an almost demonic force – they pursue Babar and Lucky to get revenge for the botched petrol station robbery. Towards the end of the film, the gang attacks Babar, throwing stones at him and even killing his dog, which they leave outside his apartment door.

Yet despite its dramatisation of youth delinquency, *Terrain vague* places most blame for this state of affairs on the older generation. There is only one positive adult character, Big Chief (Lesaffre), a kindly shopkeeper who helps various youths. We are introduced to him as he sells a jacket to a young man, who has scars on his hands because of his job working with chemicals, which prompts Big Chief to sell the coat for a reduced price. Mainly, we are presented with a succession of adults who are inept or completely unconcerned about the welfare of the younger characters: at the film's beginning we see a cold, unsympathetic social worker; Babar's father sits at the dinner table, reading a paper, paying absolutely no attention to his son, or his wife for that matter; Dan's stepfather has sexually abused her. There is even a caption at the film's conclusion stating: '… pour que les adultes prennent leurs responsabilités envers la jeunesse' ('… may adults accept their responsibilities towards the young'). In certain respects, then, the film can be seen to contain progressive discourses through its critique of aspects of the modernisation of France – the way the older generation in particular does little to help certain sections of society.

On the other hand, if we focus on gender, the film is more ambiguous. Here it is particularly useful to consider the character of Dan. As with Mic in *Les Tricheurs*, the film dramatises a young woman's experience of the modern world. She is presented as having a degree of freedom: she is a tomboy (the film is based on *Tomboy* by Hal Ellson (1950)), who wears trousers, plays pinball with her male friends, and like Mic in *Les Tricheurs* has adopted a male version of her name. In addition, she is initially the leader of the gang, which is mostly comprised of young males (there are a couple of women). However, the representation of Dan comes round to a conservative vision of femininity. Not only does she lose the leadership of the gang to Marcel, an alpha male, she is also shown to mature into a conventional form of adult womanhood. Towards the end of the film as Dan and Lucky begin their relationship, she tries on a flowery dress, eschewing her tomboy identity. She enters the room where Lucky is sitting and the camera lingers on her feminine beauty, stressing that she has now found her 'rightful' place. To emphasise further the shift towards conservative gender roles, the film concludes with the heterosexual couple – Dan and Lucky – walking away into the distance together, with Big Chief smiling paternally after them.

Although *Terrain vague* was not as popular as *Les Tricheurs*, it performed relatively well at the box-office, with 1.9 million spectators. In addition, François Truffaut, hitherto one of Carné's most virulent critics, enjoyed the film, writing a postcard to him to tell him how much he admired his depiction of the youth gang. However, this private correspondence did little to change Carné's critical standing, which had been irreparably damaged by the *Cahiers* writers. *Terrain vague* has consequently become yet another forgotten postwar Carné film, but, as I have shown, it deserves greater attention: as a film that makes astute observations about the nature of youth in postwar France it needs to be included in a wider new wave canon, and as a document on dysfunctional new housing it is a valuable early example of the nation's *banlieue* cinema.

The classicist continues as the new wave breaks

The duration of the French new wave has been conceptualised in different ways. At its shortest, it has been seen as lasting only from its emergence in 1959 to around 1961. Another periodisation sees it as lasting until 1968, when the political upheavals of May brought about huge changes in French society and its cinema. Either way, we can certainly see the new wave as exerting significant and lasting influence on the French cinema of the 1960s, and during this time its most famous directors continued to make films that are classed as belonging to the movement, such as Godard's *Alphaville* (1965) and *Pierrot le fou* (1965). Turk closes his chapter on Carné's relationship with the new wave after his discussion of *Terrain vague*. I will however continue with the new wave focus as I discuss the three subsequent films he made during the 1960s: *Du mouron pour les petits oiseaux*, *Trois chambres à Manhattan* (1965) and *Les Jeunes Loups* (1968). While these films have interesting connections with the new cinematic context, they are all also distinctive for their continuation of classical form and style. Even though the classical period, at least according to historians such as Colin Crisp (1993), lasted between 1930 and 1960, it is clear that the classical aesthetic continued on a parallel track during and after the new wave, and has informed mainstream cinema up to the present day (albeit with modifications). Carné is one of the directors at the heart of this tradition.

Du mouron pour les petits oiseaux

Following *Terrain vague* Carné again had problems getting a project off the ground, with him failing in his attempts to film Bernard Eschassériaux's *Les Dimanches de Ville-d'Avray*, which would have been another film about the Parisian *banlieues* (Ville-d'Avray is one of Paris's suburbs), a version of Zola's *Germinal*, and an adaptation of *La Dame aux camélias*. He was finally successful in bringing about a comedy adaptation, with Jacques Sigurd, of *Du mouron pour les petits oiseaux*, based upon the novel by *série noire* author Albert Simonin (1960). The cast includes Roland Lesaffre, Suzy Delair, Paul Meurisse, Suzanne Gabriello, and Dany Saval, and was supposed to star Arletty, in the role of a concierge, before she was involved in an accident with eye drops, which left her almost blind. The story centres upon an apartment building in Paris, following the lives of its various inhabitants, including: a gangster, Armand (Meurisse), who keeps birds and is hiding money from his accomplice, who is in jail; Le Siphonné (Lesaffre), a dreamy, religious animal lover, who objects to Armand keeping birds in cages; the concierge (Gabriello); and a number of other characters, such as Lucy (Saval) and Renato (Franco Citti), who are involved in complicated love affairs.

While the film is a comedy, making it distinct from most of Carné's films (aside from *Drôle de drame* and *Le Pays d'où je viens*), it continues to explore the director's familiar themes, particularly entrapment and escape. Through Le Siphonné (which means 'the crazy one' in slang) it includes the dreamy romantic character common to Carné's cinema (other examples include Billy in *Drôle de Drame* and Baptiste in *Les Enfants du paradis*). At the end of the film Le Siphonné lets the birds free, shouting 'liberté!', which aligns him with similarly free-spirited characters. Indeed, the entrapment of the birds in the cage is a broader symbol for confinement that we find elsewhere in Carné's films – in *Les Enfants du paradis*, for example, Garance is compared to a caged bird. However, Le Siphonné is also mocked for his behaviour and outlook. When he goes to see the supposedly wheelchair-bound old woman upstairs, Mademoiselle Pain (Jeanne Fusier-Gir), he sees that she is out of her wheelchair. We have already witnessed that she can walk (a fact she hides from everyone), but it takes him a while to even realise that she is standing up, unaided. She quickly makes an excuse, claiming that it is a 'miracle', which he instantly believes. The film also draws upon the theme of 'escape', which we have witnessed in earlier films such as *Le Quai des brumes, Hôtel du Nord,* and *Le Jour se lève*. This theme is most evident in the narrative involving Armand. Because he is being pursued by his accomplice, who has left prison and is searching for him, he makes the decision to escape to the Côte d'Azur. One review of the film (R., 1963: 12) states: 'L'air de Paris est devenu malsain pour lui: il achète la voiture que convoite Lucie et part avec elle et son magot pour la Côte d'Azur.'[2] This clearly recalls Edmond in *Hôtel du Nord,* who seeks both a change of atmosphere and an escape from a former criminal accomplice (the sentence also evokes the Carné film title *L'Air de Paris*). Thus Carné explores his familiar theme of entrapment and escape, but does so in a comic register.

Du mouron pour les petits oiseaux also contains elements of modernity, like those found in the films discussed so far in this chapter. In addition to jazz music on the soundtrack, the young pop star Dany Logan appears in the small role of a butcher's assistant. We are also presented with a cosmopolitan Paris, with Renato as a prominent Italian character. While this is related to the fact that the film is an Italian co-production, it also reflects changes in the demographics in France at this time. However, what is striking about the film is its

2 'The air of Paris became unhealthy for him: he buys a car that Lucy covets and leaves with her and his cash for the Côte d'Azur.'

strong connections with Carné's old-fashioned aesthetic and subject matter. Thus we find several features of Carné's classicism, particularly its finely crafted look: it was shot in a studio, with the inside of the apartment block recreated on a sound stage, an aspect of the film that was complimented in *Film Français* (R., 1963: 12), which described the decor as 'remarquablement reconstituée en studio' ('remarkably rebuilt in the studio'). The story's premise also harks back to films from the heyday of Carné's 'golden age'. By being set in a building with a concierge and centred on a small community of inhabitants, it has clear similarities with *Hôtel du Nord* and *Le Jour se lève*. Carné (1996: 306) himself points out the similarity to the former film in his autobiography: 'L'idée de montrer la vie des locataires d'un immeuble, leurs rapports intimes, souvent cachés, commençait à faire son chemin. Je ne me faisais aucune illusion: nous étions loin des *Enfants du paradis* mais, après tout, pas tellement de *Hôtel de Nord*.'[3] (If Arletty had played the role of the concierge, this would have enhanced this dimension further.) In addition, the film announces its classical identity with its stars, in particular Suzy Delair, famous for her role in *Quai des orfèvres* (Henri-Georges Clouzot, 1947), and Paul Meurisse, who starred in *Les Diaboliques* (Henri-Georges Clouzot, 1955).

The aspect of *Du mouron pour les petits oiseaux* that connects it most clearly to the mainstream genre cinema of the time is the fact that it is a comedy, evocative both of Carné's earlier films such as *Hôtel du Nord* and of René Clair's cinema of the 1930s. Much of the humour relies on people in the local community conforming to particular types, such as the hairdresser, the butcher, the criminal, the dreamer, the old woman, the policeman, the postman, and the glamorous Parisienne. They are all shown to be flawed in a variety of ways, particularly through their numerous fallouts over romantic issues, but at the same time they are treated affectionately, indeed in part because they are flawed. The Parisienne for example is stylish, spoilt and squeals at various points, revealing her vulnerability, but also her extravagant, performing nature. Part of the humour also comes from how characters diverge from these types, behaving in ways we wouldn't expect. For instance, the gangster keeps birds, revealing a sensitive side to his character and the old woman acts in an infantile way, stealing

---

3 'The idea of showing the life of the tenants of a building, their intimate relations, often hidden, began to move forward. I didn't have any illusions: we were far from *Les Enfants du paradis* but, after all, not so far from *Hôtel du Nord*.'

biscuits and generally possessing more energy than she lets on – as in the wheelchair episode discussed earlier. One stereotyped character who is particularly noteworthy in the context of Carné's cinema is Monsieur de Fleurville (Jean Parédès), a gay resident in the apartment block. As I argued in my discussion of *L'Air de Paris*, de Fleurville betrays a negative (and possibly homophobic) attitude on Carné's part towards the representation of a camp gay man: he tries to lure young postmen to his apartment, until one of them gives him a black eye in what is meant to be a humorous moment.

With just under one million spectators, *Du mouron pour les petits oiseaux* did less well at the box-office than *Les Tricheurs* and *Terrain vague*. Perhaps its relatively limited success betrays Carné's uneasiness with comedy. Indeed, in one review, Marcel Martin (1963) wrote of the film: 'Comique laborieux, situations rebattues, dialogues insupportablement plats' ('Laborious comedy, trite situations, unbearably flat dialogue'). It is also a clear departure from Carné's engagement with the youth culture that represented his main point of contact with the new wave. However, his next film, *Trois chambres à Manhattan*, would return to more overt connections with new wave cinema.

Trois chambres à Manhattan

Trois chambres à Manhattan follows François (Maurice Ronet), a French actor who moves from Paris to New York when his wife Yolande (Geneviève Page) leaves him. Initially he lives a lonely and secluded life, until he meets Kay (Annie Girardot), with whom he begins a romantic affair. The project, which was the only film Carné shot in the USA (he went to Manhattan for the location shots), came about when the producer, Charles Lumbroso, suggested he adapt Simenon's eponymous novel (1946). Originally Jean-Pierre Melville had planned on making the film, which would have been an interesting accompaniment to his earlier *Deux hommes dans Manhattan* (1959), which Ginette Vincendeau (2003: 121–5) discusses as a film that balances formal and stylistic features of new wave cinema with techniques more commonly associated with classicism. Though less overt in its use of new wave features, *Trois chambres à Manhattan* can be characterised in a similar way.

Significantly, the film saw the return of former members of the Carné *équipe*: Eugen Shüfftan returned as Carné's cinematographer for the first time since *Le Quai des brumes* and Léon Barsacq came back as set designer for the first time since *Les Enfants du paradis* (he had worked on the film's sets alongside Trauner). Both figures had careers associated with the classical period and *Trois chambres à Manhattan* would be, in each case, one of their final films. Carné's classical style maintains his characteristic control over his framing and staging of his subjects.

At the same time, *Trois chambres à Manhattan* includes elements found in new wave cinema. In this dual – classical new wave – approach, Carné shares similarities with Louis Malle, a filmmaker commonly discussed as a transitional figure between classical and new wave film. *Trois chambres à Manhattan* in this respect is particularly close to Malle's *Ascenseur pour l'échafaud* (1958) and *Le Feu follet* (1963). In both these and in the Carné film, the lead male is played by Maurice Ronet, who, as Sellier (2008: 132) writes, was one of the actors favoured by the directors of the new wave. In his films for Malle he plays vulnerable characters; in *Ascenseur pour l'échafaud* because he is stuck overnight in an elevator and in *Le Feu follet* because he is an alcoholic. In *Trois chambres à Manhattan* he embodies a similar type, and there are particularly strong connections between *Le Feu follet* and *Trois chambres à Manhattan* on the level of narration. In both films Ronet plays a heavy drinker and in both he is estranged from his wife – in *Le Feu follet* he is in Paris while his wife is in Manhattan; in *Trois chambres à Manhattan* it is the other way round. The film's other lead, Annie Girardot, is discussed by Sellier (2008: 198) as a popular cinema equivalent of Jeanne Moreau, the star who appeared alongside Ronet in *Ascenseur pour l'échafaud* as well as starring in other Malle films, such as *Les Amants* (1958) and, famously, in Truffaut's *Jules et Jim* (1962) (intriguingly, Melville also wanted to cast Moreau in his version of *Trois chambres à Manhattan*). It is significant, though not surprising, that Carné chose Girardot, thus signalling his allegiance to popular cinema. Parallels to the new wave, and Malle's films in particular, can be found in the scenes depicting Ronet and Girardot wandering around the Manhattan streets to the accompaniment of jazz music (Mal Waldron and Martial Solal, who also provided music for *À bout de souffle*), reminiscent of similar scenes in *Ascenseur pour l'échafaud*, as Moreau walks around Paris to the sound of Miles Davis, looking for Ronet.

In *Trois chambres à Manhattan* we are presented with a dark and lonely vision of New York, in which the city is used to explore personal, rather than social, concerns (as in Melville's *Deux hommes dans Manhattan* (Vincendeau, 2003: 119)). In its noir aspect, the film also bears striking similarities with Carné's earlier cinema. For instance, the theme of alienation is evident when we witness François alone in his hotel room in New York, particularly as this comes after scenes depicting him in Paris in which he drives an expensive-looking car and returns to an opulent home. His isolation is stressed further when he wanders the streets alone, before going to a diner where he suffers xenophobic insults from the owner.[4] The scenes of him walking the streets are also evocative of *Le Quai des brumes* when Jean arrives in Le Havre: while that setting is full of mist, New York, in *Trois chambres à Manhattan*, has an equivalent in the steam that rises from the vents in the streets. The similarities between the two films are particularly evident when François meets Kay; like Jean and Nelly, they are an alienated couple, who wander aimlessly together, and embark upon an intense and romantic relationship.

The film's combination of various influences and intertexts forms the basis for its representations of gender, an aspect of the film that helps us understand further Carné's relationship with the French new wave. To some extent, the film contains progressive attitudes through its interest in exploring male vulnerability and weakness, a common feature of Carné's cinema, challenging the idea of macho, patriarchal strength. Thus François is rejected by his wife (for a younger man) and is presented as lonely and alienated in New York It is also a product of the star image of Ronet, who, as I discuss above, played a number of similar roles. On the one hand, there is criticism of François's wife for her betrayal – at the beginning of the film we see her smile at her lover when François isn't looking, which casts her in a duplicitous light. On the other, Kay is presented much more positively, as a compassionate, intelligent, and sexually liberated woman. While François is initially put off Kay when he learns she has a sexual history, by the film's resolution he has come to accept it, thus challenging society's idealisation of 'pure' femininity. It is interesting that this acceptance originates in the Simenon novel, one of his most progressive works in terms of gender and in stark contrast with his general attitude to women which was notoriously not so enlightened: 'For his part, Simenon clung to the old fashioned notion of male virility and female virginity' (Becker

---

4 Robert De Niro appears in the diner scene as an extra.

2006: 31). Indeed, his next novel, *Lettre à mon juge* (1947), concluded with the male protagonist, jealous of his lover's previous affairs, killing her. While 'pure' women populate Carné's early work, in the films without Prévert such idealisation is less common. In *Thérèse Raquin* and *Les Tricheurs*, in particular, women are more grounded, as is the case in *Trois chambres à Manhattan*, which, in addition, shows concern for representing a female point of view. In part this is related to Carné's classical approach which privileges a more omnipotent, less subjective, style than in the new wave, which Sellier characterises as a cinema in the first-person masculine singular. It is also related to stardom – as critics have observed, Girardot was able to bring a strong personality and female subjectivity to many of her roles through her acting skills and popular image. As we have seen, while many of Carné's films contain conservative notions of gender, he is frequently attentive to female subjectivity and emancipation. In these respects, the film differs in a positive way from the films of the French new wave, which tend to be male-oriented and misogynistic. However, the film's lack of success – with only 400,000 spectators, it was Carné's least popular film to date – is linked, as Vincendeau (2008: 217) argues, to its progressive view of women.

Les Jeunes Loups

Carné's final film of the decade was *Les Jeunes Loups*, a colour production released in 1968 (from this point on all his films would be made in colour). The film's story, a loose adaptation of Antoine François Prévost's *Manon Lescaut* (1731), with the genders of the main characters switched, follows Alain (Christian Hay), an attractive young Parisian, who is maintained by wealthy older women, such as Princess Linzani (Elizabeth Teissier du Gros). He begins a relationship with Sylvie (Haydée Politoff), but problems develop because of his infidelities. The couple also make friends with Chris (Yves Beneyton), a young hippy, who turns out to be from a very affluent background. The film ends with Alain claiming he is fully committed to Sylvie, but in the final moments, unbeknown to her, we see hints that this is not the case, as he flirts with an older wealthy-looking woman in a shop.

As in his previous films, Carné in *Les Jeunes Loups* sustains his classical style through his characteristically restrained *mise en scène*. At the same time, the film refers to the new wave in several ways. Aside from the casting of Politoff, who had just had a leading role in Rohmer's *La Collectioneuse* (1967) (Beneyton also had a role in Godard's *Deux ou trois choses que je sais d'elle*), the film places great importance on the theme of youth. Like *Les Tricheurs* it focuses on a group of privileged young Parisians who live a hedonistic lifestyle. The film's marketing emphasised such similarities with titles on the film's trailer stating: 'après vous avoir révélé *Les Tricheurs*, Marcel Carné vous présente les nouveaux *Tricheurs* ...'[5] A key part of my consideration of Carné in relation to the new wave has focused on gender and sexuality, and *Les Jeunes Loups* is particularly interesting in this respect. There is evidence of progressive discourses, with the switching of genders from *Manon Lescaut* in the sense that it is older women who have economic power and the young man who is defined by his attractive appearance, thus transforming cinema's conventional approach to gender. In addition, the film was supposed to have a pronounced bisexual narrative centring on Alain, including a scene implying he has slept with a rich male character called Ugo Castellini (Maurice Garrel). This would have been part of the broader challenge to heterosexual normativity we have seen in previous Carné films. However, Carné was forced to make cuts, so this aspect of the film is less in evidence than was originally planned. Mainly, though, *Les Jeunes Loups* is conservative in its representations of gender. For instance, although Sylvie aspires to be independent, she ultimately hangs on to traditional ideas. Her desire for a committed relationship with Christian means that she puts up with his bad behaviour and throughout the film is constantly duped – he cheats on her, but she keeps returning to him.

Another significant dimension of *Les Jeunes Loups*, which has received little attention, is its connections with the events of May 1968, a period of significant political unrest that involved a wave of protests against de Gaulle's government and the nation's largest general strike. Because *Les Jeunes Loups* was released in April 1968, it cannot make reference to the events. However, the film would have been in cinemas as the tensions were escalating and it documents significant features of the broader social context, drawing on some familiar iconography of the period. For instance, the scene that introduces us to Chris centres upon a number of hippies sitting on steps, singing and playing guitars. Police vans arrive and, although the youths are

5 'after having revealed to you *Les Tricheurs*, Marcel Carné introduces to you the new *Les Tricheurs* ...'

not engaging in any disruptive behaviour, they are rounded up and taken to the police station. While the police do not behave in an overtly violent way, the film is clearly antagonistic towards their intervention, which is symptomatic of an increasingly negative attitude towards the police at the time. By May the situation would have intensified, as Ross (2002: 27) explains: 'Sometime around the middle of May 1968 ... the policeman's club or *matraque* had become for the insurgents in the streets a pure synecdoche for the State.'

The scene above is also in keeping with Carné's long-standing preoccupations, with the police representing the oppressiveness of society, a familiar Carné theme that is explored, for example, in *Le Jour se lève*, in which Gabin is surrounded in his room by armed police, representatives of a cold state machine. By contrast, and also common in Carné's work, *Les Jeunes Loups* contains moments of transcendence and escape. A particularly vivid example of this occurs when Alain and Sylvie go to a swimming pool, where they swim together naked. At one point they are filmed from below, with blurred light above them, the shot presenting them as paradisiacal abstract male and female silhouettes.

While *Les Jeunes Loups* has an oblique relationship with the events of May 1968, Carné was more directly involved in the period's disturbances through his role in the 'Langlois Affair'. In February 1968, Henri Langlois, one of the founders and head of the Cinémathèque Française, was sacked by the French Culture Minister André Malraux. Langlois's passion for cinema, and especially for *showing* films, rather than keeping them locked away, made him a very popular member of the cinematic establishment. Carné was involved in attending protests and sit-ins, with countless other filmmakers and intellectuals, to bring about a reversal of Malraux's decision, and was a member of the Comité de Défense de la Cinémathèque Française (Committee for the Defence of the Cinémathèque Française), along with Robert Bresson, Rivette, Godard, Truffaut, and presided over by Renoir. Paradoxically, then, at the end of the decade Carné stood united in a common purpose with members of the French new wave (not to mention Renoir, with whom he had had disagreements in the past). Henri Langlois, who was reinstated in April, was very grateful to Carné for his involvement and gave him honorary presidency of the Cinémathèque Française. Despite this, when *Les Jeunes Loups* was released in April 1968, it was, again, poorly received by *Cahiers du*

Cinéma, with the majority of the journal's writers giving the film bad scores in their weekly table of critics' results. Although these were a new generation of critics and not the members of the new wave, such a poor reception is indicative of Carné's continuing problems with certain sections of the French cinephile critical establishment. Indeed, the legacy of this poor standing has been enduring, despite his productive role in the Langlois Affair: in Bernardo Bertolucci's *The Dreamers* (2003) a scene takes place at one of the demonstrations, in which Theo (Louis Garrel) tells his friends which film personalities are there. When he mentions Carné, one of them replies: 'Carné? Qu'est-ce qu'il fait là?' ('Carné? What's he doing here?').[6]

Carné was unhappy with how *Les Jeune loups* had been censored, because of its nudity and Alain's bisexuality. The film had been changed beyond what he felt was acceptable and as a consequence he disowned it (the only film he was to disown) – he didn't even attend the premiere. However, despite this unhappy production context, and the film's lack of critical or popular success (it only attracted around 700,000 spectators), *Les Jeunes Loups* remains an important part of Carné's output, owing to its connections with the new wave and its relationship with the broader political context and build up to May 1968.

This chapter has dealt with an important but generally overlooked period in Carné's career. His production of films focusing on youth culture represents his last major innovation, or even reinvention, in his career. These films are important because of how they help us understand his relationship with the new wave, a movement that essentially signalled a significant challenge to the classical French cinema, at the centre of which Carné had stood for three decades. His films from this period share interests with the new wave in their exploration of youth culture, even though Carné positioned himself at a distance, as a social observer. While Carné's classicism was viewed negatively by *Cahiers* critics, it is through this approach, coupled with his use of realism, that he was able to capture fundamental socio-political moments in a way that reached large audiences. Moreover, his treatment of gender deals with the *female* experience of changes brought about by modernity, especially in *Les Tricheurs*. In this

---

6 Coincidentally, Garrel's grandfather, Maurice Garrel, appears in *Les Jeunes Loups* in the minor role of Ugo Castellini.

respect, his films give key insights into the period lacking from many of the new wave films, and as such deserve their place in the postwar cinematic canon.

Carné and the new wave would be – almost – reconciled with each other. On 14 April 1984 Carné and Truffaut were the two guests of honour in Romilly, where they were to witness the opening of two cinema screens: a 278-seat 'Salle Marcel Carné' and a 166-seat 'Salle François Truffaut'. They didn't have much of an opportunity to talk to each other, but, despite his earlier criticism of Carné, Truffaut stated to the people gathered there: 'I have made twenty-three pictures. Well, I would swap them all for the chance to have made *Les Enfants du paradis*' (Truffaut cited in Turk, 1989: 390). However, by this time, the damage had been done – as Carné entered the 1970s his struggles to make films intensified.

References

Alexandre, J.-L. (2005), *Les Cousins des tricheurs: de la 'qualité française' à la Nouvelle Vague*, Paris, Harmattan.

Anon. (1956), 'L'élève Gilbert Bécaud fait ses classes de cinéma avec le professeur Carné', *Cinémonde*, 119, 19 January, p. 11.

Austin, G. (2003), *Stars in Modern French Film*, London, Arnold.

Becker, L. F. (2006), *Georges Simenon: 'Maigrets' and the 'Romans Durs'*, London, Haus.

Benayoun, R. (2009), 'The emperor has no clothes', in P. Graham, ed., with G. Vincendeau, *The French New Wave: Critical Landmarks*, London, British Film Institute / Palgrave Macmillan, pp. 163–86.

Carné, M. (1996), *Ma vie à belles dents*, Paris, L'Archipel.

Crisp, C. (1993), *The Classic French Cinema, 1930–1960*, Bloomington, Indiana University Press.

Martin, M. (1963), *Cinema 63*, 75, April.

Neupert, R. (2002), *A History of the French New Wave Cinema*, Madison, Wis.; London, University of Wisconsin Press.

O'Shaughnessy, M. (2000), *Jean Renoir*, Manchester, Manchester University Press.

R. (1963), '*Du mouron pour les petits oiseaux*', *Film Français*, 978, 22 February, p. 12.

Ross, K. (1995), *Fast Cars, Clean Bodies: Decolonization and the Reordering of French Culture*, Cambridge, Mass.; London, MIT Press.

Ross, K. (2002), *May '68 and Its Afterlives*, Chicago; London, University of Chicago Press.

Sadoul, G. (2009), '*Le Quai des brumes 1960: À Bout de souffle* by Jean-Luc Godard', in P. Graham, ed., with G. Vincendeau, *The French New Wave:*

Critical Landmarks, London, British Film Institute / Palgrave Macmillan, pp. 231–7.

Sellier, G. (2008), *Masculine Singular: French New Wave Cinema*, Durham, NC; London, Duke University Press.

Tarr, C. (2005), *Reframing Difference: Beur and Banlieue Filmmaking in France*, Manchester, Manchester University Press.

Thompson, D. (2009), 'The devil of detail', *Sight and Sound*, 19:12, pp. 22–4, 26.

Truffaut, F. (1956), '*Le Pays d'où je viens* de Marcel Carné: une consternante pochade', *Arts; Lettres; Spectacles*, 31 October and 6 November.

Truffaut, F. (2009), 'A certain tendency in French cinema', in P. Graham, ed., with G. Vincendeau, *The French New Wave: Critical Landmarks*, London, British Film Institute / Palgrave Macmillan, pp. 39–63.

Turk, E. B. (1989), *Child of Paradise: Marcel Carné and the Golden Age of French Cinema*, Cambridge, Mass.; London, Harvard University Press.

Vincendeau, G. (1997), 'Paradise regained', *Sight and Sound*, 7:7, pp. 12–16.

Vincendeau, G. (2003), *Jean-Pierre Melville: 'An American in Paris'*, London, British Film Institute.

Vincendeau, G. (2005), *La Haine*, London; New York, I. B. Tauris.

Vincendeau, G. (2008), *Les stars et le star-système en France*, Paris, L'Harmattan.

Williams, A. (1992), *Republic of Images: A History of French Filmmaking*, Cambridge, Mass.; London, Harvard University Press.

6

The end of a long career

Although Marcel Carné's final films did not receive the critical acclaim or box-office success of his earlier cinema, they remain interesting as late manifestations of the core concerns that define his work across the decades. One of the central aspects of his cinema, which has been considered throughout this book, is the tension between his interest in the grounded, physical, social world and the transcendent world of poetry and metaphysics. These opposites have implications for a number of aspects of his cinema: they have formal and stylistic implications, with the social tendency being articulated through his use of realist cinematic devices, and the fantastic dimension being expressed through his capacity to create film 'poetry'. They inform his explorations of political concerns, with some films engaging with social issues and others centring more upon aesthetics and fantasy; they also influence his representations of gender, with there being a tension, throughout his cinema, between individuals, men or women, who are grounded and physical and those who are ethereal and otherworldly – such a division, as we have seen, is put to a range of ideological uses. What is striking about Carné's last films, *Les Assassins de l'ordre* (1971), *La Merveilleuse Visite*, and *La Bible*, is that they each belong at one extreme or the other.

Carné's last films

Les Assassins de l'ordre

Les Assassins de l'ordre, released in 1971, was a controversial examination of police corruption, based upon Jean Laborde's novel (1956), telling the story of real-life events that occurred near Bordeaux in 1951. One of its main features is that it stars the Belgian-born Jacques Brel, who had started his career as a singer in the 1950s, working with Georges Brassens, before appearing in a number of films as an actor, as well as turning his hand to directing, with *Franz* (1971) and *Le Far West* (1973). This, then, is another example of Carné working with a top star. According to Carné's autobiography (1996: 332), Brel was very keen on working with him: 'Nous avions bavardé assez longue-ment et il m'avait dit que son rêve d'adolescent avait été de tourner un jour avec moi.'[1] With Brel's music centring upon doomed romance as well as the exploration of social issues, it is easy to see why the two would be keen on working together. In *Les Assassins de l'ordre* Brel plays Bernard Level, an examining magistrate in a small provincial town trying to prosecute a police commissioner, Inspector Bertrand (Michel Lonsdale), and two detectives, Rabut (François Cadet) and Benetti (Serge Sauvion), who killed a man, Saugeat (Roland Lesaffre), during an interrogation. However, in the final court case the policemen, who are clearly guilty, are acquitted, with the assistance of their lawyer, Graziani (Charles Denner).

Les Assassins de l'ordre, one of Carné's most politically engaged films, fits within the then fashionable genre of the political thriller. It also draws upon a number of his familiar themes, particularly through its exploration of the oppressive forces that exist within society. As with *Le Jour se lève* and *Les Jeunes Loups* it shows the police in a highly negative light. In part this is evident through its narra-tive, which is essentially concerned with police corruption and the misuse of state power. It is also evident through the way the police are represented: they are large, bulky, tough-looking men, with aggressive faces, and are essentially portrayed as thugs. The *mise en scène* plays a key role. Using stark realism, Carné depicts the police station as grim and lifeless. The film was shot in colour, but, while *Le Pays d'où je viens* and *Les Jeunes Loups* use a range of bright colours, for *Les Assassins de l'ordre* Carné uses a duller, bleaker palette. This is particularly the case in the scenes set in the police station, which are confined to a range of greys, dark metallic colours and deep greens.

These characters and environments stand in opposition to Level (Brel), who is shown, by contrast, as intelligent, gentle and sensi-

---

1 'We had chatted at length and he had told me that his dream as a youth had been to shoot with me one day.'

tive. This is conveyed through his relationship with his son, François (Didier Haudepin), with whom he spends time working on fixing up a boat, and with his girlfriend, Laura (Paola Pitagora). At one point, with the pressure of the case rising, he drives to the nearby town where Laura has an antique shop. When he arrives, he falls into her arms, his head resting on her chest, placing him in a passive position and Laura in a maternal and nurturing one – the same pose that is struck by Baptiste and Garance towards the end of *Les Enfants du paradis*. Level's vulnerability is also expressed in the numerous scenes depicting him at court, where he is placed in surroundings that dwarf him. For example, in the final scene we see him leave the courthouse after losing the case: he appears small and vulnerable in relation to the large building, with its towering pillars, placing him in opposition to a construct that signifies the strength of the legal system, a system we have seen to be flawed. This aspect of the film is enhanced by Brel's vulnerable appearance thanks to his thin physique, large eyes, and largish teeth, which make him appear slightly awkward and clumsy. Indeed, Brel's performances as a singer had stressed his ability to enact such states with expertise, something that is particularly evident from his singing of 'Ne me quitte pas', one of his all-time greatest hit songs, in which he pleads with a lover not to leave him.

While these elements are in many respects typical of Carné's cinema, the film also has interesting connections with the broader context and again, as with *Les Jeunes Loups*, it relates to the climate of May 1968. A few years had passed since these events and the production of the film took place in a more liberal environment. As Carné discusses in his autobiography, the Pompidou government in power at the time took measures to adopt a more relaxed attitude to film, meaning that *Les Assassins de l'ordre*, to Carné's and Michel Ardan's (the film's producer) surprise, avoided censorship. In the years after May 1968 there was still a significant amount of political activity. In his autobiography Carné (1996: 333) discusses how during the filming of *Les Assassins de l'ordre* in 1969 shooting was interrupted by a strike. Carné and Ardan had secured the help of a number of students to perform as extras, but one day when Carné arrived on set there was a large sign reading: 'Carné, tes figurants sont en grève' ('Carné, your extras are on strike'). Ardan tried to reason with them, though he was unsuccessful, much to his displeasure, particularly as he felt that the film was contributing to the students' political cause. Carné

(1996: 334) quotes Ardan's response to the situation: 'Comment! se lamentait-il. On fait un film qui risque d'être censuré! Un film pour eux! Et ils nous empêchent de tourner!'[2] The film strongly evokes this moment of recent French past, partly through the negative representation of police brutality and the broader state corruption for which they stand, partly because of the final scenes depicting political activism, with youths demonstrating in support of Level's attempts to bring the police to account.

While the film has, like most of Carné's postwar work, been critically neglected, and although according to Carné it received little attention by the press (Carné, 1996: 340), it actually performed moderately well at the box-office, with 1.1 million spectators. In addition, it was well received in the Soviet Union, winning a Special Prize at the Moscow International Film Festival. Turk (1989: 416) explains that this was part of a broader appreciation of Carné's work in the Soviet Union. A number of years earlier Joseph Stalin even presented him with a gift – a model of a doll that looks like Baptiste from *Les Enfants du paradis* – to show his appreciation of the director and his most celebrated film. *Les Assassins de l'ordre* is a significant work as one of Carné's most politically engaged films, tackling the issue of police corruption head-on. At the same time, the film continues Carné's characteristic fatalistic tendency. It ends with Level being defeated, making it as bleak and pessimistic as many of Carné's earlier films. In these respects, as both the most politically engaged, but also in many ways a typical, Carné social film, it is a fitting final example of this key strand of his cinema. With his next two films Carné would move towards the opposite extreme, exploring the fantastic realms also common in his work.

La Merveilleuse Visite

In his autobiography Carné comments on how difficult it was for him to make his next film, *La Merveilleuse Visite*, which took him three years to complete, even longer, he observes, than the production of *Les Enfants du paradis*. The project was stalled by various financial problems and at one point filming was held up for three months. Based upon an obscure H. G. Wells novel, *The Wonderful Visit* (1895), Carné's film, adapted by Didier Decoin, follows an angel (Gilles

2 'What! he cried. We are making a film that risks being censored! A film for them! And they are preventing us from shooting it!'

Kohler), who is washed up on a beach in Brittany. He is discovered by the village Vicar (Lucien Barjon) and his sexton, Ménard (Roland Lesaffre), who look after him. While the Vicar is sceptical about the angel's claims that he is indeed an angel, Ménard is enchanted by the idea. In the village some people welcome the angel's arrival, but others start to feel threatened by his presence and unusual behaviour. For instance, he demonstrates ignorance about how money works, paints a house in psychedelic colours and at one point releases many of the villagers' animals on to the streets, causing a moment of anarchy. He is finally pursued by a mob who drive him off the edge of a cliff. However, the film closes with him transforming into a white seagull and flying away from the people below.

As this synopsis suggests, *La Merveilleuse Visite* belongs to the cinéma fantastique strand of Carné's work, a form he had earlier worked in with *Les Visiteurs du soir* and *Juliette ou la clef des songes*. However, it should first of all be noted that *La Merveilleuse Visite* is distinct from these works in that it is in many ways also a continuation of the realist approach he had been using since the 1950s. Whereas the earlier films drew on elaborate sets to create magical worlds, in *La Merveilleuse Visite* Carné uses a significant amount of location shooting, of countryside and coastal areas, and is attentive to the details of life in the village. It is not, however, the gritty realism that he uses in *Terrain vague* or *Les Assassins de l'ordre*, as many of its scenes focus on the beauty of the natural world: Carné shows us the sea, beach, cliffs, fields with grass and with wheat, blue skies, and various animals, elements that are in contrast to the drab, grey village. At the same time, as with the earlier films, and departing from this realism, he has recourse to special effects to create the film's fantasy – for example in the scenes in which mirrors suddenly mysteriously break when the angel looks at them. Also at one point when the angel throws grey paint he has found at a building, it transforms into a range of psychedelic colours. Not only does this use of special effects contribute to the film's 'magic', it also emphasises its place within its historical context, when psychedelia was prominent.

The main way in which the film creates fantasy, though, is through the use of the angel character. Indeed, one of the effects of the film's realism is that it makes this one magical element even more fantastic. The film, then, is different from Carné's earlier poetic realism in which the poetry *permeates* the realism; in *La Merveilleuse Visite* the realist elements are distinct and separate from the film's fantasy, which comes in the form of the angel. We have seen that throughout Carné's cinema there are ethereal characters, initially in the form of the women of poetic realism, and then André in *L'Air de Paris*, who has an angelic quality to him. With the angel in *La Merveilleuse Visite*, this element of Carné's cinema is taken to an extreme: as an angel who has fallen from the sky to the earth, he is quite literally an otherworldly character. This is emphasised through his very striking appearance, which makes him stand out from his surroundings: he has bright blonde hair, blue eyes, a defined jaw, and a pale, smooth, toned body. His costumes also add to his distinctive appearance. At the beginning of the film, we see him naked when he is washed up on the beach, and throughout the rest of the film he wears little clothing – at one point wearing nothing but a large poncho; at another just a pair of white trousers with a red heart on them. Above all, though, it is his behaviour that sets him apart. As a stranger to the earth he responds to everything with great innocence, not understanding such concepts as money or the need to wear clothing.

The significance of the angel's masculinity is explored through his relationship with the locals in the community. To some extent his presence is welcomed, particularly by Ménard and Delia (Deborah Berger), who are both enchanted by his purity, as well as by other members of the community, such as the Duchess of Quéfélec (Mary Marquet), who admires his exquisite violin playing. However, there are others who are less keen on him, such as François (Jean-Pierre Castaldi), a lorry driver and Delia's boyfriend, who is in many ways the angel's opposite. He is a little older, has dark hair, a large, strong jaw, and a bulky physique, and embodies a more physical masculinity, evident when at one point he roughly grabs and shakes Delia, believing her to be having an affair with the angel. His personal antagonism towards the angel, who remains passive throughout, becomes shared by other male members of the community – at the end of the film they pursue the angel and ultimately drive him off the edge of a cliff. It is noticeable that the progressive class dimension of Carné's cinema is less pronounced here, with the working-class characters forming a malevolent and oppressive force. At the same time, the opposites represented by the angel and the community are used to explore other familiar Carné concerns. For instance, Carné places the naturalness and innocence of the angel, who sees the world afresh from an asocial position, in opposition to the repressive community, who stand for an unimaginative and constrictive status quo. Moreover, underpinning the tension between the angel and the male members of the community are competing visions of masculinity: the unimaginative thugs are pitted against the sensitive, innocent male.

What is also clearly at stake in the marginalisation of this different type of masculinity is the issue of sexuality. Like earlier examples of Carné's cinéma fantastique, *La Merveilleuse Visite* has a gay subtext, in large part through the angel. As Dyer (2000: 134–6) has discussed, and as we saw in Chapter 4's analysis of *L'Air de Paris*, the angel has an important place in gay iconography. Indeed, it is significant that the only other adaptation of Wells's novel is in the form of an opera, written by Nino Rota, a gay composer. Carné's representation of the angel, as has already been hinted, has a strong homoerotic dimension to it. He is young, slim, and attractive in a delicate and androgynous way, and is naked or semi-naked throughout the film.

The film's gay subtext is also evident through the relationship between the angel and Ménard. Turk (1989: 422) remarks that when Ménard first sees the angel lying naked on the beach, the camera suddenly zooms into his body from Ménard's point of view, which presents his discovery as a jarring moment, and one that possibly represents the sudden awaking of his gay sexuality. When he witnesses the angel walking with Delia, Ménard appears upset, believing that they are involved sexually or romantically. His disappointment, which leads him to call François to tell him what he has seen, could be related to him feeling let down by the angel's apparent loss of purity. On the other hand, it can be interpreted as jealousy that the angel is with the woman rather than him. For Dyer (2000: 131), one of the most significant moments in the film, in terms of its gay subtext, occurs when, in a conversation with Delia, the angel claims 'Ça peut prendre des milliers des milliers de couleurs, l'amour' ('Love can take thousands and thousands of colours'). When Delia asks 'Quelle est la couleur du tien?' ('What colour is yours?'), he replies 'La transparence' ('Transparency'). This evokes Carné's recurring concern with metaphysicality, which in *Le Quai des brumes* is represented through the transparent raincoat worn by Nelly. Undoubtedly this notion of 'different types of love' is one that challenges the narrow parameters of heterosexual monogamy – thus opening up the possibility for forms of gay love, particularly the transcendent forms that Carné's films advocate. In *La*

Merveilleuse Visite ethereality and transcendence are conflated with an expression of gay sentiments, emphasising further Carné's representation of his homosexuality in elevated, spiritual terms.

One of the most distinctive features of the film is that it ends with a moment of genuine escape. While the majority of Carné's films conclude in bleak and pessimistic ways, *La Merveilleuse Visite* possesses an optimistic, uplifting finale – indeed, arguably the most positive ending to any of his films. When the mob from the village drive the angel off the edge of the cliff, he escapes by transforming into a seagull. The look of awe on Ménard's face underlines the specialness and magic of the moment. As with *Les Assassins de l'ordre*, then, the film possesses elements that are typical of Carné's cinema, but also pushes certain features to their extreme – in particular through its treatment of homoeroticism and transcendence. However, despite – or perhaps because of – its innovative features, the film did not perform well at the box-office and was badly received by critics, with Jean de Baroncelli, for example, attacking the film for its 'affectation and puerility' (cited in Turk, 1989: 420). As a result of its negative reception, *La Merveilleuse Visite* would be Carné's final feature film.

La Bible

La Bible, Carné's final film, is a ninety-minute documentary made for television, based upon stories from the Bible and told through the mosaics in the Monreale basilica in Sicily. A couple of years after the failure of *La Merveilleuse Visite*, Carné visited Sicily to appear on the jury for the Festival Cinématographique de Taormina, and while there visited the basilica. Later, in Paris, he told the producer André Tranché about it and it was suggested that he use it as a subject for a documentary. While Carné was not keen on making documentaries (*Nogent, Eldorado du dimanche* being his only one), he was so moved by the basilica that he agreed to make the film. While *La Bible*, as a documentary, is not part of the cinéma fantastique trend several points link it to this strand of Carné's filmmaking. Most clearly, *La Bible* is shot in his familiar style: through the careful, controlled use of framing and editing, and by adding music, sound effects and a voiceover, Carné uses the mosaics to tell various stories from the Bible, occasionally adding other images, some of which were filmed on location in Israel, to embellish the storytelling. Carné's presentation of the basilica emphasises the building's formal beauty and exquisite craftsmanship, establishing a parallel with his own perfectionism and the importance he placed, throughout his career, on the nuances of his craft.

While Carné himself was not religious, as we have seen, many of his films explore the theme of transcendence. *La Bible* shares this concern and, through stories from the Bible, examines familiar tensions between the physical and the spiritual realms. In Carné's cinema, the notion of transcendence is frequently conveyed through the use of ethereal characters. To a certain extent, such characters efface the physicality of their own bodies, their otherworldly quality suggesting they belong in a metaphysical realm, beyond the concrete world. In *La Bible* this is pushed to the extreme: aside from a few extras, characters are rendered entirely through mosaics. At a number of points, as the story is being told, we are also presented with empty spaces, filmed on location in Israel, which leave us to *imagine* the people occupying them – significantly reducing the film's impression of corporeality. Combined with his formal perfectionism, the heavenly orchestral music, and the religious subject matter, *La Bible*, then, presents us with one of Carné's fullest expressions of transcendence.

The final years

Carné's last three films demonstrate interesting continuities with his earlier work. Indeed, in certain respects they provide the most extreme explorations of some of his key concerns: *Les Assassins de l'ordre* is his most overtly political film; *La Merveilleuse Visite* is his most homoerotic work and, with *La Bible*, provides his fullest exploration of transcendence. This highlights Carné's remarkable consistency and, in the face of difficult circumstances, his determination to continue exploring the moral, philosophical and aesthetic issues that were important to him.

Following *La Bible*, Carné struggled to find work and experienced financial difficulties. He tried to sell his personal archives to the Cinémathèque Française, but – extraordinarily yet revealingly – was turned down. The archives were bought by the French Library in Boston, where Carné officially opened the collection during a visit in 1981. While his career almost ground to a halt, he did, however, finally begin to receive official recognition for his contribution to French cinema, after the long period of neglect: amongst other distinctions, in 1980 he was the first film director to be admitted to the Académie des Beaux-Arts and in 1996 was made Grand Officer of the Legion of Honour.

While he was finding it difficult to get film work, Carné wrote his autobiography, *La vie à belles dents*, which was published in 1975 (it was renamed *Ma vie à belles dents* when reprinted in 1996). Between 1980 and 1988 he produced five 'spectacles audiovisuels' for tourist centres, which he called: *Lourdes*; *Toulouse Lautrec et Albi*; *Martinique, île des fleurs*; *Rome éternelle*; and *Paris*. These video installations are computer-programmed non-narrative pieces consisting of multiple projections with surround-sound systems. Turk (1989: 429) points out that, with these tableaux-like spectacles, Carné was in certain respects returning to his first-ever projects: the magic lantern shows that he made for his neighbourhood friends.

While these pieces gave him a degree of creative satisfaction, Carné continued to try to make another feature film and in the early 1990s almost succeeded with one last project, which was to be an adaptation of Guy de Maupassant's story 'Mouche' (1890). He completed two days of filming before the project was abandoned. The film was to focus on the milieu of the French Impressionist painters, centring on seven friends who fight over a young woman, referred to as the *mouche* (fly) of the title. Jill Forbes (1993: 8–9) writes: 'This recreation of the world of the Impressionists would have taken Carné full circle, back to the milieu of punts and riverside cafés lovingly evoked in the first film he ever shot *Nogent, Eldorado Du Dimanche* (1929).' Even though the film was never finished, it is indicative of another familiar Carné talent – his ability to identify star quality. In addition to Roland Lesaffre, the film was to star, in the title role, Virginie Ledoyen, an actress now famous for her roles in *The Beach* (Danny Boyle, 2000) and *8 femmes* (François Ozon, 2002). This authorial continuity is stressed by Danièle Heymann (1992) in *Le Monde*, who compares Carné's discovery of Ledoyen, with his use of Michèle Morgan. Carné, then, had not lost his gift for identifying future stars right to the end of his career. Sadly the film was not completed, initially because of bad weather, before problems with insuring the ageing Carné (who was eighty-six) finally put an end to the project.

Carné died on 31 October 1996 and was buried in the Saint Vincent cemetery in Montmartre, Paris. While he struggled to find work in the last years of his life, his lasting appeal since his death has been evident in a number of ways, particularly through the regular screenings of his films. To mark the centenary of his birth in 2006 there were retrospectives in Toulouse and in Paris, followed by seasons of his work in, amongst other places, Lyon (2008), London (2009), and Stockholm (2010). In 2009, in an ironic twist, the Cinémathèque Française bought Carné's archives from the French Library at Boston, bringing a wealth of letters, scripts, and film paraphernalia back to France. Carné's significant contribution to French cinema, then, finally began to receive the acknowledgement it deserved, following years of neglect and critical hostility.

Conclusion

This book shows that, contrary to the established view of an uneven career (brilliant work in the 1930s and during the war, and decline after), Carné's work as a whole displays consistency and continuity. This is evident on a thematic level with his exploration of entrapment, alienation, loneliness and marginalisation on the one hand and transcendence and the redeeming power of romantic love on the other. These themes are of course central to his poetic realist films, but, as we have seen, they continue to play an important role in his work right up to films like *Les Assassins de l'ordre* and *La Merveilleuse Visite*. Throughout Carné's cinema such themes find their complement in his controlled, classical style. This 'closed' aesthetic generates the sense of suffocation that enfolds the Carné protagonist, while the beauty of the compositions and the romantic love stories hint at the possibility for salvation. Such core concerns and continuity structure Carné's cinema and audience expectations of it and emphasise his talent for creating a distinct cinematic vision. They also testify to his 'auteur' credentials despite the *Cahiers* critics' contention that he was a mere 'metteur en images', suggesting that the claims that Prévert was the dominant creative force behind his early work have been greatly exaggerated, if not wrong all along.

At the same time, there is no denying the changes and developments in Carné's work. His early films undeniably constitute the core of poetic realism. These critically respected and largely very popular films centre upon fatalistic and romantic narratives, embedded in poetic transformations of quotidian spaces. With the postwar films there is a break with this type of cinema, though the transition is not entirely clear-cut. The films of the Occupation years, *Les Visiteurs du soir* and *Les Enfants du paradis*, with their huge scale, high production values, and more 'distanced' aesthetic, already represent the beginning of a shift from the intimacy of poetic realism towards the 'academicism' of the tradition of quality. Although Carné made 'fantasy' films in the postwar period, such as *Juliette ou la clef des songes*, and later *La Merveilleuse Visite*, prompting Bazin (1983) to predict a shift towards 'disincarnation', Carné's films generally move away from the *idealisation* of poetic realism. While a number of his films retain a certain poeticism, notably through the atmosphere of *L'Air de Paris* and *Trois chambres à Manhattan*, the defining feature of the postwar aesthetic is a classical approach to realism. Although the tradition of quality, and Carné's contribution to it, has suffered great critical neglect, Carné's films from this period are illuminating pieces of work, well deserving of better recognition. Of particular importance is the fact that, contrary to the cliché view of Carné's decline, several of his postwar films were extremely popular, especially *La Marie du port*, *Thérèse Raquin* and *Les Tricheurs*.

Also crucial to the shape of Carné's career as a whole, as we have seen throughout this book, is his treatment of gender. To a certain extent here again we can see continuities throughout his career. A crucial element in this respect is his emphasis on male vulnerability and weakness. This dimension goes through some interesting developments: we have, in turn, the doomed proletarian hero incarnated by Gabin in the 1930s, the sensitive androgynous characters played by Cuny and Barrault during the Occupation, the transcendent, almost angelic Lesaffre in *L'Air de Paris*, and the vulnerable youths of the films from the new wave period. While this image of vulnerable masculinity remains relatively constant, there are major changes in the representation of women. In Carné's poetic realism the main female characters possess modern qualities, but their defining feature is their transcendent otherworldliness. This is the case right up to Malou in *Les Portes de la nuit*, Juliette in *Juliette ou la clef des songes* and to a lesser extent Corinne in *L'Air de Paris*. However, with the end of poetic realism Carné's women come down to earth. Concurrently, the later films privilege, to greater and lesser extents, a female point of view, as we have seen with *Thérèse Raquin*, *Les Tricheurs*, *Terrain vague* and *Trois chambres à Manhattan*. This is to a certain extent related to the stars Carné used (Signoret and Girardot in particular) as well as to the absence of Prévert, who significantly influenced the romanticised (but problematic) notion of femininity found in their poetic realism. The example of *Les Tricheurs* is particularly instructive: in contrast to the frequently male-centred films of the new wave, the film places emphasis on the female experience of the emerging youth culture. Carné's treatment of gender is also significant in the complex ways it relates to his identity as a gay filmmaker. Of particular importance in his early films is their emphasis on androgyny. Aside from the overtly gay character of Adrien in *Hôtel du Nord*, such ambiguities constitute one of the main indexes of Carné's sexuality and represent a significant challenge to the patriarchal contexts he worked in. However, in the postwar period a few more overt representations of gay characters gradually begin to appear. Here *L'Air de Paris* is a key film, but also of interest are *Les Tricheurs* and *Les Jeunes Loups*, which feature bisexual males, as well as *La Merveilleuse Visite*.

The final key aspect of Carné's cinema that I have been discussing throughout this book, concerns his films' relationship with broader society and politics. Throughout his career Carné's work engages with these contexts in complex and challenging ways. While he was politically of the left we see little direct engagement with politics on screen, in the way Renoir, for example, was engaged in the mid-1930s. Many of his films avoid dealing directly with major political events, such as the Popular Front or the Occupation, both of which are registered obliquely. In addition, Carné's films tend to be extremely fatalistic, making them profoundly pessimistic about the possibility for any positive change, and are thus, for some, 'reactionary'. Yet many of Carné's films contain a strong sense of working-class solidarity and populist sympathy with 'ordinary people' and popular communities, features that are in evidence in his films from the 1930s to the mid-1950s. In the later years such portrayals of populist Paris, while becoming less frequent, still characterise *Terrain vague* and *Du mouron pour les petits oiseaux*. The later films also have political significance and, indeed, to a certain extent often engage more directly with politics. In this respect it is high time for *Les Portes de la nuit* to be rescued from critical oblivion. In a way which is unique for the period, the film interrogates the issue of wartime collaboration, and, with 2.6 million spectators, the claims that it was a box-office failure are clearly more a reflection of the critical distaste for the film than of its appeal to spectators. As for *Les Tricheurs* and *Terrain vague*, they deal with the issue of postwar youth culture, and more generally with problems relating to the modernisation of France, in a way that signifies their – albeit oblique – relation to the new wave. *Les Assassins de l'ordre*, as an exploration of police corruption and the potentially oppressive nature of state power, is one of Carné's most politically engaged films, and fits perfectly within the popular trend of the 'political thriller' of the 1970s.

In a more diffuse way, Carné's films provide interesting insights into the broader social contexts from which they emerge. In particular, a consideration of the development of Carné's populism, from the 1930s to the 1950s, emphasises significant changes in France as the nation entered 'les trente glorieuses'; in these films we witness France's increasing modernisation, wealth and cosmopolitanism and see evidence of the tensions, fears, and pleasures generated by the modern world. While his early poetic realist films have rightly been celebrated for the insight they give into France in the 1930s, Carné's ability to encapsulate important societal moods and discourses is one that continues beyond the masterpieces of the early years.

Undoubtedly, and rightly, Carné will continue to be celebrated for his contribution to poetic realism and for making some of the greatest films of the 1930s and the Occupation period. At the same time, I hope to have shown that there is also much to be gained from the quality and pleasures of his later work, and what it can teach us about Carné, French cinema and postwar French society.

References

Bazin, A. (1983), 'The disincarnation of Carné', in M. L. Bandy, ed., *Rediscovering French Film*, New York, Museum of Modern Art, pp. 131–5.

Carné, M. (1996), *Ma vie à belles dents*, Paris, L'Archipel.

Dyer, R. (2000), 'No place for homosexuality: Marcel Carné's *L'Air de Paris*', in S. Hayward and G. Vincendeau, eds, *French Film: Texts and Contexts*, 2nd edn, London, Routledge, pp. 127–41.

Forbes, J. (1993), 'Surreal eye in the city', *The Guardian*, 20 August, pp. 8–9.

Heymann, D. (1992), 'Marcel Carné, le retour', *Le Monde*, 15 May.

Turk, E. B. (1989), *Child of Paradise: Marcel Carné and the Golden Age of French Cinema*, Cambridge, Mass.; London, Harvard University Press.

Filmography

Nogent, Eldorado du dimanche (***Nogent, Sunday Eldorado***) (1929)
17 min., b/w.

Assistant director: Michel Sanvoisin
Music: Bernard Gérard provided music for a 1961 release of the film
by L'Avant-Scène cinema

Jenny (1936) 95 min., b/w.

Production: Réalisations d'Art Cinématographique (Albert Pinkéwitch)
Screenplay: Jacques Prévert, Jacques Constant, from *Prison de velours*
by Pierre Rocher
Photography: Roger Hubert
Editor: Ernest Hajos
Set: Jean d'Eaubonne
Music: Joseph Kosma, Lionel Cazeaux; American spiritual sung by
The Five Kentucky Singers
Principal actors: Françoise Rosay (Jenny Gauthier), Albert Préjean
(Lucien Dancret), Lisette Lanvin (Danielle Bricart), Charles Vanel
(Benoît), Jean-Louis Barrault (Le Dromadaire), Robert Le Vigan
(L'Albinos)

Drôle de drame (***Bizarre, Bizarre***) (1937) 105 min., b/w.

Production: Édouard Corniglion-Molinier
Screenplay: Jacques Prévert, from *The Lunatic at Large: His First Offence*
by Joseph Storer Clouston
Photography: Eugen Shüfftan
Editor: Marthe Poncin
Set: Alexandre Trauner

Music: Maurice Jaubert
Sound: Antoine Archimbaud
Principal actors: Françoise Rosay (Margaret Molyneux), Michel Simon (Irwin Molyneux/Félix Chapel), Louis Jouvet (Archibald Soper, Bishop of Bedford), Jean-Pierre Aumont (Billy), Nadine Vogel (Eva), Jean-Louis Barrault (William Kramps), Henri Guisol (Buffington)

Le Quai des brumes (*Port of Shadows*) (1938) 91 min., b/w.

Production: Grégor Rabinovitsch (Ciné-Alliance)
Screenplay: Jacques Prévert, from the novel by Pierre Mac Orlan
Photography: Eugen Shüfftan
Editor: René Le Hénaff
Set: Alexandre Trauner
Music: Maurice Jaubert
Sound: Antoine Archimbaud
Principal actors: Jean Gabin (Jean), Michèle Morgan (Nelly), Michel Simon (Zabel), Pierre Brasseur (Lucien), Raymond Aimos (Quart Vittel), Robert Le Vigan (Michel Krauss)

Hôtel du Nord (1938) 95 min., b/w.

Production: Joseph Lucachevitch (SEDIF)
Screenplay: Henri Jeanson, Jean Aurenche, from the novel by Eugène Dabit
Photography: Armand Thirard
Editor: Marthe Gottié
Set: Alexandre Trauner
Music: Maurice Jaubert
Sound: Marcel Courmes
Principal actors: Annabella (Renée), Arletty (Raymonde), Louis Jouvet (Edmond), Jean-Pierre Aumont (Pierre), André Brunot (Émile Lecouvreur), Jane Marken (Louise Lecouvreur), Paulette Dubost (Ginette), Bernard Blier (Prosper), Andrex (Kenel), François Perier (Adrien)

Le Jour se lève (*Daybreak*) (1939) 87 min., b/w.

Production: Sigma (Pierre Frogerais)
Screenplay: Jacques Prévert, Jacques Viot
Photography: Curt Courant
Editor: René Le Hénaff

Set: Alexandre Trauner
Music: Maurice Jaubert
Sound: Armand Petitjean
Principal actors: Jean Gabin (François), Jules Berry (Valentin), Arletty (Clara), Jacqueline Laurent (Françoise)

Les Visiteurs du soir (*The Devil's Envoys*) (1942) 120 min., b/w.

Production: Scalera/Discina (André Paulvé)
Screenplay: Jacques Prévert, Pierre Laroche
Photography: Roger Hubert
Editor: Henri Rust
Set: Alexandre Trauner, Georges Wakhévitch
Music: Maurice Thiriet, Joseph Kosma
Sound: Jacques Lebreton
Principal actors: Arletty (Dominique), Marie Déa (Anne), Jules Berry (the Devil), Fernand Ledoux (Baron Hughes), Alain Cuny (Gilles), Marcel Herrand (Renaud)

Les Enfants du paradis (*Children of Paradise*) (1942) 195 min., b/w.

Production: Société nouvelle Pathé-Cinéma
Screenplay: Jacques Prévert
Photography: Roger Hubert
Editors: Henri Rust, Madeleine Bonin
Set: Alexandre Trauner, Léon Barsacq, Raymond Gabutti
Music: Maurice Thiriet, Joseph Kosma; pantomime music by Georges Mouqué
Sound: Robert Teisseire
Principal actors: Arletty (Garance), Jean-Louis Barrault (Baptiste Deburau), Pierre Brasseur (Frédérick Lemaître), Marcel Herrand (Pierre-François Lacenaire), Louis Salou (Count Édouard de Montray), Pierre Renoir (Jéricho), María Casarès (Nathalie), Fabien Loris (Avril), Étienne Decroux (Anselme Deburau), Gaston Modot (Fil-de-Soie), Jane Marken (Madame Hermine)

Les Portes de la nuit (*The Gates of the Night*) (1946) 120 min., b/w.

Production: Pathé-Cinéma (Raymond Borderie)
Screenplay: Jacques Prévert, from *Le Rendez-vous*, a ballet by Jacques Prévert, Joseph Kosma, Roland Petit and Brassaï
Photography: Philippe Agostini
Editor: Jean Feyte

Set: Alexandre Trauner
Music: Joseph Kosma
Sound: Antoine Archimbaud
Principal actors: Yves Montand (Diego), Nathalie Nattier (Malou), Pierre Brasseur (Georges), Serge Reggiani (Guy Sénéchal), Saturnin Fabre (the Sénéchal father), Julien Carette (Quinquina), Jean Vilar (Destin), Raymond Bussières (Raymond Lécuyer)

La Marie du port (*Marie of the Port*) (1950) 88 min., b/w.

Production: Sacha Gordine
Screenplay: Louis Chavance, Georges Ribemont-Dessaignes, Jacques Prévert (not credited), from the novel by Georges Simenon
Photography: Henri Alekan
Editor: Léonide Azar
Set: Alexandre Trauner, Auguste Capelier
Music: Joseph Kosma
Sound: Antoine Archimbaud
Principal actors: Jean Gabin (Henri Chatelard), Nicole Courcel (Marie Le Flem), Blanchette Brunoy (Odile le Flem), Julien Carette (Thomas Viau), Jane Marken (Café du Port owner), Claude Romain (Marcel Viau)

Juliette ou la clef des songes (*Juliette or the Dream Book*) (1951) 106 min., b/w.

Production: Sacha Gordine
Screenplay: Marcel Carné, Jacques Viot, from the play by Georges Neveux
Photography: Henri Alekan
Editor: Léonide Azar
Set: Alexandre Trauner, Auguste Capelier
Music: Joseph Kosma
Sound: Jacques Lebreton
Principal actors: Gérard Philipe (Michel Grandier), Suzanne Cloutier (Juliette), Jean-Roger Caussimon (the Personage and Monsieur Bellanger), Yves Robert (the musician), Roland Lesaffre (the Legionnaire)

Thérèse Raquin (*The Adultress*) (1953) 105 min., b/w.

Production: Robert and Raymond Hakim for Paris-Film Production, Lux Films (Rome)

Screenplay: Marcel Carné, Charles Spaak, from the novel by Émile Zola
Photography: Roger Hubert
Editor: Henri Rust
Set: Paul Bertrand
Music: Maurice Thiriet
Sound: Antoine Archimbaud
Principal actors: Simone Signoret (Thérèse Raquin), Raf Vallone (Laurent), Sylvie (Madame Raquin, Camille's mother), Jacques Duby (Camille Raquin), Roland Lesaffre (the sailor)

L'Air de Paris (*The Air of Paris*) (1954) 100 min., b/w.

Production: Silver Films (Robert Dorfmann), Del Duca Films (Paris), Galatea (Rome)
Screenplay: Jacques Viot, Marcel Carné, Jacques Sigurd
Photography: Roger Hubert
Editor: Henri Rust
Set: Paul Bertrand
Music: Maurice Thiriet; song by Francis Lemarque and Bob Castella sung by Yves Montand
Sound: Antoine Archimbaud
Principal actors: Jean Gabin (Victor Le Garrec), Arletty (Blanche Le Garrec), Roland Lesaffre (André Ménard), Marie Daems (Corinne), Jean Parédès (Jean-Marc), Simone Paris (Chantal)

Le Pays d'où je viens (*The Country I Come From*) (1956) 94 min., col.

Production: Clément Duhour, Gilbert Bokanowski
Screenplay: Jacques Emmanuel, Marcel Achard
Photography: Philippe Agostini
Editor: Paulette Robert
Set: Jean-Denis Malclès, Jean Douarinou
Music: Gilbert Bécaud
Sound: Jean Bertrand
Principal actors: Gilbert Bécaud (Julien Barrère and Éric Perceval), Françoise Arnoul (Marinette Hardouin), Claude Brasseur (Roland)

Les Tricheurs (*The Cheaters*) (1958) 125 min., b/w.

Production: Silver Films (Robert Dorfmann), Cinétel (Paris), Zebra Film (Rome)
Screenplay: Jacques Sigurd, from an idea by Charles Spaak and Marcel Carné

Photography: Claude Renoir
Editor: Albert Jurgenson
Set: Paul Bertrand
Music: Recordings by Ray Brown, Fats Domino, Roy Eldridge, Herb Ellis, Stan Getz, Dizzy Gillespie, Norman Granz, Coleman Hawkins, Gus Johnson, Oscar Peterson, Buddy Rich, Maxime Saury, Sonny Stitt
Sound: Antoine Archimbaud
Principal actors: Pascale Petit (Mic), Andréa Parisy (Clo), Jacques Charrier (Bob), Laurent Terzieff (Alain), Jean-Paul Belmondo (Lou), Dany Saval (Nicole), Roland Lesaffre (Roger)

Terrain vague (*Wasteland*) (1960) 100 min., b/w.

Production: Gray Films/Films Rive Gauche (Paris), Jolly Films (Rome) for Louis Dolivet
Screenplay: Henri-François Rey, Marcel Carné, from *Tomboy* by Hal Ellson
Photography: Claude Renoir
Editors: Henri Rust, Marguerite Renoir
Set: Paul Bernard
Music: Michel Legrand, Francis Lemarque
Sound: Jacques Carrère
Principal actors: Roland Lesaffre (Big Chief), Danièle Gaubert (Dan), Jean-Louis Bras (Babar), Maurice Cafarelli (Lucky), Constantin Andrieu (Marcel), Le Râleur (Dominique Dieudonné), Alfunso Mathis (Hans)

Du mouron pour les petits oiseaux (*Chicken Feed for Little Birds*) (1963) 91 min., b/w.

Production: CICC (Raymond Borderie), Champs-Élysées Production (Paris), Variety Films (Rome) for Jules Borkon
Screenplay: Jacques Sigurd, Marcel Carné, from the novel by Albert Simonin
Photography: Jacques Natteau
Editor: Albert Jurgenson
Set: Jacques Saulnier
Music: Georges Garvarentz, Charles Aznavour
Sound: William Sivel
Principal actors: Dany Saval (Lucy), Paul Meurisse (Armand), Suzy Delair (Antoinette), Jean Richard (Louis), Dany Logan (Jojo),

Suzanne Gabriello (Madame Communal), Roland Lesaffre (le Siphonné), Franco Citti (Renato), Jean Parédès (Monsieur de Fleurville)

***Trois chambres à Manhattan (Three Rooms in Manhattan)* (1965) 110 min., b/w.**

Production: Montaigne (Charles Lumbroso)
Screenplay: Jacques Sigurd, Marcel Carné, from the novel by Georges Simenon
Photography: Eugen Shüfftan
Editor: Henri Rust
Set: Léon Barsacq
Music: Mal Waldron
Sound: Jacques Lebreton
Principal actors: Annie Girardot (Kay), Maurice Ronet (François Combe), Roland Lesaffre (Pierre), Geneviève Page (Yolande)

***Les Jeunes Loups (Young Wolves)* (1968) 110 min., col.**

Production: SNC (Paris), West-Films (Rome)
Screenplay: Claude Accursi, Marcel Carné
Photography: Jacques Robin
Editor: René Gillet
Set: Rino Mondellini
Music: Jack Arel, Guy Magenta, Cyril
Sound: Antoine Bonfanti
Principal actors: Haydée Politoff (Sylvie), Christian Hay (Alain), Roland Lesaffre (Albert), Yves Beneyton (Chris)

***Les Assassins de l'ordre (Law Breakers)* (1971) 110 min., col.**

Production: Les Productions Belles-Rives (Michel Ardan)
Screenplay: Paul Andréota, Marcel Carné, from the novel by Jean Laborde
Photography: Jean Badal
Editor: Henri Rust
Set: Rino Mondellini
Music: Pierre Henry, Michel Colombier
Sound: René Longuet
Principal actors: Jacques Brel (Bernard Level), Catherine Rouvel (Danielle Lebègue), Charles Denner (Maître Graziani), Didier Haudepin (François Level), Michel Lonsdale (Commissioner Bertrand), Paola

Pitagora (Laura), Roland Lesaffre (Michel Saugeat), François Cadet (Rabut), Serge Sauvion (Bonetti)

La Merveilleuse Visite (The Wonderful Visit) (1974) 100 min., col.

Production: Mandala Films, France Films Productions, ORTF (Paris), Zafes (Rome)
Screenplay: Didier Decoin, Robert Valey, Marcel Carné, from the novel by H. G. Wells
Photography: Edmond Richard
Editor: Henri Rust
Set: Louis Le Barbenchon
Music: Alan Stivell
Sound: René Longuet
Principal actors: Roland Lesaffre (Ménard), Gilles Kohler (Jean, the angel), Deborah Berger (Delia), Lucien Barjon (the rector), Mary Marquet (the Duchess of Quéfélec), Jean-Pierre Castaldi (François Mercadier)

La Bible (The Bible) (1977) 90 min., col.

Production: Antenne 2, André Tranché (ARC Films)
Screenplay: Didier Decoin, Marcel Carné, from *La Sainte Bible* by Don Raffaello
Photography: Jean Collomb
Editor: Maurice Laumain
Music: Jean-Marie Benjamin

Select bibliography

Books and articles

Andrew, D. (1995), *Mists of Regret: Culture and Sensibility in Classic French Film*, Princeton; Chichester, Princeton University Press. Andrew's study of poetic realism contains extensive analysis of Carné's important contribution to the movement.

Aurouet, C., ed. (2001), 'Jacques Prévert qui êtes aux cieux …', *Ciném-Action*, 98. This special issue on Jacques Prévert includes articles that explore his partnership with Carné and the films they made together.

Carné, M. (1988), 'When will the cinema go down into the street?', in R. Abel, *French Film Theory and Criticism, 1907–1939, Vol. II 1929–1939*, Princeton, NJ; Guildford, Princeton University Press, pp. 127–9. Carné's most well-known article, which was first published in *Cinémagazine* in 1933, can be seen as a manifesto for his vision of populist cinema.

Carné, M. (1996), *Ma vie à belles dents*, Paris, L'Archipel. Carné's autobiography is in places a polemical and bitter response to the criticism he received, making it an important contribution to the critical debates surrounding his work.

Morisson, P. (2005), 'Marcel-Carné.Com', www.marcel-carne.com. This website, which first went online in 2005, is a treasure trove of archival documents on Carné, his films, and his collaborators, and includes copies of articles, reviews, press books, and promotional materials.

Quéval, J. (1952), *Marcel Carné*, Paris, Les Éditions du Cerf. This first full-length book on Carné was not liked by the director himself, but holds interest as an early response to his work.

Turk, E. B. (1989), *Child of Paradise: Marcel Carné and the Golden Age of French Cinema*, Cambridge, Mass.; London, Harvard University Press. Turk's seminal study was the first – and, until now, only – full-length Film Studies book devoted to Carné. Drawing upon a psychoanalytical and gender-based approach, while remaining attentive to aesthetics, politics, and discourses on Carné's sexuality, Turk provides an exhaustive analysis of the director's cinema, particularly of the early work, up to and including *Les Enfants du paradis*.

Various (1972), 'Revoir Marcel Carné', *Les Cahiers de la Cinémathèque*, 5. This special issue on Carné contains essays on topics and films that fall, refreshingly, outside the conventional emphasis on his poetic realism and the masterpieces produced before his 'decline'.

Vincendeau, G. (1997), 'Paradise regained', *Sight and Sound*, 7:7, pp. 12–16. Vincendeau gives an overview of Carné's career and films, and, in particular, argues for the value of his neglected postwar work.

Work on individual films

Bazin, A. (1979), '*Le Jour se lève* ... poetic realism', in Le Jour se lève *a Film by Marcel Carné and Jacques Prévert*, London, Lorrimer Publishing, pp. 5–12. This landmark article on the aesthetics of poetic realism, originally published in 1953, focuses specifically on *Le Jour se lève*.

Bazin, A. (1983), 'The disincarnation of Carné', in M. L. Bandy, ed., *Rediscovering French Film*, New York, Museum of Modern Art, pp. 131–5. Bazin's discussion of *Juliette ou la clef des songes* makes useful observations about developments in Carné's aesthetic and gives insight into his postwar critical reception.

Dyer, R. (2000), 'No place for homosexuality: Marcel Carné's *L'Air de Paris*', in S. Hayward and G. Vincendeau, eds, *French Film: Texts and Contexts*, 2nd edn, London, Routledge, pp. 127–41. This chapter on *L'Air de Paris* is one of the only works on Carné to explore the relationship between his sexuality and his cinema.

Forbes, J. (1997), *Les Enfants du paradis*, London, British Film Institute. This analysis of *Les Enfants du paradis* discusses in particular the film's representation of French history and its relationship with the context of the Occupation.

Sellier, G. (1992), *Les Enfants du paradis*, Paris, Nathan. Sellier's book provides an overview of the film's aesthetics, its politics, and, in particular, its representations of gender, concluding with close analysis of a number of key sequences.

Turim, M. (2000), 'Poetic realism as psychoanalytical and ideological operation: Marcel Carné's *Le Jour se lève* (1939)', in S. Hayward and G. Vincendeau, eds, *French Film: Texts and Contexts*, 2nd edn, London, Routledge, pp. 63–77. This essay examines the psychoanalytical, political, and melodramatic aspects of *Le Jour se lève*.

Index

EU authorised representative for GPSR:
Easy Access System Europe, Mustamäe tee 50,
10621 Tallinn, Estonia
gpsr.requests@easproject.com

www.ingramcontent.com/pod-product-compliance
Ingram Content Group UK Ltd.
Pitfield, Milton Keynes, MK11 3LW, UK
UKHW021815150726

7214IPUK00016B/136